The Market Lads
And Me

A 1980's Memoir

Contains Strong Language

Table of Contents

Ai Free Publication is a UK Registered Trademark.
Trade Mark No: UK00003915810.
No Ai was used in the publication of this book.
QR Code & Trademark supplied by aifreepublication.org

A sad end to put the weekend to bed, but never the less, I'd found myself here again. The last two standing. Fully tuned in, totally oblivious, and well worse for wear. Trudging down the rain sodden street.

Slowly, but surely finding our way home, sheepishly drunk, and more than a little sideways, on a cold, miserable and soaked, Sunday night. Me, after a hectic afternoon, unloading at the market and him, having run his sock off at football training. But both with a gallon of beer afterwards. 1 find myself thinking deeply, and sinking heavily, back into work thoughts all over again. Would I even make it there! And even if I did, could I carry it off? More to the point, would I hear my alarm clock, anyway?

Monday looming. It so quickly comes around. After a very costly and short, alcohol induced weekend. At least it seemed that way, judging by the amount of coppers, weighing down in my pockets. Either way, it didn't seem to matter now.

Out enjoying myself, with my other like-minded individuals, as if there was no tomorrow. The pub finally shut, less than half an hour ago. Very heavily on the illegal side, but with such an obliging landlord, and they are, when you're lining their pockets. Who was to know or care any different? I'm just hoping I'm home soon. I'm followed closely, by the last of my 'Brothers in Arms' left, Birdy. A good mate from the estate, and my high school years. The newest, almost a fully initiated, and paid up fledgling member of the gang.

"Ste hold on, wait for us!" He shouted, now lagging heavily. At one point he was well ahead, due to my thorough 'watering' of a hardy perennial

"You goin the long way home Ian or what?"

Bad sense of direction had Ian, or birdy to the chosen few. Especially with a gallon of 'The Tippings Arms' finest, and the other nights libations inside him. He disappeared from my view, into some knee-high grass, behind the housing estate's shops. "You can get.... through... a no a short burfi!... pardon, cutere." Ian slurred and burped, walking into some trees at the same time. I swished through the overgrown grass, and edged closer to his pole position, and promptly overtook him. An easy manoeuvre, due to his staggering and unzipping and a heavily listing bladders imminent release. We still hadn't a clue where we were going.

We surfaced from heaven knows where, straight into a private back garden. On the opposite side to our intended destination, the shopping parade. Strange territory, made even worse in my double vision. God only knows how he got us to this place. I stopped to do a quick ordnance survey. We were now at least a quarter of a mile in the wrong direction. I put it down to his head in the clouds boredom and alcohol abuse on both our parts. After quickly exiting the private property I soon found myself lagging well behind Ian. Cigarette duty always slows progress. Not for Ian though. He was now bounding through the scrub like a dog on heat, but still heading the wrong way. More to the point, I was following him. I paused, to figure his logic or reason and ultimately his destination. I felt a crankshaft click, or a light bulb switch on in my head. This was all for the girl... a very pretty girl at that! Everything in my head now dropped into place. An hourglass figure, blue-eyes and long, blonde hair. Jealousy creeps. Need I say more? I shook my head and smiled to myself, 'Julia,' I said aloud. Now agreeing with his tempters.

The most sought-after girl in her year at college. And not too young for me to have a dabble either. Dare I say so myself.

The love of Ian's life, apparently? This much of a pledge he constantly claimed. He never shut up about her. The simple fact that she already possessed a boyfriend, was courting strong, and was currently on holiday in Spain, with her hunk, couldn't be accessed by Ian's well-pissed floppy disk brain. He remained completely undeterred and continued in his slowly uncovering goal.

"Ste... see that house down there. Wos that say...? Glenbrook Avenue,

that on with, wite, conservatory fing? That's where she lives. . . Burp! Ser rouse that is."

"What?... say that again Ian, you slurring bastard." I look down the dimly lit road for visual clues, flicking my spent stump into the air.

"There look.... stood on its own, the big one, see? With a red Volvo in the drive?"

"Detached Ian, the detached house?"

I sighed and shook my head despairingly "Yeah, whatever."

"Look ste, she must be in, yes.... lights are all on yes, yes aaahhhh!"

"Bloody hell! Ian listen pal, People always leave lights on when they're away. It makes thieving bastards like Tommo think someone's in. So, they won't........"

Ian wasn't listening. He reminded me of the happy rabbit in the cadburys caramel advert. Euphorically in love, but with added drunken grin. Or possibly, he just had a bad case of trapped wind after downing a more than a considerable amount of lager.

"Do's a fav Ste, knock for us, go on... just say I'm here like, want a word like. Go on.... please. Go on mate, I'll wait on't corner........"

Ian, when sozzled, had a memory like a sieve. I had to get him up to speed.

"Fuck off Ian...! You've forgotten haven't you, you docile dick-head! She's away, abroad, in Spain. Even if she was in she wouldn't answer. Think about it Ian, were more than half cut, knocking after twelve in the pissing down rain. Come on, be serious. Even If she was in, what if he answered or worse her Mum or Dad?"

I gave him a minute to digest the information.

"Now come on. Let's fuck off home before they call the filth or sommat. We've already been pissing and loitering in someone's back garden."

I gave him another minute to think. He looked to be struggling on the Spain bit. I started walking, leaving him furiously scratching his head.

Putting some space between us might help speed him up. My bed had been calling me since way before closing time. I was knackered after unloading at the market too.

I shouted back. "Listen dipshit! I'm at work in a few hours, and you're in kindergarten later too.... That's If you decide to fuckin turn up that is? Let's get bloody home and get some kip."

"Woah! hold on Ste, I'm fucked!" I turn around to see him slowly picking himself up from the rain-soaked flags, then slouching up at me from a wet garden wall, where he'd unhappily settled for what looked like the duration. Thanks to his drunken fall, he now looked like he'd just done a shift down the pit. He slowly rose up to his knees, then his feet. Running his fingers through his rain-soaked mass of black wedge cut hair, to get it out of his eyes.

"Aw fock! Shit! I forgot abart Spain, basterd."

The reality had bit. *Ouch!* I laughed to myself. It must've had rabies when it bit him.

Ian was the youngest in the gang, and three years my junior. Still schooling, and studying art at college, on some sort of flexi- time. That was whenever he could be bothered going, or when Julia was definitely in art class, and he could go sniffing. Apart from that, he rarely made an appearance. Couldn't take his ale either. At this point, he definitely seemed to be struggling with his nights mega-alcohol ingestion. They don't make drinkers like they used too, I thought. Didn't matter. He would soon be whipped into shape. He had me, and the rest of the lads schooling him in that department. With such a reliable bunch of drinking (never miss a shift) mentors he couldn't fail. We'd have him transformed into a young Ollie Reed, in no time at all. I lit another cancer stick and waited. After another failed attempt to get going again, Ian had totally stopped, and was now silently hunched over. Hands on his stomach, and staring at the flags, as if he was waiting for something un-miraculous to happen.

He looked auspiciously across at me and quickly turned back to the garden. With his head down, and leant precariously forward over the wall, he wrenched, and spewed his guts for all he was worth. He shuddered and shook, in-between his sick bouts. Looking possibly as if he was going to lose his balance and follow his sick, straight over the wall.

"I told you not to touch that Pernod, you dick-head! That stuff's lethal Ian. If you have a drink of water as soon as you wake up, you'll be drunk again. Pernod can do that!" He silently looked at me. Apprentices I mused.

"Ffuuuckotfh, you baassstard. Blaahhh, tuigh, yeuch oh-that's euch........!"

He spat out what looked like the cheese and onion crisp, he'd added to his stomach's alcohol mix earlier.

I could smell them from two feet away! I decided to let him alone, and get on with it, and sat smoking, at the other end of the garden wall, until he'd finished.

"Look at you Ian? You look like you're going in for a male wet t-shirt sick contest! Your piss-wet through with your own vomit. Why didn't you bring your coat out with you anyway, you numpty? It's been raining all night."

Normally, I tried to be home at a reasonable time. Mam liked it that way. House rules. Especially week days. Mam, always early to bed, early to rise. Even more so on Sunday's with religion and all. She'd held a job down since she was fifteen. Her generation had hard graft Instilled in them. Probably since birth. There were three mouths to feed. Four if you count Shamus.

Even when I was running around in nappies, Nanny Peggy used to look after us, while mam went to the sewing factory. And at work, as at home, she was head down, arse up busy. I think she enjoyed work. Never complained, just got on with it. No questions asked. I don't think they make them like me mam anymore either? She paid the mortgage, and the rest of the bills and we needed to eat. It was as simple as that. Apart from my older brother John, and my pretty poor work pittances. She was the main house income now. This was all thanks to my Dads, nonchalant disappearance to pastures new. Another woman. According to our John, Dad had been unable to tie a knot in it for quite some time now. Which was quite an eye-opener for me? Particularly when he really did bite the bullet, divorced me Mam, and finally flew the coop.

Ian had relinquished himself from his stomach drinks cocktail and had almost managed to catch me up. Mumbling his bad luck continuously as he neared. I didn't have a key to get in, I wasn't allowed one. I looked at my watch as the rain got heavier. Time was moving swiftly on. With no further closure on getting to my pit. Another ten minutes, a wet arse, and two more cigarette's walking went by. Stuff this, I thought. Enough's
enough.

"Ian, I'm going to cut down Balfe road in a bit. That'll be quicker for me. Yours isn't far now, I can see your Dads car."

This was just a wee 'Giddy up' rouse. I'd already tried the 'bomb up his arse' routine.

"Wait... am comin nar... What's yer rush, yev never bothud befoure? Yeuch, that tastes orrible."

"Yeah, I know Ian. But Mondays a really busy day. Worst one of the week, and a late finish too. If I've had no sleep, a day feels like it's never going to end. Plus, I've gotta get in the bloody house yet?"

"You mean tomowwo?"

"No Ian, today. It's after midnight Ian you berk! Tomorrow is today?"

"Shit, here we go again.... Is it worth, it, I thought?"

"Look, you pillock! I need as much shut eye as I can get, and that'll be next to nothing at this rate!"

"Your John will be up on his CB radio, won't he?... He'll let you in. The bionic man. He never sleeps haha."

"That's if he's in, yeah, I just don't fancy waking me mam up. Do you know what I mean Dodo?"

God this is hard work I thought. Was I talking in space, via broken satellite link up, in Welsh? Even though Ian was slightly more legible after his most recent sick up. He was still making little sense.

After another further five minutes, listening to his Julia ramblings, we reached my cut off point.

"See you sometime tomorrow then Ste? Soz bout the wild goose-chase like.... Ooh, I think I'm gonna be sick again?"

"Yeah, you probably will until all that green Pernod shit's all out. I'll speak to you later then, Ian."

I headed left and got about fifty yards further on. Behind me, mixed in with the constant pitter patter of the un-ending rain, the un-dulcet sound of Ian singing Simply Red's 'holding back the years' chorus, repeatedly in the dark. What a shit end, to a good night that turned out to be.

Some five minutes later, I thought I was walking faster. But not gaining any ground. One foot forward, two- back! The alcohol had really kicked in. Oooh, I thought. Now I know how Ian was feeling. I really don't need all this messing to get in now either. I wish I could just walk up to the door and turn a key like every other normal person. I suppose that's what I get, for getting regularly slaughtered, and losing three keys in succession. Mam had said she couldn't afford to have the locks changed again. She probably couldn't though. It always boils down to money, or lack of it.

Things were always very tight in our house. But we never went without. Not to worry, I thought as I slid over the back-garden gate latch. Little incidentals, like keys don't matter either. Even if our John's not home, I can get in. I always get in. When you want something bad enough, you'll always find a way.

Most weekends and drinking nights, I'd leave the locking arm, on the kitchen window off. With the pane pushed closed, it looked locked. Since the frame wasn't fully square, it was still hard to open, unless you had the knack. It was a ritual I always went through before I went on a binge. The other most important, and flawless security device was; as Johnny Morris said 'Animal Magic'. Shamus, our trusty, long haired German Shepherd. He was eleven stone in growl alone. But a big softie once you got to know him. A proper dog!

Another crucial point being that, after many thoughtless, pointless beatings, from my recently defunct Dad, Shamus was now transformed. A pure man hater. Present company accepted of course.

He was totally devoted to his female owner, me Mam. Let's just say; I wouldn't like to be the thief breaking into our house. Once home, I quickly hushed his barking and yawning up. Feeling slightly aggrieved, I did the usual; climb through the window to get in routine. Closed it over, grabbed the biscuit tin, and left him happily crunching on some digestives, as I silently creeped up the stairs, to exit earth.

TWO

I woke startled, to the blare of my radio alarm. My head was a self-instigated spinning haze. I fumbled madly around, for the clocks snooze button. I was still fully clothed, but now totally dried out. The radio alarm music had gained Illegal-security clearance. I'd denied any access to my REM sleeping brain, but it still shook my half-alive head awake! To my angry head, the sound of pure melancholy bullshit, emanated blankly into my senses;

"Morning has broken, like the first morning, Blackbird has spoken, like the first...."

BANG!

I thumped the insidious machine to silence. At the same time, launching into a full on, but whispered expletive ridden rant.

"Aaarrghhh shit!... shut the fuck up... cat fuckin Steven's... you happy, mundane fuckin bastard!" I knew at this point, his tune was threatening to stick in my head, endlessly for the rest of day. I'd probably be annoyingly singing it at customers, and not even know I was doing it.

I scratched my head and sat up. Realising what lay ahead of me. Things could only very quickly go from bad to worse. I stood up and turned on the light as everything went south and headed toward the bathroom. The full blown, whispered conversation with myself continued.

"Oh no, no, fuckin no! What a friggin job. You must be totally off your chomp!" I turned on the hot water tap and waited. *"You loser...! Even the Milkman doesn't get up this early."* I splashed the warm water into my face. *"Ooh, I still feel drunk. Some bloody chance of driving a forklift today. I'll probably be over the legal limit, pulling a bloody handcart? Knowing you, which I fuckin do. You'll probably end up, running over yourself. Or someone else? You're a fuckin glockenspiel!"* I sat down on the toilet seat. Angrily yanked the towel from the rail at

the back of the door and dried my face and hair. Listening in to my brains internal hidden good and evil tempters counselling. I grabbed the toothbrush and laced it with Maclean's. Sleepily gathered my thoughts again and rubbed at my eyes.

"Stuff this, I'm not goin in."

"You're not?"

"I'm not."

"You sure about this are you?"

"You watch me."

"I'm watching."

"I can't, I can't face it. Face them!"

"Customers, the selfish bastards. Coming to destroy my day. Coming to annoy the shit out of me. I hate the fruit market. I hate my life!"

"Oh, come on now?" My good tempter appeased. *"Surely It's not that bad?"*

I stood and turned back to the sink mirror, and squinted at my half awake, gaudy reflection. Grabbed the hairbrush and pulled it through my hair. Replaced the toothbrush, into its holder. Gargled and spat.

"I know, I'll ring in sick, that's what I'll do yeah, that's it!"

At that moment, Reality knocked sharply on the side of my head.

"But there's no one going to be there until YOU get there, dummy!... Shit!" I walked back into the bedroom and lied back down on the bed. Closed my eyes, thinking for a minute. The minute must have radically increased tenfold. I must have nodded back off as the clock came back from its snooze. 'Return of the zombie alarm clocks (part deuce) this time it's personal'. The music this time was suitably better.

A more soothing ditty, Madonna's song 'Rain', strangely lifted my ill mood. As I lay there, I echoed her words in my head. I opened my eyes. Is there a touch of 'déjà vu'? There could well be? I thought. I sat up, stretched forward, and reached over the bedside cabinet, peeping through the curtains, to view the impending situation outside. *"Ten out of ten Madge"* I mumbled. Madonna was right. It was still pissing down.

Despite the cats and dogs weather, I decided I'd walk to work. It'd be much safer. Biking it last week, I'd very successfully managed; to hit a stationary car and snapped one of my pedals. Buckled the front wheel, so much so it would hardly turn. And last but not least; ripped both knees out of my best going out jeans. How I came to be wearing them on the way to work was the usual story.

The market wasn't far from home. But sadly, all uphill. I'd have to forget my usual departure coffee. 1 was already running late. This was nothing to do with me of course. It was his fault. *"Yes you, cat bloody Stevens!"* Stephen, you're talking to yourself again I mused. I put my cigs and lighter, and five quid in shrapnel, back into my pockets. Donned my tea cosy bob hat and made a sharp exit.

This time unlike my entrance. In style, through the front door, resembling Benny from Crossroads. Minus miss Diane. I could usually get to work at a steady pace in fifteen minutes. That's from the front door, to the main gate. I quickly grabbed a cheap can of caffeine laden coke and fag before I shut the front door. The brisk rain and a cold breeze hit me. Thanks Madonna. Walking fast, I was soon feeling a tad more alive, compared to the lethargy I'd greeted when I woke. My thoughts were fleshing out the premise of a typical Monday morning at the Market. If there were such a thing? The pending customers, their wants, needs, ideal prices to make a sale, with adequate profit margins. So, on and so forth. Mmm blah, blah, fuckin blah. The usual bollocks I thought.

My needs, to get me through the expected car crash of a Monday were, minimal and straightforward. Cigarettes, coffee or tea or sometimes in the freezing or snowy winter months, Oxo. Things were always so hectic on the stall, and market, it was sometimes a trapeze act choosing when to take onboard and dispense of said refreshment in peace.

I'd made up for the lost snooze time and was now almost at the top of Fulbeck avenue but bursting for a piss. I quickly crossed over the road, and made my way down the small alleyway, in-between the Ben Johnson back yard wall, and the old terraced houses. The Ben Johnson was a local boozer which stood at the top of the housing estate. I looked around stupidly as if there was going to be an audience down a back alley at this time of a morning. I quickly pissed, like I was on a parking meter. Then zipped up and crossed back over the main road again. Glancing back with a wry grin. I'd be in there later, with Paul and Tony. Sooner than later! with a bit of luck. *The Market lads and me.*

When **I** arrived at the market, the main gates were closed. Mmm I thought, *"I know you're twenty minutes late Stephen, but this is a first"*, I said to myself. Terrible habit, that talking to yourself. This wasn't on the morning's schedule? This could push the whole day, further into utter turmoil. I'd have to have a fag and think about this. I looked up at the over imposing wall. 1 could scale over that, to get in and get the ball rolling. I lit my smoke, and looked over at the silent, lifeless stall. An even bigger concern, quickly dawned. The way twenty tons of bricks does! There was no movement, lights on, or usual sign of life. Where the hell was our nightshift? I had to do something quick.

I looked again, at the daunting, smiling rusty barbed wired wall. I threw my spent ciggie and slowly and unwillingly, began my ascent up and over. After three testing and traversing minutes, I'd somehow made it up, to the top of the brick gateposts. Mmm, I thought, panting. Halfway there. I carefully straddled over the sharp, rusted wire. Some headlights appeared. As if tracking my unsteady movements. A black car pulled up.

I glanced down. Out got a familiar face, Bob Higham. The ever-organised swine, even had a torch in his hand. The most self-opinionated salesman on the market. Worked from another pitch, exactly opposite 'Churches'. Unlike myself Bob, a teetotaller who could be trusted was with his key. Too late for me though, I was almost over. I didn't fancy climbing back down either. I grabbed in-between the barbed spikes, closed my eyes and hoped for the best. I dropped to the concrete, on the other side of the wall to find my footing. My left leg chose to re-join terra-firma on top of a rotten spud. As I landed, it *squelched* and twisted my ankle in the process. *"Aaarrghhh Shit, Bastard!"*

Thank you so much Monday.

"Good morning Stephen?" Instantly came the cockney, sickly smarm, from the other side of the gates. He grabbed the lock and chain to put the key in.

"What's good about it Bob? Ouch, my fuckin ankle! What time D'you call this anyway, your fuckin late?" I checked my hands for muck and wire punctures.

"Yes, must apologize. Sorry, Stephen. But Marjorie blocked me in with her car Stephen. Bloody women eh," he moaned, pushing open the gate and smiling, as if he was enjoying my predicament.

"Blocked you in? Should have nailed you in a bloody coffin too! Will you stop calling me Stephen? Only my Mother is allowed that luxury."

"That is, your christened name isn't it?" He needed seriously correcting.

"Now really isn't the time Bob, so listen very carefully. Inge or Steve will suffice. Fuckin got it, pal!"

My patience had now left the situation.

"Oh, erm, okay erm. Now then Steve." You could hear the uncomfortable tone in his voice.

"Are you ready to seize the day Stephen?" He felt his error.

"Just great, it's like talking to a brick wall with a personality defect this is."

I muttered under my breath. I felt something pulling as if attached to the back of my coat.

"Seize, Seize˙ The only thing I want to seize is my bed, or alternatively, your fucking neck Bob! What the fuck is that pulling my c —?"

"I beg your pardon?"

Bob looked up from the lock to see me wrestling with some anaconda loose barbed wire embedded in my coat.

"Fuckin neck I said! Are you deeef too Bob?"

"Language Stephen, it's a virus ... Oops... sorry Steve."

I got the distinct feeling, he'd not listened to a single word I'd said.

Just like Birdy on the way home earlier.

Bob was one of those people, who really enjoyed the sound of his own voice.

Smarmy bastard. He needed to be made fully aware of the seriousness of my situation.

"I'd really love to chat Bob but I'm a bit fuckin busy here, if you hadn't noticed." As I pulled on my coat and released the wire from the material it sprang back on itself back toward the wall.

"My nightshift hasn't turned in either."

"Dear oh dear, so I see, that's a bit of a problem for you, Isn't It Stephen?" He smiled.

"Are you taking the piss, you cockney shit?"

My rain-soaked coat was now ripped thanks to the barbwire and Bob's yakking.

"What is this; Breakfast with Frost? Just fuck off Bob!"

"Not very reliable that Brother of yours is he Stephen?" He's loving every minute of this I thought.

"Erm, no, you can't get the staff these days can you Bob?" He had to be humoured, just to get him to shut up, then I could get a move on. I walked away from him, and over to the stall shutter and shouted a dig back.

"Good luck selling your overpriced, rotted shit today pal."

Today was already becoming a nightmare.

At Churches we were usually well organized. But with the morning's events so far, and zero nightshift to boot, it now had to be.............. Lights! Camera! Action!

After a two-minute, welter-weight bout with the shutter doors, that even more fuelled my anger, I made a bee-line straight for the phone.

"Mam, where the hell's, nightshift, I mean our John?"

Earlier, I didn't want to wake her. That was then this is now. She paused to brush her sleep cobwebs away.

"He stayed out last night at Karen's. What's the matter?"

"Shit! Do me a favour. Just get hold of him somehow? Tell him to get to work pronto! Preferably yesterday, ok mam? taarraa!"

I didn't wait for a reply and bashed the phone down. Half in anger, half in haste.

THREE

I quickly jumped into my bright yellow, PVC pants and jacket, and started stacking the over-night deliveries, quickly onto pallets. shell peas, beetroot, cress, mushrooms, etc. The deliveries had an annoying habit, of always materialising in the completely wrong place. Either slap bang, in the middle of the fruit and veg display veranda. Or worse, on next doors pitch. As I finished stacking the last of the boxes, it started to pour down even harder. Wet and soaked all day again. *"Bloody great this Is"!* I thought, pulling down on my hat. *"Fuckin splendid!"*

I always talk to myself. Probably much more than the average person. Let's be honest, everyone does it? Sometimes, you're the only one around making any sense!

Maybe it's an old family trait? Something we inherit from our parents? Wherever it comes from, It's always very orately visible, In all of my actions. I could be either, trying to entertain an audience pissed. Or in a club, trying to get into someone's knickers, and laying on the charm. Make an important sale at work. Or under pressure, From Dad. John, Mum or customers. Anything in that vein, 1 would simply sing, or just mumble nothingness to myself, or anyone who would be around listening.

Alternatively, even whistle. No set tune or melody. That usually hides my little un-sureness or nervousness. It just happens, without actually happening, if you get my drift? Maybe I'm just mental? It's probably just family mentality, genes or idiosyncrasies? <u>Don't sit there reading this and tell me you're any different? Don't tell me you don't have good and evil Tempters either?</u> Cos you know that that's not true!

I continue my nonsensical ramble, as I slide open the rest of the shutter doors, and jump onto the fully charged, and already pallet full forklift;

"Well steveo, moving fast today boy, you cool dude you. Flying along, my old stringus beanus. (Bob cockney speak) But you must seize the day! Crack the whip my dear boy! Take the bull by the horns. Let's get this stall sorted. Think Ben hur hyah! Hyah! Do, do, do, do de...................."

Just as I was emptying the perishables from the fridge cold store, I hear the faint revving of a Motorbike engine in the middle

distance. I look over to the other side of the market, to see Bob, only just opening the doors to his stall. *"Bloody hell! I wonder if he's that slow on the job with the Marjorie? Probably, the tosser!"* I carry on rushing out the paletted stall stock, as John switches his motorbike off, and parks it under the stairs. At the side of the coffee machine. My carrier pigeon had been swift and reliable. John arrived in less than ten minutes.

"What fuckin time do you call this John? Shagging all night again?" I could see him concocting.

"Yes, no. Well erm... I was at Karen's. Forgot to set her clock like. Oh, and erm, I ran out of petrol about half a mile away. Anyway, I don't have to answer to you. You're not my boss. Peter's my boss."

After the shit I'd just endured, with Bob and getting in, a tempters voice in my head came to life. Launched into automatic rip-him-to-shreds mode. With free bonus levels, and full firepower. Including smart bombs after the first wrong word.

"Oh, right I see, and pray dear brother, forgive my confusion, but how did you sort this minor petrol hiccup out? There's no fuckin garage open at this time of a morning!"

It would be so much easier, to teach him how to lie properly. i.e.; big believable story, etc. Just like the one about going fishing and catching a whale (you know the one). Then be able to carry it off. Always remembering, whenever questioned, every last detail, of the complete pile of shite you've just uttered. But then, that would take away all the fun, wouldn't it?

In the bullshitting instance, my Brother was terrible. Too honest a soul. And yet somehow, always ended up convincing, no one else but himself, the whole story was true. Aren't you supposed to look up to your older siblings? What a load of old bollocks that is!

"Simple Ste. I siphoned some out of a car on the way here. Clever bastard me you know?"

He smiled to himself as if he'd pulled it off. Mmm, I thought, think you're clever do you John. About as clever as fuckin Bob. Too much self- importance this twat's, I enthused to my tempters.

I began to goad him. Too obviously really.

"Wa haay! Good thinking John. But how did you manage that when your bike tank is clearly higher up than any cars petrol tank? What did you do? reverse-gravity feed it? What are you? some kind of fuckin magical Genie, you thick twat!"

"No, I sucked it into a coke can first you, shithouse!" Suitably annoyed, he kicked his helmet down under the bottom office desk, where he kept his motorbike crap. Aha, a reaction. I've got him. Our John was easy to wind up. Just like candy from a baby.

"Oh, and the siphon tube, you had one of those with you, did you?"

"Course I did. I carry one with me all the time."

"Aaah, would that be the one you told me is stashed under your seat?"

"Fuck off, smart arse, or I'll fuckin belt you!" He would too. Done it many times before. Mmm, I'd have to be pretty careful with his biting point here. He was rapidly getting pissed off with me.

'Good' said my devil side Tempter. 'Good, good, good!'

I looked over at him and smarmily smiled like Bob.

After a couple of minutes, John had seceded to the work ethic, and was zipping his skin-tight leathers off.

"Hang on John. One final question if you please?"

He turned to face me.

"Stephen, enough now, or I'll fuckin hit you."

I ignored his threat. This is a real question after all, **I** thought.

"Ok then. Let's say I believe you. But how the fuck does four-star, car petrol, run a two-stroke motorbike engine?" He looked up and shrugged his shoulders.

"Don't know Stephen but it does. Terry Conway showed me. Besides, it's cheaper robbing it and I'm skint. I took Karen to the 'Hawk' last night. There was a band on. Spent up. She cost's me a small fortune she does. Bloody women?"

"It's a good job she's alright in the sack then isn't it hahaha...?"

Hmmm, good choice of question. I congratulated myself as he rambled on meaninglessly to himself.

"So, your engines fucked now too then?" He pondered my question, climbing into his blue overalls. "Probably is...? don't care, anyway. It's goin soon. Getting a bigger one. A fuckin monster! Yamaha RD 350lc.

Mmm, Is that so......? Shouldn't have told me that now should you John? I mused to myself.

"Oh good, wait till **I** spill the beans on the estate then. You won't get a buyer for that fuckin boneshaker, this side of next year'. His winning smile dropped. Like the Hindenburg, on its maiden flight to Lake Hurst. He frowned like a road map and went to grab me.

"You keep your gob shut D'you hear. Or I'll fuckin batter you!"

Oh John, what sledgehammer wit, and repartee I thought.

"Oooh, batter me, really? what big eye's you've got grandma."

My last snide comment had done it. He'd snapped, and chased me up and down the stall, three times, before cornering me behind the onion racks.

"Ouch! get off, you, fuckin soft sod, I was only winding you up! I won't tell a soul if you pull your fuckin finger out. Get some work done, John and sharpish! We've fuckin loads to do yet and were running around like a pair of fuckin kids here."

"Yeah, well, just fuck off, you wind up merchant."

Reluctantly, I had to agree.

And so endeth the lesson. Did him good though. It all ended with sibling smiles from both of us. Thinking he'd won the last word, he turned and walked to jump on his forklift. He always needed winning around when he'd lost a war of words. I was better with him on my side than against me.

COME ON JOHN! I funly shouted, lets KICK ASS! with this stall. Make it look like we're ready for them when they come. Or at least that you've been here all along, know what I mean?'. He Ignored me.

About half an hour later, John had speedily fork lifted most of the stock out, under the stall verandas out of rains way. Perishables had to be kept dry too. But easily inspectable to customers. The stall housed umpteen rack areas. In separate rows. Running from one end of the building to the other. They had just enough space between them, for a tight forklift access. Potatoes, onions, carrots and other veg filled one side. Tomatoes, all fruit and the walk-in fridge filled the other. I was putting the final touches to the display. A concept borrowed from the main fruit and veg market in Liverpool.

A simple, but effective visual statement of fruit and veg quality and availability. As I walked back in from the rain, John was huddled in the downstairs office. Shiftily sipping a coffee, near the small blowing heater, sat on a box of bananas. After what seemed to be the minimum amount of forklift work.

"Is that you finished is it? Where's my fuckin brew you tight sod?"

"In the machine shit-head! Peters here. I've just heard his car, round the back."

The un-mistakable wheel spin of his speed machine easily identified. A dream car. 2.8 Injection Capri. Or metallic blue 'Babe' magnet. John necked his coffee and got suddenly busy again. Doing tangibly nothing what so ever. Rearranging stock for the stocks sake as ever with his forklift. The stock must have felt pissed, it was being moved around that much. As long as it wasn't physically challenging, and could be done by forklift, John was your man. Two minutes later Peter walked in.

"Morning Peter?" I let him know I was alive.

"Alright Inge, that's 24,32,96. Sorry Paul... I mean Inge. Where's the night delivery tickets? Was everything there? John! Get me a coffee lad. Inge, did we get any more restaurant orders in? Here's the one's I've got for this week. I mean, oh, not them ones. Sorry, hang on where did I put them now? At this point, Peter or H as he preferred to be called, was on another planet. Making no sense, to himself or anyone else. Frantically rummaging through his pockets.

"Shit, where's them glasses now? I've forgotten my glasses? Ah no, here they are, got em. Where's that coffee John? Inge, while it's quiet, make a start on these orders here." He handed me a crumpled bunch of tickets. While it's quiet? Humph. I've not fuckin stopped since I climbed over the fuckin wall, I thought.

"John! forklift the finished orders over to the onion store, when they're done. Oh, hang on,

there'll be fresh stuff on the wagon to add to them. Do not forget to finish them off when you get the other bits from the wagon. Start fosters order soon as you can. Just nipping to my car. Forgot my smokes. Back in a sec?"

Soon as Peter was out of sight, John stopped. Got off his forklift and walked toward me.

"What a fuckin arsehole. Foster's friggin order. He's already doin my head in! What does he want fuckin blood? I've just about had it with this place, I'm gonna Jack and look for another job." He angrily marched away. I was temporarily stunned into silence.

"Erm, come on John, give him a few minutes to calm down. He'll settle down in a bit. It'll be fine." He wouldn't of course. With Peter, you can run, but you can't hide. John was just pissed off he'd have to do some more work. Couldn't hide or pretend anymore. He'd now have more than plenty to do. Peter came back from his car, furtively smoking. John looked over at Peter. Peter looked back at him and was readily given a dark scowl. If looks could kill, Peter was being lowered into the ground.

"You know what he's like John, anyway you were late remember." I whispered to him as he stormed past me. I watched them both, as John walked away into the office, flashed through his handful of fosters tickets, obviously trying to will the order to nothing. He walked back out the office, looking totally thwarted. He glared again at Peter, then disappeared toward the toilet, to have a good old chinwag with the cistern. I continued to amble away, regardless. Stacking sacks of carrots, onto an already overflowing pallet. I did feel a bit bad for our kid. Mondays order for Fosters was always massive. Seven tickets worth today. In all the time I'd worked here, Peter had put a lot of trust in me. Above most other

porters really. I'd made it to the sales book surprisingly quickly. God knows how? I was more often than not, half cut from the night before and half the time really didn't care, if I sold my soul, or nothing at all. Maybe I was just a good actor, or a damn good liar.

Being in a position of trust meant more work, and longer hours. Therefore, starting before anyone else did.

Opening up so on and so on. But with all the responsibility, came that bit of extra money. Beer tokens. This took the form of a brown envelope. Quietly and neatly dropped into my back pocket, usually around pay-day.

FOUR

The big market clock was showing four fifty-five. Paul and Tony were due in any minute. Two more motorbike graduates. The amount of times I'd pulled the three of them up, for talking motorbikes instead of working, couldn't be counted on centipede's feet.

Paul was a human machine. A born grafter. Ask, give, or show him anything and no matter how big or small, a job or order, he'd make mincemeat of it. No questions asked. Tony, on the other hand, was the complete opposite. A totally psychotic individual. I was convinced of it. The missing patient from a hospital 'yellow van'. Asking him to do a bit of work well, waste your time and breath why don't you.

He always had to answer a question with a question. He would purposely leave Items

missing from orders, in the hope that in the end, you wouldn't ask him to do anything again. On the grounds, that you'd took enough 'fuck-up' cannon fodder from Peter, to kill a small army.

The market clock said five. Soon we'd have a full staff crew. All hands-on deck. Thank god. I could hopefully grab a coffee and smoke in partial peace.

The early customers appeared in dribs and drabs. From far and wide all over Wigan, Lancashire and then some. Vehicles pitch parked in their usual places. Some customers opted for the far end of the market. Or even around the back, in complete darkness. Heaven knows why? It wasn't as if they were harbouring a fruit and veg nuclear secret. Loading up specially cloned vegetables, Or semi-precious mushrooms!

Some customers would buy one or two items, from the closest stall to where they'd parked. Then walk 200 yards and buy a ship-load of gear from us.

Obviously, this meant more legwork for us barrow boys. Except the illustriously work-shy John and Tony of course. Everything they did was with the forklift. The quickest way. So, John and Tony always led me to believe. Paul and I christened them the lazy brothers. Peter called them glass-backs. They're forklifts would get where water can't. Their lazy un-founded forklift actions, on a busy morning would more often than not, cause constant mayhem. If two of the stalls four aisles, were blocked at any one time, it would result in total chaos. They would both often win amazingly varied levels of vocal abuse from both customers and staff alike. In some cases, un-happy or potential customers, would just hurl a torrent of abuse at them, and exit the stall in protest, and alternatively take their trade to Conroy's or Highams.

Five hours of 'good mornings' and plying our trade had simply flown by. Things had been going extremely well. The usual suspects, customers and clients had been in, and out and left reasonably happily, with their fresh cache. Orders had been rapidly compiled, stored and put ready for despatch. I was even enjoying my third cup of coffee. Work was still flowing as normal, until without warning, we became grid-locked, when sod's law was fully tested.

"Tony... move your fuckin forklift?" Tony looked straight through Paul as if he wasn't there.

"Fuck off why should I? I've got this lot, and at least two more for Connors. And his wagon's round the back. You'll have to go around Paul, I'm too busy." Paul glared at Tony in pure disgust. There were only four items on Tony's lonely pallet. Then came the voice of God.

"TONY! you heard Paul, shift it now. Right FUCKIN NOW!" Let's just say Peter had recently shown a more than vested in Tony. All events, concerning Tony's conduct were not good at all. In this particular instance, you could see Paul's point of view though. He had three full tickets, and he was loading by hand, on his own. From the floor, to the wagon. Then he'd have to jump on the back, and stack everything neatly, in such a way, that it couldn't fall off in transit. He'd got a pretty bad draw.

Greenways' of Ashton. They would kindly take pallets but wouldn't swap them for anything less than pristine. Pallets were the markets highest commodity. Goldust. And always in big demand for speed, and a fast turnaround. But as in the Good Book, you have to give to receive.

This was a strict rule of the market, and particularly at Churches. Sometimes, if the rule was kept in good stipulation; 'Fruit and Vegetable' by-laws- Paragraph 2, section Three [updated 1982, by Mr Peter Hill] (Churches LTD). Or the law according to H. You could find yourself fork- lifting orders into the back of transit vans. Easy life. But some smart-arse buyers came in with what could only be described as matchsticks for exchange. Such vagabonds were kindly advised to 'FUCK OFF!' by our Illustrious leader. Some days, we could get a late delivery or twenty! and have no spare pallets. It would be wise to think ahead, to avoid twice the work.

With no set break time, coffee times only came into play, if and when, or where. Or If at all?

But were mostly achieved in hiding or secretly. But I was on the book. Once again, a good place to be. Sometimes tea breaks came almost via conveyer belt, on a customer to customer basis, or just fast and furious. On a good day, I didn't put my hand in my pocket once.

In between the sales, I would be compiling orders. Got together for our drivers. Bill, Frank, Fat Bob and Me.

As in the aviation industry, how planes have a designated flight slot. So, did the bulk of our deliveries. Drivers were wholly responsible for correctly collating items and getting them from 'A' to 'B'. Market, to shop, supermarket, a beach, a brothel? Etc. If a single item was accidently omitted from a delivery. So were you. Verbally and orally, and almost with Peter's size nine up and down the market! *"Always double check everything's present and correct, ship shape and Bristol fashion."* Another quote from Peters compressed, and concise, pretend Bible. In the case of Tony orders, *"double and triple check?"* Before shutting doors, sheeting up and leaving.

There were set routes for best fuel efficiency, and they're even time coordinated. Frankie and big Bobs double drop's, are to Wigan's and Leigh's retail markets. They're wagons are always over full. Bordering on Illegal. By far, the whole markets biggest deliveries, and they drove both wagons down together, for an easier two-handed turnaround. Bill the 'fossil's' run was basically just a leisurely day out for him. You could call it, entertaining friends, on a free and easy casual, ad hoc basis. With no concept of time involved whatsoever. Because he'd been here donkey's years, most people turned a blind eye to It, and he'd blatantly got away with murder since 'Adam' was a lad. Or at least before I'd contemplated leaving my father's sac.

If Bill were furniture, he'd be worth money. As a delivery driver, or human being come to that, he was well past his sell by date. His forty something, years on the markets had gained him respect from most quarters. But not from where 1 was standing. His lazy bullshit had all worn a little too thin for me. As far as I was concerned, he'd milked it until it was empty. I'd already made my own mark, with the smallest but most expensive orders. I was the hotel, restaurant, and eating house, fruit and veg specialist.

FIVE

The market was now packed. Jonny Chu, our huge wagon driver had parked in his usual drop zone. As drivers go, Jonny was steady. A mountain of a man scouser, with a heavily receding hair line. Akin to a plump Bobby Charlton. A quiet man really. But fussy about his job description, He always arrived, with a make-shift, untidy load. Pallatted in typical dodgy Liverpool style. A float his recently acquired new wheels. Because of this, Jonny had a Mothers urge. To look after his new baby. He dictated every move around his offspring, to whoever was given the job of emptying it. Tony was allowed only limited access, to the bright, red and white, sign-painted super ship. Unless allowed otherwise, by Peter the higher power.

CHURCHES LTD [a B + R company] Wholesale Fruit and Vegetables.

A little fish in a big pond. This was our position, in the infrastructure of our parent

company. They bought us out, less than eighteen months ago. This was our trump card over our competitors. We looked small, or just a mediocre, tin-pot stall on the market. But we had the strength of a Roman Garrison, and the advertising power of Saatchi + Saatchi hidden in the wings. B & R were a massive conglomerate. We could buy our produce in bulk, from our partners internally. Then it was dished out, to all our other market branches. We simply dealt, direct with the main man. Therefore, increasing our margin of profit, twofold, sometime threefold! We went dealt directly to the farmers, in the same way. The bigger the order of produce, the cheaper the price. Our wagon arriving daily helped too. We looked 'fresh' every single day.

I looked over at the full to bursting wagon as Jonny pulled back its curtains. The pallets loads were very high today and looked risky.

It needed a softly, turned hand at the forklift controls. I decided drinking my tea was more Important. After he'd done his curtains, Jonny Chu was soon cab bound again, with no forklift license. He just claimed he couldn't drive forklifts. Which was a total lie? I'd been second man with him, picking up loads of times and seen him in full action on a forklift. Besides which, he was well into his tea flask now.

"Tony, go and unload the wagon please?" He looked at me like I had four heads.

"You must be jesting Inge, have you seen all these orders? I'll be here a fuckin week!"

Tony pulled out a handful of tickets and thrust them wildly in my face. With his last, aggrieved comment, Peter looked up from his sales book, and gave a look of thunder Tony's way.

I quickly snatched them from his hand, to look what meagre amount of stuff he had. They

somehow didn't look right.

"Who they for then?" I quickly eyed the tickets. "They're virtually blank you lying git! What's your game?"

"No! No Inge, they're not, look?" Tony looked shiftily over at Peter, then reached into his jacket pocket, to try to save himself from losing his mortal coil. He didn't say another word when his eyes met with Peter's.

Peter never said much unless he had to. But even so, he always knew exactly what was going on around him. In my opinion, Tony was already on his last thin ice. Peter would only take so much and that was you out the door. Sacked and promptly, Fucked off. Finished and out of a job for wasting God's valuable time.

"Excuse me please, but when's the fresh stuff coming off the wagon Inge? I'm in a bit of a hurr..."

"Erm, any minute now Mr King." Kingie. A little pushy but not a pure bastard.

"Tony where's.......... Paul?"

"You fuckin blind Inge? he's doing the wagon." I looked across the market again.

"Oh yeah... so he is. Tell Paul what you want, and he'll sort you out Mr King."

"Yeah, he is doing the fuckin wagon, but on my shagging forklift! Why couldn't he fuckin use Big Bertha? I'm sick of this." Tony's got everyone's attention with his big mouth now, I thought.

"Because he wouldn't get it in that gap-width fuckin ways, you stupid ginger prick!"

Peter interjected. Making his point and rapidly losing his temper.

"Just get on with your tickets Tony, and shut it, or **I**'ll really fuck you up with orders."

Tony no longer had the forklift mechanics and knew he now had to get physical. Soon his tension would be at boiling point. Excellent, I thought, I'm loving this.

French Cauliflower's are doing well today. Flying through the roof actually. I thought, sipping my tea. 1 could almost sense another load being ordered for Wednesday. Not a pleasing thought to look forward too. Suppose the Beer money would come in handy though. We'd got the cash in hand job of unloading them last year. We had a great payment plan with Peter too. We'd insisted on getting the readies, the day before we'd actually offloaded them. Never holding on to the dosh any longer than pub though.

We unloaded for all the market stalls. Five independent firms in all. We'd recently invested in another stall. So, storage wasn't a problem. And as cheap labour, we were the obvious choice.

The storage stall, was on the other side of the market, In-between Conroy's and Higham's crap emporiums. They usually came in around eight, or nine o'clock at night on an arctic.

Keeping our speed up, and with all cylinders firing. We could usually get the job knocked off, and just make it for last orders at the Ben Johnson. Just like we had last night.

31

"**L**et's get some extra crates Inge. Come on eh? Beer money. The thick French prat won't cotton on."

Tony had arrived pissed and swigging from a quarter bottle of whiskey. God only knows how he got to work without crashing his motorbike. Paul however, was fed up with his usual mental behaviour. Thanks partly to a recent bust up with Karen his girlfriend. Or 'bitch' as he affectionately called her and proceeded to rip into Tony

"Listen to me smart arse. What's gonna happen when he counts them up then thicko? He'll see there's some missing and report it. Then Peter will find out from the haulage company. Then we've got no jobs, right? Oh, then low and behold, I get angry, cos I even listened to you. And then I kick ten colours of shit out of you. And to put the Cherry on top, you eat hospital food. D'you get the message prick!"

Paul had made a particularly valid point. Here was Tony bladdered, and not content with his lot. Hatching stupid schemes to overthrow the French government. Not quite, but how very novel.

Tony had quite a temper too. As he later decided to show. We were about seventy-five boxes, or three pallets from finishing. Paul and I were on the wagon, lashing boxes in unison for all we were worth. Tony was sat on his sucker, on the forklift, swigging at his whiskey totally, regardless. Biding his time, for us to fill another pallet,

"Ok Tony take it away!" Immediately after Paul shouted this, the pallet lifted from the back of the wagon, and disappeared into the onion stall. Paul pulled another pallet from the side into its place, and we carried on. The space between the end of the wagon and our picking spot, was now well distanced. Too far, to just throw boxes into their final resting place. I'd made a partial stack, halfway between us, so Paul didn't have to keep bending so much. After another five minutes of solid humping, Paul hooked the last box of the twenty-five up into place and shouted again.

"Come on Tony, that's another. Take this next fuckin pallet away and hurry up about it. It's getting scarily close to last orders."

A couple of minutes had passed. I'd lit a smoke. We couldn't carry on until the last full pallet was shifted. Paul had walked to the back of the wagon to look.

"Where is he Inge...? TONY! Did you fuckin hear me? move this bloody...."

"I'm here, old yourrorses I'm comin. I was just makin a bit more room in the stall like."

"Just move your arse and shift it, you idle get! Throw me another pallet up we're one short," Paul said looking just about ready for a pint. I know I was.

After throwing up a pallet, Tony climbed back onto his seat. He was smiling and rubbing his hands together. It wasn't that cold was it? Mind you, I was sweating, thanks to the nonstop box humping. A strange little face appeared, at the side of the wagon.

"Escusee, you do have many to go please?"

"Who the fuck's that Inge?"

"Erm, not many now old pal. Two more pallets, I think. It's just the driver Paul." The driver acknowledged me with something like; "It's good ya- ya, I'm to Preston. Good, good."

Paul frowned and went into a Fawlty Towers sketch. "Hallo, hullo? hullo? I read it from a book. I Manuel, I come from Barcelona haha."

"Paul, he was Spanish." Paul was laughing loudly.

"Who's Spanish?" As I picked up another crate and turned around, I could see the nearly full pallet moving out of the back of the wagon. Paul was still throwing and smiling away at the French driver.

He went to launch his crate at the now empty space.

"Paul, LOOK OUT! There's no palle........!"

I was too late. Both Paul, and the crate he was still holding, flew out of the back of the wagon and landed in a crumpled heap, some six feet below, on the cold and wet but very solid concrete market floor.

"Shit, Aaaarrrgghh." he yelped. I closed my eyes and winced. Listening to a painful sounding crunch as our oblivious and pissed forklift driver left the scene. A moment or so later, Tony returned and promptly jumped off his forklift. "What's goin on? Are you okay Paul?"

"We did say take It away. But Paul hadn't thrown the last crate on." I told him.

Tony honestly hadn't a clue what had happened. He looked a bit upset about it. Despite this, 1 still had to get in-between them very fast.

"You fuckin.... ouch! You stupid, reckless, lazy, thick cunt! I could've broken my leg then. Shit! look at my hands. My bastard back's killing me." Paul was a little too injured to advance on Tony. There was roughly five minutes of arguing shouting apportioning blame. Mutual drinking of whiskey and wiping of blood. I firmly mentioned the possibility of missing last orders.

The French driver returned. Probably confused by all the commotion. He'd played no part, nor done nothing wrong. But he was going to get it, anyway. Probably just because he was French too. Talk about being in the wrong place at the wrong time. Fuck this, I thought. I'll leave them to it. Such is life I said to myself, shrugging my shoulders. I jumped back up onto the wagon and carried on stacking the final pallet of caulis. Thank fuck we'll be finished in a minute. I can almost taste the nectar.

After locking up the stall, I walked toward Jack's burning shed, to hide the stall key under the red brick. Jack was another of the market's part time madmen. When I arrived at the Ben, Tony and Paul must have been already in, about twenty-five minutes or so. They seemed to be in a better humour now. Tony was in full flow. Dribbling intently and laughing with a mouthful of lager.

"It's a good job you didn't throw my empty bottle too Paul."

"Why? I know you'd have ducked."

"Probably, but you might've hit the French frog, hahaha."

"I might too, hahaha. I didn't even know he was standing there?"

"Oh, alright Inge?" Tony spotted my entrance. As Paul relived the accident.

"Right behind me he was hahaha you piss-head."

"Paul here." I interrupted. "Here's that money you wanted. Who's got me this?"

A Guinness was adorning the table and begging for my attention.

"I've just got the round in Inge, No hard feelings mate?"

"Nothing to do with me Tony? I'm not the injured party. Look at his hands? cut to ribbons thanks to you?"

"Just grab your pint Paul, the cold will ease the pain. The taste will help ha ha-ha. There's plenty more where that came from, Tony said.

"But he's ugly though. What about that? Does that count Tony? haha."

"I don't know, but he can get the next round in. Fuckin Peter's pet hahaha."

"Your hilarious, real variety performance stuff Tony." I laughed.

"That's very funny, your very funny Tony. Thanks a bunch mate, thanks a lot." Tony was drunkenly enjoying his own comedy. But by the looks of things, Paul was seeing the funny side now too. His earlier serious stony-face was readily replaced with a scary white grin. A Hannibal Lecter kind of smile. Paul had realised he wouldn't be dipping into his own pocket at least for a little while yet. Come to think of it neither would Tony. I'd ordered a round as soon as

I walked in. Shit. Forgiven probably. Forgotten Never. All's well that ends well. We left the pub via the back door around midnight. Staggering well and professionally pissed.

SEVEN

Tuesday morning came. Work was always a bit easier to deal with after getting the first one out the way. Despite my on-going excesses of the previous night. John was in fine form. Even half my display was done.

"Morning Stephen. I got in earlier for letting the side down yesterday. We're all out of Coffee. Do you want tea or a soup?"

I surveyed John's nifty lay out of the stall.

"Mmm I'm Impressed John you've done well."

"You've didn't shit the bed, did you?" I smiled.

"Fuck off Stephen, you ungrateful sod. I can't do right for doing wrong. I should have kept my mouth shut while the going was good. Get your own fuckin drink," he replied storming off yet again.

"Sorry John, only joking. Got any change for the machine then?"

"Don't need change," he humped. "I put it on free."

I walked over to the machine and pressed for oxtail soup and went into the bottom office.

"John will you make sure you put it back onto pay before Peter gets here. He'll only lose the head if you don't."

"Yeah, yeah, right? What happened unloading last night Ste?"

John must've been inquiring about Tony and Paul's fracas. Best not say too much I thought. "Not a lot, nothing John. It was nothing. Minor disagreement that's all. It's sorted."

"Oh? it's just erm, what do I do with the pallet of caulis, behind Conroy's? I'll bring them around in a bit." He zoomed off.

"You what! what did you sa...... Oh fuck?" I was gobsmacked. Tony had done it. *"He said he would the bastard. He's robbed them? Shit, I didn't even see it coming? Or the Driver. Tony, you bastard! I didn't think he was sober enough? I bet he's forgot about them too? Fuck!"*

"Ste. who you talking too?" John was back on his three-wheeled walking attachment. As I told him the story, he just laughed in evil glee. He knew this was now my problem. "What do we do with them now John?"

"Less of the *WE*, Stephen. It's now't to do with me. If you don't tell me where you want them I'm not even touching them again. You could sell them on behind Peter's back. Dodgy Derek or even Alan Lightfoot? Make yourself a few quid?" John had a point. He's probably half right there, I agreed to my tempter.

In all walks of life, there's rogues, villains, or rip off merchants. The market was no

different.

"Good thinking John. We won't get much, but as long as Peter doesn't find out we're golden." I said trying to goad him into my plan.

"I've told you once, less of the wee Ste. I'll bring em round. After that I'm having nothing to do with it."

"Ok, just stick them over in the onion stall. I'll deal with it later."

As he scooted away, my brain shifted up a gear and bounced questions off itself, as I rambled aloud.

"Alan will want them delivered. I wonder if I could put them on a wagon? Is he due a delivery today?" Yesterday was pretty bad. But now with this, today was heading in exactly the same direction. *'Fuck it'* I decided. I'm not carrying the can for Tony. I'd say I miscounted. That was the only way. Then the whole sorry shit, would fall on Peter's back.

I'd just finished off the display and went to the comer of the market to look. Until then, I only had John's word the caulis even existed. The craftily hidden anomaly was sandwiched between Jack's burning shed, and my old scrapped Viva. I'd parked It up there months earlier. Romantic trips out for me and Linda. Good idea at the time. But instead just left to rot. Suddenly, I heard Peter's car pulling up. I may as well strike while the irons not. He might be in a more controlled and relaxed mood than yesterday. That wouldn't be hard.

"Morning Peter?"

"Morning Inge. Everything go alright last night?"

"Well, erm yes, erm I mean, no." His expression never faltered.

"Good, what time did the Arctic turn up? Was it late again? I'll fuck them on the phone later. Are the Caulis alright? We've had some crap off them in the past?"

"No Peter, the wagon wasn't late, and the cauli's are good. It's just, erm, the amount really." I waited for a reaction.

"Fuck, don't tell me we're short. I'll ring them now the French bastards."

Peter as ever, was jumping in at the deep end, and drowning.

"We're hardly short, were erm, over."

"Over? by how many?" I fastened my safety belt and closed my eyes.

"A pallet full. Twenty-five crates."

"Fucking excellent Inge. How did you manage that? At this point, I wasn't complaining either. I'd survived. I decided to milk the cow. There must be a good few gallons available here, I thought.

"Oh, I just miscounted. Added up wrong. Sorry won't happen again."

"Don't be fuckin sorry Inge. You can do that again, any time. Just don't get caught. Here, go and get two coffees Inge. There's the right change." I walked away, happily flicking the money into the air. It suddenly dawned on me we had none of the magic drink that kept Peter bearable. I hadn't taken a bad word yet? Apart from off John. Coffee-less a sad looking? I'd probably be ripped limb from limb now, slowly?

"Peter, we're all out of coffee. I forgot to tell you to order some more sorry."

He smiled. "You did remind me Inge here." His car keys came flying toward me. I cupped my hands to catch them.

"Big fob one opens the boot. There's a box of refills in the boot, under my raincoat. Hurry up. Customers will be wanting a hot drink shortly. Bring the forty fags out the front too."

I made my way to the far end of the market where Peter parked his 'beast'. Well out of any harm's way. Such as, weaving Tony driven forklifts. Damage limitation, or simply using his brains. Peter trusted no one, near his pride and joy. I was lucky, even to be holding the keys. As I opened the boot, the car let out an ear piercing 'shrill'. 'Waoowh waoowh'.

"Sorry!" I shouted. *How was I to know your fuckin alarm was on'* I muttered. I went quickly back to the stall, fully laden with tea, coffee, soup and hot chocolate. At the machine, I re-stocked the empty Innards. Pressed for two coffees and locked back up. Remembering to flick the free switch off. I slid his thirty pence into my jeans and resumed the morning. Peter had decided, he could get away with the extra twenty-five crates, and promised a drink in it for me. All I had to do was keep quiet. Mouth wide shut.

"I'll just blag the haulage company Inge. They owe me one anyhow."

Who was I to doubt him? If I could sell fruit and veg, half as well as him, I'd be doing well. John walked back on the scene after a lengthy visit to the toilet. He probably didn't even need to go. Not even for a crafty smoke. It was just laziness, or possibly a little tiredness setting in at the end of his shift.

"Ste, have you sussed out your little situation with Peter then?"

Very inquisitive my brother when he wanted to take the piss. But more especially when money or his personal gain was concerned. Either that, or he'd seen us talking.

"Yeah, he said he'd erm, make it right with the erm wagon people."

That should keep him off fuckin the scent, I agreed to myself.

"Oh good, so have I." John smiled.

"I, you what?" Calm yourself Stephen. I said to myself. Play it cool.

"How do you mean John?"

"Peter said he was pleased about the stall, and the three big Wigan orders I'd got

ready."

"So, what, it's what you're paid for?"

"Yes, I know, but he found out about yesterday remember? I was late thicko."

"Oh, oh that's right."

He shook his head in confusion.

"What did you think I meant?"

"Nothing John nothing. Erm, well done Bro, well done."

Tony hadn't shown up this morning. Even Paul was late. Things were really pushed, to say the least. Looking around though, you wouldn't think so. Peter was sharing a joke with Alan Lightfoot. Possibly being cauliflowerd to death. Paul was swimming in oxtail soup, with John Fellows, as John's wife looked on steely eyed. Loading up their van, alone and uttering torrid, un-complimentary expletives, as no one listened.

John Fellows, a very strange man indeed. God knows how his wife puts up with him. A weird, but likeable, country bumpkin. Very hard to stay on his wave-length, even for me. He always talked about telly documentaries, In his own, strange and inimitable way. Since he obviously existed, on another planets astral-plane. He'd made up, unfathomable, pet names for everyone. Tony was the 'wood gnome'. I could never figure out why. The only one I could ever make sense of, was 'The Broomraker' A word twist on the James Bond film and nickname, to Jack the market cleaner.

As I was serving the Fellows clan, who I soon learned, were in with their baby boy, tucked in the front seat and wailing loudly. Due to the rapid thrashing around, of the lone Mrs Fellows in the back. In strolled Dave Wilson, right between us. Severely dislocating my conversation with John, who wasn't his best fan either. As Dave walked past, John swung his leg mock- kicking Dave up the arse, as he passed. "Lookie there, it's inspector gadget. Put your hands up you're under arrest."

John mentally announced.

"Fuckin wanker." I sanely agreed,

A pure arse-licking creep. Wilson or spongy, slimy, shitbag to his friends. He always insisted, only being dealt with, or served by Peter. Dealt with he was, on a regular basis. Took to the fuckin cleaners more like. Peter hated him. You could see, the negative candour and body language Peter afforded him.

"Morning Peter a nice selection of stuff today."

Peter slowly looked around, scribbling into his sales book. A very long pause later.

"Erm, yeah, morning David. Inge I'm just off for a burst. See to David while I'm gone will you."

Peter said it loud enough, so Dave would get the subliminal message, and he sloped off like a Cheetah on acid. Dave looked on, harangued and snubbed, as I waved the fellows clan off.

"Right then John, I said slamming his van door. That's the lot, you old reprobate. See you again the morrow."

"Morning Dave, can I help you?"

"Erm no thanks, I'm just going to get myself a drink Inge. Peter might be back by then."

He sloped off. leaving a shiny slug trail behind him.

"The feeling's mutual, I don't want to serve you either!" I turned and grabbed a hand cart to load up another order. *"Stuff you, you fuckin leech."* I muttered.

Just then, Roy walked into the stall. Our second most prominent salesman.

At once, Dave miraculously re-appeared, like a broken record.

"Good morning Roy. Nice selection of caulis today. You haven't got ten pence spare for a good customer have you Inge?"

"I've no change Dave, sorry." He was getting fuck all from me. Roy, ungratefully came to his aid.

"Let me get my coat off first David, I think I've some, erm, change here somewhere?"

"Right you are Roy right you are. hahaha." Roy quickly called me into the office.

"Where's H Inge?"

"He's gone the bog Roy."

"Bollocks, serve that greasy, low-life for me Inge."

"Sorry Roy, no can do. I'm on with Mr J's stuff for tomorrow. Just started it." I smiled walking away.

"Bollocks!" Roy mumbled a loose comment in. "Why do I always get the vomit suckers?"

"No one wants to know what keeps your ears apart, Roy, haha." Tony piped up.

"Shut it Tony. Or I'll have your job, you ginger tit."

Roy hung his coat, very studiously. Then fished into his pocket and threw twenty pence in Dave's direction.

"Here, I'll have one of same too."

Roy, or 'Brillo', due to his uncanny likeness to one, was the top fruit buyer. In fact, our only fruit-buyer. I didn't really count.

Dave soon sluggishly attached himself to Roy's side. Roy in Dave's

eyes is; as high and mighty as Peter. Not like us underlings.

"There you are Roy, one coffee. This one's on the house hahaha."

I looked over at Roy and gave him a piss-taking thumbs up. He gave out a visibly reluctant smile. As I caught his eye, I could read his silent lips, mouthing me to 'fuck off'. I greeted it with a piss-taking wide smile.

The markets toilet block, was just behind the fish stall. As I gazed over, I could see Peter on his way back. With his usual JPS, cancer stick, hanging from his lips. Usually, H couldn't escape Dave. He'd got away with serving him today though. H had cunningly, just used delay tactics. He'd slowly, waltzed back and was chatting to anyone who possessed a heartbeat, or who, had absolutely anything at all, to say to him, until Dave, finally succumbed to Roy's sales patter.

By the time 10-30 had arrived, most of the stale-warts had been in, and done their shop-shopping and left. Back to their-own retail outlets. Stalls, supermarkets, shop's, and even garages. Our deliveries were in full flow, and I was about to leave too. I was just studying and checking my last tickets when Peter strangely appeared from the upstairs office. We never saw him after ten or so? He was usually up to his eyes in paperwork, or organising the following days new stock, and processing sales tickets, smoking, farting and drinking coffee.

He came down the stairs and shouted toward me. Rapidly, cupping his words, with his cigarette loaded hand, as if he were secretly selling drugs.

"Inge, a word." I suddenly found myself, whispering and selling drugs as well.

"Yeah, what's up H? do you need a fix man? Do you want some good shit? I've got some good skunk'.

There was no acknowledgement whatsoever.

I started laughing. "Some crack-cocaine then?"

He smiled. "Stop dicking about Inge!" He tried to stay serious. "Listen Inge, this is serious. Have you any mates who want work? got to be reliable though?"

"Why, H? I thought we had enough bodies?" Peter got very serious. As if he'd, just secretly soiled himself. That was what was stupidly going through my mind, anyway.

"I don't want more bodies, new bodies. I think you know what I'm talking about."

In fun, I winked at him. "Ooh saucy, I suppose I do, big boy," I said, as he reluctantly smiled.

"Stop pissing about Inge!" I stopped grinning and straightened my Tempter ridden face. "Why don't you give him a warning first, he might get the message then, and wise up?"

"Warning? I'm sick of giving him warnings. Already tried that, three times... and a fuckin written one! Not to mention, threatening to re-arrange his fuckin ginger face. There's no more last chances, I've fuckin had it with him. He's out the door. And he fuckin knows it. Give him this envelope. It's his final notice letter."

Mmm I thought, Tony had kept this lot quiet. Wonder if Paul knew Tony's had his marching orders and hadn't let on to us? "Well H, I could erm, have a word with little Eric to come back, full time, Instead of just cash in hand. He's out of work at the minute."

"Right Inge, Eric'll do. That sounds good enough to me. He knows the score here. Just sort it as soon as possible, for fucks sake. But keep this under your hat too, right?" Peter lit a shit stick up. "Anyway, you shouldn't be here, go and get your stuff delivered. Don't be long though. Bill's on his way back with the butties." Peter sullenly climbed back up the office stairs. "Oh. by the way Peter, I meant to ask you yesterday. Are my holidays booked in now?"

"Yes Inge, you're off from Friday, this week. Just like you asked for. All the more reason to get Eric in as soon as possible."

"Righto, erm brilliant, thanks for that H."

Mmm, Bill's on his way back already? Wonder what's up with him? I'm fuckin starving too. If I decided to wait for Bill, I really would be late. That would please Ken Green Immensely, said my Tempter.

I knew my bacon and egg would be stone cold when I returned. Stuff it, I thought, I'll get a pie out on my rounds.

The radio didn't work in our transit. Fat Bob had brought a portable radio-cassette in to compensate. Despite his bad taste, he did love his music. Only last week, I found myself decapitating a Rolling Stones cassette. My left foot had found it accidentally, just pressing the clutch.

I climbed into the dusty, chip-paper ridden cab, and slammed the door. The driver door window-glass dropped completely out of sight. *"Fuckin heap of shit"* I grumbled.

As I started the engine to leave the market, a Tomato made a squashing *thud!* on the windscreen, Followed by Pauls familiar voice.

"Inge Inge!"

"What d'you want? I'm fuckin late!" I played with the defunct glass in the door as Paul spoke.

"Do us a favour Inge. Will you nip to my mums when you're out please? Go on, you can do it on your way back."

"Jesus, what the fuck for Paul?" I wasn't keen.

"Just tell her to give you a tenner out my savings. Go on, I'll tell her your coming."

"Tut, fuck.................... erm, Ok. Does she know where to lay her hands on your dosh when I get there?"

"She should do... it's in her fuckin purse. I just can't save up at all, so she does it for me."

"Hmmnn, what's it for Paul, that is, if she asks?"

"You know damn well Inge."

"I do know damn well, but if she asks I mean? am I talking Swahili again?" I moaned.

"Oh, right erm... petrol, that'll do."

"Ok, if she's not in, I'll lend it you." I reached over for the seat belt, to show him my avid willingness to go. "By the way Paul, My time off's sorted for next week. I can't bloody wait haha."

"Good. Just don't forget my money Inge." He didn't give a damn about my hols. All he was Interested In was his beer dosh.

I was fast becoming Paul's personal money lender or loan shark. I'd have to invest in a baseball bat soon. "Where are we going after work anyway Paul?"

"The Freemason's Inge." With that, I turned on the van engine, geared up, and shot out of the main gate, like an F1 car on pole position, to the words;

"DON'T FORGET!" ringing in my ears.

EIGHT

There were four drops on today's run. Carrington catering, Ken Greens shop, Stokes's shop and last but not least, The Beech's restaurant. Not a bad round trip, and all pretty close together. The van was low on diesel, due to the fact that the van was never still. Hence the wrecked interior. I decided to fill up first, not just the van, but also my five-gallon drum. Hidden very well, in the rear spare tyre compartment. More essential beer money, when I sold a full drum to our next-door neighbour, mad Mick, the digger driver. I quickly filled the drum and van at our B P account garage. Then headed off to my first port of call Carrington's.

"Good morning Rupert, alright mate?"

"No not really. Where have you been? I wanted this lot an hour ago?"

Rupert Carrington. Rich and posh, with a perfect English speaking voice. He put me in mind of Sir Alec Guinness. What it might say on his CV? Friend of Politicians, local bigwigs, celebrities and maybe Royalty. Much of that, and maybe more. He was probably a secret Freemason as well. Personally, I just thought he deserved a hammer on his head occasionally, or at regular intervals.

I never in two years, had I heard him swear, let alone, raise his voice.

Apart from the obvious chivalry and pots of dosh, ok fine.

But then I would say that? Knowing I could always make a good few quid out of him. Lightening lies, were always omnipresent, in my sales patter to Rupee-babe. Another John Fellows conundrum?

"To tell you the truth Rupert, It's because of your order, I'm late old pal."

"Because of my order, sorry, I don't understand?"

"Asparagus pal, asparagus! I had to wait for it. Roy was late back you see."

I was quickly emptying the van. Easier and more rapidly when you've got a totally confused ex-private school helper.

Rupert was the catcher as I threw.

"But that really isn't my fault Stephen. I ordered the asparagus last Friday?"

"Ah well, not to worry Rupert, it's here now."

Rupert had opened the asparagus box, to check the condition of the costly green Elves spears.

"Yes, it is, and good it looks good too. Very good and fresh, well done Stephen. Well done that man" He said, as we off-loaded. I launched into a random, impromptu, ad-lib song; "Oh Rupee baby, you foxy lady, you drive me crazy, I want your babies!" He looked on, both frowning and smiling, as I continued to overpower him with the thrown boxes. His ill mood had eased as he stacked his last box of

tomatoes on the floor.

"Right Stephen, is that everything?" He eyed his ticket, and then his order, marking off each item as seen. I walked toward the van passenger door.

"Mushroom's? Where's my mushroom's oh darn it, they're not here? I can't see them? You'll have to go back and quickly. I've to prepare......"

"Wow... wow! Rupee, calm down. I've got them over here in the front."

"Where? I can't see any?"

"Front... meaning the cab.... in the cab Rupert!"

Rupert boldly threw himself into the van, and poked his head over the seats, like shamus did, out the window, on a car journey.

"But they'll get hot in the front and blacken. You don't understand Stephen... what I do........ It's all about the look, and the presentation......, see if you......"

Rupert was about to go into one. An all-out lecture, on the rise and fall of five perfectly good boxes of mushrooms. I had to curtail his mushroom-brooding, emotional state.

"The heater's fucked!"

"Pardon?"

"The heater.... It doesn't work Rupert...... comprende?"

"Yes but...."

"Oh God, I'll say it again, slowly with gaps! The-heater-doesn't-fuckin-work!" he stopped suddenly, as if been hit by a Star Trek Stun ray.

Rupert was comparable to Basil Fawlty when he'd done something terribly wrong and Sybil had just found out.

He sat down, on what he thought was an empty red box. Sadly, for him, this turned out to be a box of Ken Greens tomatoes.

A large *squelch* quickly ensued, as the packaging collapsed, into its contents.

"Oh dear, oh no" Rupert slowly picked himself up, and quickly climbed out the back of the van.

"I'm so sorry I must apologise. I went a bit silly then, didn't I? I must have looked a right fool?" *Just looked,* I thought.

"I never saw a thing Rupert. Just sign this ticket for me old pal." He readily obliged. I couldn't be bothered consoling him, I'd enjoyed the incident too much.

"Right, I've got to get on Rupert. People will be ringing up, wondering where I am. See you next time. If you need any more asparagus or 'special's' give us a bell."

"Here Stephen, something for all your trouble. Once again, I'm very sorry."

Rupert was pretty high up on our customer tip list. Today was no exception. I was on a winner, or crushed tomato hush money? He'd palmed me a five-pound note.

I was just finishing off the last remnants of an apple as I arrived at the Beeches. A well-renowned posh local restaurant in Standish. With a menu, and reputation that went well before it. For me, and other similarly working-class folk, so did its prices.

Serving dishes, I'd never even seen, let alone tasted before. Venison, quail and grouse.

Even fish delicacies, lobster, crab, squid, and even caviar. Jimmy, the

owner, got these in fresh, every day. Picked up from Wigan train station. Bought direct, from a large London supplier. "My fish-man sells to the Savoy you know lad." This statement, Jimmy, was quick to ram this statement down my throat-sideways, every time I served him. But he was proud, and happy of his little empire. Who wouldn't be? Driving around in a top of the range BMW and living in an enormous house, on the posh-side of Wigan

I was hoping he wouldn't be about? I was lucky. Five minutes in and out. I left his ticket nestled in his mange-tout. Normally, it would be half an hour delivery, minimum. 'Lad' this, 'lad' that. That's expensive 'lad'. When I'm in my villa In Spain 'lad'.

Sometimes I was never sure if he even knew my real name?

Away to Stokes's now. I'll get the motor-mouthed, know it all 'younger' stokes son out

of the way before Kens, I resolved.

After his old man's retirement, Brian had just taken over the reins. Being some-what

green, after years as a taxi driver, he was still finding his way as the top man of Stokes's. He had to pick it up quickly. His dad was taking a weekly wage for the hand over. Plus, for his thirty years trouble, keeping it afloat. At the maximum hourly rate to boot. Who could blame him? With five other full-time staff as well, Brian was finding it a bit of a struggle, to say the least. Daddy had dropped in today though, to keep things selling in the right direction. The fact that he was just bored with retiring, was obvious. But the older customers liked to see him, still kicking around the shop. Reminiscing of the old times; 'Before the war don't you know?'.

Stokes's had an old brick outhouse. Just a big, un-used toilet block round the back. I'd reversed in as usual, for a quick getaway. One of his staff was waiting for me to offload, then he could get his pickup in. I edged the van, in-between the wall, and door. A tight squeeze to say the least. Bill would have had no chance.

"Yo, mate here," I pulled alongside.

"Give this ticket to Brian, will you? Everything's there. See you again." I drove away and stopped at the end of the narrow alley. Quickly looking left and right. As I did,

I spotted Brian in the mirror. He'd come outside, to see what the commotion was.

I beeped on my horn, gave him the classic, two-finger salute and was gone.

Ken's shop was only about fifty yards down the same main road, in the centre of Pemberton. It was always busy around the back of Ken's. With all the other shops people, and the police station too. Like a tiny M25, With equal traffic congestion. Because of this, and the obvious bonus of customers seeing a 'fresh delivery'. Ken always gave me access at the front. This allowed me full 'blimping' rights for potential new shagging partners, both using the shop, and passing by. Well, you should always keep your options open.

"Wee bit late Ken, sorry mate. There's temporary traffic lights near Rupert Carrington's. I nearly hit a car coming through." Any excuse or lie, for an easy turn around delivering.

"I bet you did Inge." Ken twitched his nose like Samantha Stephens in Bewitched.

"Was you out on the motion lotion again last night Inge?" I'd been rumbled. Good job he was kidding. "Phew, I'm lucky you're not in your full sergeant's uniform today Ken." I laughed.

"Just get my stuff off quick Inge? They're waiting for more Bananas in there.

Inge, your couple of beers, would put me out of commission for a week! With the shop, and as for the wife well.... I'll say no more."

Yeah, quit while you're ahead Ken I thought. She's a fuckin dwarf any way and a fuckin ugly dwarf at that.

Ken was a cash man, and meticulous to the last. Once, I even found him putting pen

marks on the sides of his chosen boxes of produce. If you turned up with his delivery, with unmarked boxes, you were simply made took them back Pronto! and told in no un-certain terms. Then you had to make a fast return, with his original marked up ones. With a thousand apologies. As well as selling fruit and veg. Ken had a few other side-lines in his shop. Crisps, casserole sauces, oxo, milk, etc. And lastly, my favourite. Hot Twiss's pies.

"There you go, all present and correct Ken.

"It is Inge..., it is, good man." He'd already checked! "There're some apples to go back though? Through, into the shop on the left." He ushered me forward.

"I've spoken to Roy, he knows about them, Ok?" I loaded the incriminating bad apples into the van, then went back inside. "Ken, give me a meat and potato please."

As I reached into my pocket to get some loose change, he interrupted.

"Here Inge, there's two. Good and hot. Favour for a favour Inge."

"You're really not as bad as they make out Ken. I don't know why they call you haha. I think you're really a decent cha.......!"

"Get off with you Inge and sling your bloody hook."

He walked back into his shop with a wry smile. At least Ken could take it as well as give it. I couldn't imagine the last exchange of words with Dave stinge-bag Wilson. Talk about miserable. Scrooge wasn't in it. I said my goodbyes and jumped in the van, back to the market.

Back at base, I opened the side door. Paul came walking out the stall. I lifted the apples on to a handcart ready for Roy's scrutiny.

"Did you get my money Inge?"

"Oh shit, I knew there was something?" Paul's face didn't exactly light up with joy.

Neither had mine. I'd have to sub him now, just keep him happy.

"I'll sort you out Paul, no probs. Just remember, I want it straight back on pay day".

"Cheers, I might need a bit extra though. Karen's coming up to the pub, when we've finished. You should get Linda there too, we'll make it a foursome."

"Not a chance Paul! No women allowed after work. Not for me that mate. Time alone for me only. Drinking time. Besides. I see enough of her, anyway."

Paul was keen on Karen, and in my opinion, going a bit soft. He knew I only saw Linda on my terms. Besides which, it was sort of over between us. From my point, it was getting too much. I liked my own space occasionally. For drinking, smoking and going out with the boys. Generally, all acceptable forms of escapism, alcohol and self-abuse.

That was getting barely possible, with Linda's 24-7 badly attempted control of me. Now Ok, on one hand, it's always good to have your oats on tap. But there are limits.

Note; In every facet of my normal, everyday life. I seemed to have an Angel occupying my right shoulder. Doing a good job of keeping his tenancy agreement. Looking after me, helping with decisions, advising my general up-keep, to the better good really. While all the time, a mischievous Devil, was blatantly using 'squatters- rights' to wreak havoc on the other. My tempters of good and evil. On the particular Linda situation, the devil tempter was winning hands down, by more than a short-head! But there was, forever a pitched battle between them. Heavy internal conflict in my head. Maybe I should bring her along after work? Paul did have a point? But then so did the little red tempter?

"I might bring her Paul, let's just wait and see. I might be picking up lettuce today though? We'll see how I get on?"

This was my 'get out of jail free' card. Unknown to Paul, I'd written in extra options for myself. Just bending the rules to suit myself.

"Your sarnies on the heater in the office Inge. I'll carry on getting the gear in. Is there a delivery for us later or what?"

"Yes Paul, but not fruit. Jonny Chu's gone to Moluneux's, for spuds and spring cabbage. I've made extra room for them. So, he can unload himself. We won't be here will we Paul." I fixed a knowing glance to him, which was quickly intercepted, smiled, and openly given the thumbs up.

I climbed the steps to the top office. As I opened the door, the smell of charred paper, and bacon, wafted into my nostrils. Bill swivelled his chair to face me. Dropping ash on to the carpeted as he did. Luckily for Bill, going unnoticed by everyone else. He burped straight in my direction. In a feeble attempt to mask his pig ignorance, he loudly coughed, and dropped an empty brown bag from his lap, at the same time,

"There s your toasted sandwich Inge. Bacon and egg, wasn't it?" I picked up the brown bag and looked inside at the cremated remains.

"There's no brown sauce on this Bill?"

"Oh, erm, well I asked for it? There was sauce on mine lad."

"Self, self, fuckin self," I thought.

The angel and devil tempters in my head, re-animated instantly.

"Oh yes, I bet there was sauce on yours? I bet there was extra bacon too? You, fuckin fat, lazy bastard!"

"But he might have forgotten too? Forgive him he is old you know?

"Piss off good Angel, you do-good bastard!" I thought.

I had to whole-heartedly agree with the devil tempter.

What once, would be a joy to eat, was now dry pork scratching, on flat, burned, rock-hard toast. Iced over, in melted-margarine, and topped with, what now looked like, a joke rubber egg. Hote-cuisine indeed.

Peter put down his pen, looked up from his desk, and lit a JPS up.

"Inge, when you've finished your butty, start the stock will you? Oh, and do us all a favour please? Will you eat that stinking thing downstairs? Sandra's moaning about the smell."

"Are you sure it's not Bill's arse your all smelling? Hahaha." My quip was ill-advised and angrily rejected. In a trice, Roy, Peter and Bills heads spun around in unison. As if joined on a spring. They black looked me and turned back just as readily. Mmm, I think I get the message. I thought.

Even though I hadn't brought the offending article In, I still felt slightly guilty. *"Don't have a guilty conscience,"* the devil tempter said. *"Fuck them, fuck the lot of them!"*

I picked up the stock-board and walked out of the office. Slamming the door, as I went, in sheer disgust. As I got to the bottom of

the stairs, I kicked the rubbish bin and threw the charred sandwich bag in it, in anger.

Paul was sat on an orange box stack, with a cup of tea and finishing off his sandwich too.

"Are you going picking up then Inge?"

"No Paul, Bill is. He's leaving the stuff on overnight. So, throw him some pallets on his pickup. If we don't, it'll be more work hand-balling them off tomorrow ok?"

Paul duly obliged.

"Paul! I shouted, I'm gonna start the stock."

"Ok Inge, I'll finish putting the display away. That's all there is outside now." Paul was fishing through the bin.

"Are you fuckin sick or what?"

"Nope, just hungry Inge."

"You're welcome to it Paul, I had a pie at Ken's."

"I'll give you a hand when I've finished this." He crunched into the solid toast. "Two heads are better than one, know what I mean Inge?"

"Ok old pal."

I started counting in the fridge. Its full capacity was seven pallets. Today was an

unusual exception, due to the distinct lack of salad greens. Paul had also made it easier, the way he'd put the stuff in. He'd left good walking gaps. I could get in-between each pallet. The fridge was usually straight-forward, anyway.

"All done in here Paul."

"Right coming." Paul pushed in the last pallet inside, and slammed shut, the knackered door.

"Back in two sec's Inge, just add four bags of spuds on." Mmm, the display must all be

away then, I thought. Stock was pretty easy to count up. Everything was mirror stacked. The same amount on every tier. Multiplied by how many high, and how deep.

"Inge, I'll go do the onion stall, speed things up.

"No, Paul you count everything, I'll write." He agreed my way was better. There was valuable drinking time on the line now.

"Ok, you're up to here aren't you?" He pointed to my counting spot.

We walked around the stall, with Paul shouting out. Sandra watched us, through the window of her office, smiling, as if she wanted her knickers ripping off?

Mmm, let's face it, she was married to the main man of the firm, and probably didn't get much in the bedroom department. Despite her reasonably young, middle age looks. I bet she'd probably would play away from home, if she could get away with it too? That was my wishful thinking, anyway.

As we collated the stock, Bill came fatly wobbling down the stairs. Heading for his fat pickup truck, to his local fat boozer. 'The Cambridge' in Burscough. One of those place's you can't find until you realise you've just driven through it!

"You gonna give us a lift counting this lot Bill?" Paul goaded him. He hated the fact that Bill always got an early dart, almost as much as me.

"I can't lad. I've lettuce to pick up yet. I bet you two finish work well before me?"

"Yeah, I fuckin bet Bill! don't strain yourself too much, with the fuckin lettuce." Paul had another dig. Bill just Ignored him and carried on his fat penguin impression.

Where Bill picked up from, was close to his house, and local boozer.

Jim Johnson's farm. I'd been there myself, many times. The farm labourers loaded you up as soon as you drove in. Paul didn't know this. I decided, best to keep my mouth shut for fear of repercussions. Besides, I wanted this stock counted.

"86 Spanish, 145 English, 78. French and 28 Pickling onion's... SHIT!"

"What's up Paul?"

"It's these Swede's? I can't count them? they're all over the place, look at them?"

"It's ok Paul, I know how manys there. It's a full cage remember? The one you took off Jon's wagon? Peter said put them out of the way, so I hid them there, till the others have gone.

"Sound, we've only got the onion stall now Inge? Then we're all finished. I'll go and get the keys." I had to stop him in his tracks.

"Paul hold it? no need. It's all counted, look?" I showed Paul my list, detailing the stall's contents. "I did that lot while you were doing the fridge."

"So, we're finished then?"

"Yep, I just hope it all tallies, up right?"

"Fuckin great. I'm gonna ring Karen then. Get me an outside line for the phone when you go upstairs Inge?

I'd only scribbled the last few things down, and they still needed adding up.

"Hold your horses Paul? It's all got to tally with the sales tickets upstairs yet? Are you on a promise or what? Ring her up from the pub when we get there. We could be bloody ages upstairs doing that yet?"

Two hours later, and lots of thinking, arguing, shouting and excuses, to make the figures just look right, we'd finished. Peter wasn't happy, but he had to leave early, to pick up his sproggs from school. It was a bit of a let off, really. We'd have to do a lot better than that tomorrow. We quickly left the smoke ridden upstairs office, and I was left behind to shut up shop.

Terrible stock day gone. Phew! I was finally on my way to see the lovely Mary. My favourite barmaid in the Freemason's Arms. Stock hadn't gone as well as planned. Paul had already made it there on his motorbike. Leaving me, somewhat trailing behind, on my knackered, sorry excuse for a push-iron.

"Hello Paul, your late? What time D'you call this?"

"Don't ask Mary, bad stock day. Loads of stuff was missing, and nothing added up at all. I'll have the usual, please?" Mary bent down to get a pint glass.

"You'll have to have Carling instead Paul. The Stella's gone."

"Ok, and give me two Mary, I've got a thirst on."

"Where's Tony and Stephen?"

"Tony's not been in today the lazy bastard."

"Oh, dear Paul, a bad hair day?"

"Yeah, summat like that Mary, he always has a bad fuckin hair day, the ginger twa.......! sorry."

Paul bent forward, to free the loose change in his pockets. Located the crumpled up twenty-pound note I gave him, and threw it on to the bar, in front of Mary.

It came to a slippy stop in a small pool of spilt lager.

"How's the bandit situation Mary?" Paul enjoyed blowing all his money on the reels. I didn't. If he lost, I'd have to lend him more money, which I didn't really have to give.

"No one's been near it since I started. It's not switched on either. Where did you say Stephen is?" Paul picked up his first full pint off the bar. "Oh, Inge is on his way. He won't be long."

I was on good form. Flying down the dual carriageway, on what I thought was now a totally rejuvenated back tyre. Just pumped up at the BP garage, opposite the Ben Johnson. Over inflating it proved to be a really bad move.

More so, after less than five minutes into my destination, when it decided to blow after one too many rubs with the brake calliper.

"Bollocks!" I said to myself loudly, as I careered onto the embankment, rolled over twice, hit a new sapling. Stopping in a sour heap. "Bollocks, bollocks, shit!" I quickly stood up to survey the scene. Did anyone see me? Probably was on a main road. I shiftily looked up and around. Picked up the wrecked excuse for a bike and walked the remaining ten minutes to the ale house. I pushed the bike through the back gates and laid it against the empty kegs. Sometimes it stayed there for two or three days. Until which, 1 usually gave in and went to collect it, as an excuse to go and see Mary. Or just that I'd had enough of traipsing to and from work.

As I opened the double doors, I could see Mary pulling a pint. She looked me up and down.

"Here Steve love, this is yours, you mucky bugger." She passed me a full pint of lager. So full, I had to take a sip to stop it from spilling.

"Cheer's Mary."

I glanced around. Paul was totally engrossed in losing his, or my money. I decided music was needed, to cheer myself from the bike crash, and made my way over to the jukebox. The Freemasons, got new sounds in every Monday.

"Any requests Mary?"

"No Stephen, just go on with what you're doing."

Mary and I had a strange affection for each other. I couldn't describe it. A weird

affinity. Not really of the biblical sense. God, she was nearly old enough to be my mother.

It was just a nice knowing or understanding of each other. I think sometimes, other people could see it too, but rarely commented, just endured it. When we got talking to each other, people, rarely got a look in.

"You took your time Inge, why you were so long?" Paul asked.

"Yeah, I went back to give Jonny Chu a lift un-loading the spuds. I'm like that Paul. Kind-hearted."

"Yeah.... fuckin stupid that way you mean!"

I had to lie. It was just, well, easier.

If I explained what really happened with the bike, I'd be doing myself no favours.

"I've got a surprise for you Inge!"

"Oh yeah really?... go on? thrill me......? You want some more bloody money?"

"No, Karen's coming in a bit."

"Yes, I know, you've told me that once."

"Ah, I know I have, but wait for it, she's bringing her new best mate, your Linda."

I quickly took take the name in.

"You bastard....... Paul! Linda? She's the last person I wanted to see. D'you realise you've just spoilt my afternoon. I'm not going to get any sleep tonight now either! you prat! You really are a dick sometimes Paul."

Paul was deeply frowning, and smiling like a Cheshire cat, but also scratching his partially empty head, like an ape, possibly wondering about Darwin's theory of relativity.

"You, miserable sod Inge. I thought you'd be pleased? Karen and her talk on the phone all the time."

I was getting increasingly Irate.

"Is that so Paul? you don't fucking say? Well thanks a lot! That's ok then, isn't it? Yippee-fuckin-doo! You, big turd! That's me fucked." He walked away. He couldn't comprehend the enormity of my situation. The rest of my day was 'mapped' out. Probably as far as the Equator or at least infinity. I sipped on my pint as I perused my situation.

As I did, the pub double doors opened and closed behind me. I glanced around, expecting to see two pairs of adequately sized mammarys, bouncing in unison toward me.

I was wrong. It was a prick! a very big one at that. Tony.

Paul was now over at the bandit. Working out his correct nudge-moves. As Paul had gone against my wishes by inviting Linda, it was then only fair I return the compliment. To a minimum of threefold at least!

"Paul? mate, chum, buddy, you'll be pleased to know Tony's here."

Paul played his bandit game, then immediately spun around.

"Thanks, for dropping us in it today Tony. I'm knackered cos of you. I had to do all your orders again. They were all completely fucked up. Where the hell were youtoday?"

"Yeah, where the fuck was you?" I hastily added, deciding to include myself in the mini Spanish-Inquisition.

"Nowhere, just overslept that's all."

"No Tony, overslept is when your late, but still manage to make it in. What you did is having a day off you, idiot." My words were lost on him.

Just then, as if saved by the bell, or divine intervention, the bandit lit up. As did Paul's face? The sound of pound coins, filling the bottom tray. k-chink! Paul was as oblivious to my words as Tony.

As I watched Paul at the bandit, I spotted Karen and Linda walking into the lounge.

"Well done Paul, you can get me a pint now you've dropped the jackpot mate. It's your turn innit?" Paul scooped up the reams of coins and quickly lost them in his pockets.

"Fuck off Tony, you said my ale was free last night? You could have broken my leg, screwing around. I'm still sore."

Paul took two-pound coins out of his left pocket, "Inge, give us two quid?"

"What for? what you doin anyway Paul?" He looked at me like my mum did when I was in trouble.

"Don't ask questions, just do it. I've had enough of this idiot." Paul's mood was

decidedly flustered. I gave him the two pounds. Well, he was a tad bigger than me, and in punching mode as well. He lunged forward at Tony's arm.

"Here, that's for the beer you got me in last night. Don't ask for any more, I've had enough of you. Now piss off and leave us to fuck alone."

"Why should I? not good enough for you now or something?"

"Just do yourself a favour and do one Tony." I said. "We're expecting company. Look through the bar, into the lounge? There's our company."

"Inge, tell him nothing, the fuckin shithouse." As I was contemplating Pauls swift right hook landing somewhere in Tony's vicinity, tony peered over, and then smiled back at us.

"Ah, the girls, the girls, you sly bastards." With his comment, my mind wandered

aimlessly away, to Sally Webster in 'Corry'. Talking to Kevin, on a family day out: The 'girls', the 'girls

Linda and Karen had arrived, but were sat in the lounge side, and hadn't seen us.

Paul became more than insistent now with Tony. With noticeably, added volume. "SLING YOUR HOOK TONY! IT'S QUITS now. Or shall I remind you where the fuckin door is with you head?"

"OK ok, no problem no problem. I'm going Paul!" Tony had finally twigged. 'Keep your hair on'. Tony turned, and made a beeline to the bar where Mary had been watching events.

"Bloody hell Inge, he's only been here five minutes, and I'm already thinking about doin him in."

"Oh, just forget him Paul, let's go and see the girls."

I quickly remembered the brown envelope, Peter had given me earlier, with Tony's name on it. Now was the perfect time to exact a little revenge on Tony. We left the lounge through the separating doors bidding Tony a fond, 'fuck you' farewell, with both fingers aloft. My jeans muddy and ripped. Paul, in his work- leathers. Oh well 1 thought, she might like it rough today.

"Paul, we'll go back to him, in a few minutes or so, give him this little surprise." I waved the envelope like a bone under Shamuses nose.

"Is that ....?"

"Yes, it is the..........." You could see Paul's delight. His mood quickly eased. Karen and Linda were sat on the tall stools, chatting to Mary, at the bar.

"What time D'you call this, we've been here a quarter of an hour where've you

been?"

"Coming Karen....coming! Stock check was a bloody nightmare." Paul led on, and ushered them to a sufficiently hidden table, and Tony's vantage-point. As Karen and Linda sat side by side, Paul took his

respective perch facing his sweetheart. I opted for a single stool, facing the bar,

with my feet outstretched, and arms folded, not giving an inch to Linda.

Ready, with my imaginary 350 hidden troops, In full battle armour. 1000 cohort's, on an all system's back-up. And

10,000 followers to the cause, not organised, or even affiliated, but ready to fight. Let's just say, I wasn't going to be pushed around by her today

Mary looked on, regardlessly thumbing through her 'woman's own' behind the main bar.

"Stephen, why don't you sit here with me?" Oh, here we go, I thought. I remained steadfast and unrepressed. "I'm just fine where I am, thanks Linda."

She gave me a look to start a nuclear war. She knew she was pushy, always wanting her own way, and eventually, when I was too drunk to care, usually getting it. Today I

decided I'd be a little stronger. Or so I liked to think. I sat silently, watching her body language as she chatted to Karen.

"She can't be so bad, can she?" Un-knowingly I'd just disturbed my tempter**s** back to life.

"Finish your pint quick boy? then you can have another?"

"No, just take your time Samaritan, you don't want to create a bad Impression of yourself to her."

"Oh Ignore him, the winged Idiot! listen to me? If you finish your drink quick, you can go to the bar, and get another. Think about it? you'll be away from her and closer to Mary. You can make her jealous of Mary and have more beer too... why not? It makes perfect sense........?"

"Inge... Inge! When shall we give him the envelope?" Paul shook me, from my staring into space.

"What? sorry." As I glanced over at Karen, I felt Linda's hand, descending on my right leg. Karen was frowning. Looking somewhat confused. "What are you talking about? What's going on?"

Paul filled her in with the details as he finished his pint.

"So, It's his final notice then Inge?" Karen asked.

"Yep, Peter's already asked me about Eric, you know Eric...?"

"I bet he follows us in here next?" Karen added.

"Karen. we don't have to stay here? It's not the only pub."

"I suppose your right Linda. I didn't even think about that? I'm so used to being in here in the afternoons with Paul."

"We could venture up town for an hour or so? Go to the Bees Knees, or even the

Raven. How about it lads. What d'you think Stephen?"

She'd put me on the spot.

I had to revert to, 'create a problem' mode.

"It's all well and good hitting the town for a change. But were not exactly dressed for the occasion are we Linda?"

"Well no, but you could nip home if we got a taxi, it wouldn't take long. What d'you think Karen?" Karen looked over at Paul, for any signs of a reaction. This would put an end to it all I thought. Paul hated night-clubs and crowds. As a rule, any type of humans at all. That was unless of course, they wore leather, and liked rock music and bikes. Or either, he just had the unfortunate pleasure of having to endure them, because work demanded it.

"Nah, too much fucking about for me. Besides, I'm quite happy where I am."

"Well," I said. "I'm with you Paul, let's just go with the flow. If the Idiot appears, we'll have a re-think. "The Plough, or even the labour club down the road will do."

"That's not bad?" Paul piped up. "Me and Inge can have a game of snooker."

"Yep, not a bad idea at all." *I'll Just doubly, reinforce that last remark old boy.* I said to myself.

"Yeah, and the bikes are outside. can't leave them here. Or put them in a taxi."

"Yeah, they might get robbed? Doesn't matter so much about Inges though, eh, Inge? hahaha."

"Mines worth 600 smackers minimum. His push-Iron's not worth a carrot!"

Karen laughed at Paul's little pun.

"All right smart arse, it gets me from A to B! that's all I need it to do Paul. It beats walking."

"You're just making excuses Stephen, I didn't see it anywhere when we came in, did you Karen?" *Who rattled your cage Linda?* I thought.

"Listen Linda. Paul doesn't want to go up Wigan, and neither does Karen. And as for me, forget it, end of conversation okay."

Wow. I thought. *Stephen where did that personality spring from? You 'tough-love' bastard. I should be that forceful and domineering more often. She might just like it. I know I did.*

"Paul, give us the money. I'll go and get the ale in." I said as I watched Linda, looking

dumbfounded. Searching herself, for solutions to her 'uptown' problem She needn't bloody bother. The writing was on the wall.

Paul fished into his pocket, what timing. The middle door opened, and Tony walked

through, greeted by four looks of disdain. Paul quickly passed me a tenner, under the table fashion, fearing the prospect of being money stung again, by the ginger one.

"Everyone want the same tipple?" I quietly inquired, not really listening.

"Stephen, can I have some lime in mine this time please? Stephen!"

Linda had to be different. *Awkward cow!* I pondered.

"Anything for you, my little nest of vipers."

I was thinking aloud again? and getting myself into serious shit in the process.

"What did you call me then?"

"Erm.... only messing. What's up with you, anyway? can't you take a joke? I don't know women, all the bloody same."

Phew, that was a close one. Careful Stephen.

"Right, two pints and two halves, one with lime? Back in a minute." I walked away, past Tony.

"Hello girls, hope they're looking after you?" Tony placed his pint on the table and pulled up another chair from near the window. He was surprisingly chipper. Mind you, we hadn't given him his bad news yet. If it was bad news? I thought, as I stood at the bar.

'It means nothing to him! Oh Vienna!

"I beg your pardon Stephen?"

"Sorry Mary, just singing. Same again please love. I'm going for a quick burst, while you're doing the honours." I said, still rambling the Ultravox song.

Linda and Tony looked quietly on as Paul and Karen were in and out of sexual chat. Karen was giggling dirtily and whispering behind her hand.

"I'm gonna, put some vibes on." Tony said. Everyone Ignored him. "Come with me, pick some tunes Linda?"

Tony rated his chances with her. Even she wouldn't look at him twice.

"Ok, Tony, I'll come and have a look with you."

"Well come on then?" Tony grabbed Linda's chair, and pushed it away to eye her legs, as she stood up. That was my take on it, anyway. I walked from the bar, deciding to use the Vault toilets to get out of the way completely.

"Inge get me a pint of lager, I'll give you the money." Tony asked.

"No can do? Going to drain the main vein pal."

"See you in a minute Stephen, I'm just off the jukebox with Tony."

"Yeah whatever, I'm going for a piss Linda." She stopped me in my tracks. I

found myself with a freshly planted a kiss on the cheek, and my left hand holding a twenty- pound note. I walked on, now contented in a small victory, for Stephen's the length and breadth of the country.

I was fortuitously back in two shakes of a lamb's tail.

"Mary, Mary how's your hairy............ sorry?" She smiled. "That's me Mam's middle name you know?"

Linda must have made a quick selection, she was at my side, instantly at the bar. I felt her hand squeeze my arse, then make a full-reverse assault on my gonads. Then quickly appeared to my right.

"Alright babe, you didn't forget my Lime, did you?"

"Erm no, that's the one with the Li-ME I think, OUCH! Are you ambidextrous or what?"

Mary watched me being openly played with, and just laughed. Quite the opposite of how I thought she'd react. Maybe she didn't really care as much as I hoped she did. Or maybe she did and was just a damn good actress?

"Awe, leave him alone, you're embarrassing him?"

"Don't you bloody start Mary." I said.

"That's nine, sixty-four please, Stephen my love?"

"There you go sweetness. Cheers Mary." Mary made her way to the till, on the lounge side of the bar.

"You two seem very friendly?"

"Oh, erm, yeah Linda. We are. She's pally with me mam like."

"Where does she know your mum from then? Does she go the Darby and Joan club too?"

"Oi you, Mary's not that old, that's enough Linda'. I pushed her hand away from my side.

Mary walked back through the bar, and handed me my change, eyeing me the way only she could.

"There you go. I had to pour them in the lounge. The Lagers gone in here. Shall I bring them through, or leave them there?"

"Oh, just leave them where they are, we're going in that side now, cheers Mary. Hang on, I suppose you'd better give me a pint of Guinness for Tony as well, the slime that he is. He might just disappear if he gets a pint, eh Mary?'

"Stranger things have happened Stephen, stranger things'.

The unscheduled ale, was a tiny ploy, to rid us of Tony's unwanted presence. It could work quite well even if it did cost the price of a pint to extinguish the untold annoyance from the continued company of the ginger one.

"Linda, can you just take those two drinks through for me please? Karen and Paul's, oh and yours too. I'll be over in a minute or two, just hanging on for Tony's black cow's milk. You can pour that in here can't you Mary? It's fed in here isn't it my love?" Linda was cupping the glasses and making it look hard work. I leisurely leant on the bar watching.

"It would be a lot easier with a tray Stephen."

"Suppose it would Linda? Mary, can you fix her up for me?" Mary ducked down under the bar, quickly re-appearing with a round steel tray emblazoned in red and blue letters; *'Double Diamond works wonders- so drink some today!'*

"Probably worth a few quid on antiques road-show that is." I masterfully commented to Mary's giggle's and Linda's solemn stare.

I mounted all the glasses on the tray for her and walked away. Mary watched on.

"There you go, I'll even hold the door for you."

"Erm I'll just grab the tray Stephen." She turned back to the bar to see the mass of

alcoholic liquid waiting before her and braced.

I had neglected to inform her about the two bottles of Newcastle brown, and my side order of vodka and orange. It did look quite heavy. I proceeded to pull faces behind her, Mary turned away for fear of Linda seeing her laughing. As she reached the door, I casually said.

"Like I said, I'll be right with you Ok?" Not a word of reply, or even a glance, she just exuded concentration. I'd probably gone a bit too far by now. Letting her carry all that stuff. Probably? But she'll get her own back in time. Women always do. *Enjoy it while you can,* the devil tempter insisted. Good advice, I enthused. Linda went through the door and made her way back to our tables in the lounge.

"Mary! you're a disgrace? You could have given her a better bloody tray than that? Double diamond? Noah was around when they used to serve that stuff." She looked at me with an evil glint.

"I hold my hands up, guilty as charged. I don't care though? she's a snotty little cow. That's not your proper girlfriend is it?" She Inquired.

"I suppose I'm guilty as charged too? Mary topped up the glass of Guinness, until it poured over, and placed it neatly on the bar.

"Here Stephen, that's on me, for the cross you have to bear."

I couldn't quite work out if she was referring to Tony or Linda. I wasn't really bothered which. Just happy I was on the winning side for a change.

"I've another confession Stephen." Just as she said that, the door flung open, and in charged Linda. Looking fumingly angrier, than she had, when she'd left. Mary was just about to leave to serve another customer, who'd come into the other side.

"Excuse me, woman? I said excuse me? whatever your name is?" Mary turned back.

"Are you talking to me lady?"

"Yes, I'm talking to you! There's no lime in this lager, and before you say it, there's

none in the other either?"

"Right, number one; My name is Mary. Number two; you didn't ask for any lime."

"Sorry Linda, I could have sworn I'd asked for lime."

"Shut up Stephen!"

"Sorry Lin......."

"Shut up I said! or are you as stupid as she is?"

My angel stirred. *"Oh oh, I fear there's going to be trouble Samaritan?"*

The devil rubbed his hands. Mary reached for the lime splash bottle, in a rather flurried fashion, catching her cardigan sleeve on a hanging brandy optic as she did. Plucking it and making the whole row of bottles rattle at the same time. I'd never seen her lose her temper before. Even throwing people out was done with very relative decorum.

"Ok, say 'when' then...? didn't catch your name either missy." Mmm, I thought, my best course of action? Leave them well alone.

A head to head female battle of wills, and a war of words. Women fighting? great! So much better than Hulk Hogan v The Undertaker. I had a ringside seat too.

Linda was fidgeting in her handbag? Probably looking for her purse, or getting her twelve Inch blade out I grinningly thought?

"Linda, that's my name bar bitch!'. As she looked up from her purse, she realised

Mary was still pouring. And why not? Linda hadn't said 'When'?

"That's enough... Stop!... I mean.... WHEN!"

Two beer-towels and eight Heineken beer mats saturated? The bar was a bit of a mess to say the least. A fish pond of lime, dripping endlessly onto the floor.

"That's another twenty pence for the lime lady!" Mary calmly said.

How very endearing I thought. Linda angrily threw a coin onto the bar. The twenty- pence coin's, rapid trajectory was suitably slowed, as it sunk into the spilt liquid, like a pebble on Lake Windermere. Mary pulled it toward her, turned around, and dropped it into the tip glass on the till.

"Thank you, missy." Not even uttering Linda's name. Mary moved onto the new customer who'd appeared at the bar in all the commotion.

"Alright Frank. Be with you in a second. The usual love? How's Maureen, not seen her in a while. Has she got rid of the cold yet?" Linda had disappeared. I was stood there on my Jack Jones like a plonker.

As I re-joined the gang. Linda was quietly sipping her drink. She looked at me and slammed

her lager, hard down on the table, making Karen jump and look, frowning so much that her forehead looked like spaghetti junction.

"Tony, you're on my stool, shift your arse."

"Your stool Inge? has it got your fuckin name on it?" He ungraciously moved. After a couple of minutes settling back down, I realised I had to make some kind of amends to Linda. It was me that forgot to order her lime. She looked clearly ruffled and angry by the 'Mary' events. Tony was oblivious to everything, other than a personal quest, to gain entry to Linda's grassy-knoll bikini area.

"Did you get me a pint Inge?"

"Sure, I did Tony. You'll find it on the bar in the vault. That's if nobody's drunk it

already?" With this catastrophic news, Tony, immediately got up, and disappeared through the adjoining doors to retrieve his free motion lotion. I nestled closer, beside Linda.

"I suppose we could go up Wigan Linda. Nothing stopping us, no law against it." Linda stopped her throwing of random beer-mat chunks, into the ashtray and lifted her head.

"Stephen, can we? are you serious? I'd really like to? Beats the hell out of this place and its staff."

"Yeah.... why not? Even if Paul and Karen won't come, we can go on our own? Eh sweetie -pie?"

"Don't you dare call me that!"

"Sorry Chicken."

"Chicken! don't you dare call me that either! I'll bloody chicken you? A sharp nailed hand squeezed into my nether regions. I choked down a neck-full of lager in pain. Her hand stayed there as a smile found itself onto her face. I'd got her back. I'm resigned to a drinking session into the town centre though? Needs must.

The hand was still moving down there five minutes later? The prospect of getting my leg over as well as my nether regions had grown substantially. From a tiny seedling, to the champion winning cucumber, at the north west regional agricultural show.

Paul had just got back from the bandit again and him and Karen were having an all-out chat about Tony. Or rather Karen was.

"So, he's getting the sack, then is he? Does he not know yet? Wow, that'll be sommat to see Paul, are you gonna tell him now? I interrupted Karen.

"Right Paul, Karen, listen.... were having this one, then shooting downtown, for a bit of a change. Are you comin with us or what?" Karen was still clearly up for It. She gave Linda a sly wink and rubbed her hands in glee. It was Paul however, who was the one to convince.

"Fuckin Wigan... still on about that? fuckin hate the shit hole! Over-priced, watered down ale. Rubber fuckin glasses. knob heads everywhere, and fuckin crap music. Last time I went, I ended up, wasting a bouncer. I had no class he said? The cheeky fucker! He had no-glass when I'd finished. Straight through the fuckin window he went... the fuckin pansy."

"Oh, Paul let's go, come on, we can even go the John Bull?" Karen waited for his reply.

TEN

The table was quiet, Paul was staring up into the bottom of his glass, open mouthed and

gulping loudly, until the last drop of lager was drained. 1 watched his clacking throat.

Things seemed to move slower, but louder. Like a replay in slow motion. Even 1, found

myself waiting for his next word, BANG! His glass echoed down on the table, empty and drained. A bang to start the Grand National, it was that loud. Followed by the loudest burp this side of 'Burpsville'. If there were ever such a place? "BUURRRP!! Oops. Excuse moi, sorry hahaha."

"I should bloody think so too you nasty PIG!" Mary yelled over from the bar.

Even Frank, the oap, I never miss a shift 'flat cap', cast a beady glance Paul's way.

"I never expected that? it's very gassy this Lager" Paul's in-sufficient excuse was paltry in comparison with his burp. But God he was funny, more so, when he wasn't intending to be. I burst into my own personal tirade of obscene giggling. So much so, that I had to almost leave the room to learn how to speak again. Slightly weeing myself with laughter hadn't helped.

"So, can we go Paul?" Karen was still pressing for an answer.

"I suppose so. As long as the Bull is our first and last port of call. Besides. Yoda might be in, or even our Mark. I can borrow some more money off one of them. We'll have this last one, give Tony his envelope then get the fuck out of here."

"Let's just go now then, Stephen? I'll go and order a taxi. I'll even pay for the whole

afternoon if we go now?"

"What about his push-iron outside Linda? How's he gonna get to work tomorrow?" Karen had a good point. I'd left it once before, but regretted it the next day going to work

"I'm not leavin my bike here." Paul said loudly. "Fuck that, kids'll fuckin wreck it, like they did our Marks when he left his here."

"Paul, what about me, you just gonna leave me here then?"

Again, Karen was on the ball. Didn't happen much that. If she went on mastermind her chosen subject would be; soap operas on television; last week to yesterday.

"No stupid, you can come with me to me mums, drop my dream machine off, and we'll follow them up-town."

Who does he think he is? I thought to myself? *David Essex on a fuckin moped!*

"Meet them in the Bull mind."

"What! I'm not getting on the back of you without a helmet."

"Chill out Karen, you can wear my mine. We can go over the slag-heaps. Don't need a helmet that way, and there are no fuckin pigs."

As their discussion carried on, Linda quietly watched. Either visually intrigued, or just confused by Paul's continued mastery of the ape world. I found time to slope away, to replenish my dwindling pint of lager, duly greeted at the bar by Mary. Who'd also earlier expressed her distaste of Paul's neanderthal burp explosion. Along with Frank's agreeing grunts, toping of his pipe and 'half a mild' slurping. The male Ena Sharples of the pub.

So, it was agreed. We'd meet up town centre, in about an hour or so.

Taxis, buses and beer funds permitting. Linda was made up. As I returned from the bar with a replenished pint, she disappeared to make a phone call to Julie, A mate who worked uptown in the Bee's Knee's. While all this had been going on. Tony was totally engrossed in losing the remains of his coinage feeding the bandit in the hope it would redeem his flagging drinking career. "Paul's just dropped that you tit!" I shouted over.

"So, what, it could go again, Mary's not seen it go this week?"

"That's because she's not been in you dope. She only works three days now. Landlady's cut her hours down. Anyway, were making a move Tony, see you tomorrow. Here's a letter from Peter.

"Fuck! look at that, bastard. I've no more change. Inge give us a quid til I get some change. I can't leave that on," he said as I took a look. Fair comment really. If the reels held, it would go straight onto 'Best Win' feature. I'd play it too. I ruffled my pockets to get a sovereign. At the same time, moving any notes behind my wrist, to my arse pocket. Couldn't risk him clocking them I thought.

"There, that's your last, I'm off. I hope Frank gets on it after you and drops the fuckin lot. See you in the morning," I retorted in typical style. So unlike Paul and myself. Who didn't need to say very much at all? Indeed, most of the time we talked very little. Didn't need too. Even when we did, to the outsider was in complete riddles. Very often losing their interest pretty quickly. As we walked outside, I could see Linda couldn't make head nor tail of it either;

"Inge?"

"Yeah, Paul, Bull."

"Yeah, Bull, an hour or three, no problem. Taxi it?"

"Defo there."

"Yowsa, sorted."

"Sound, later."

"Later, Chongo pie."

As we left, Tony was loudly cursing, trying to kick the fruit machine, into in-animate submission.

I put my arm around Linda's shoulder and headed off for a taxi. Crusader cabs office, was at the back of Goose Green labour club nearby. We could also grab a bus if one came along the main road, anyway. We engaged in some playful rapport along the way. Or to the average eye, an adult version of 'tick'. Slapping each other, on various parts of the body, then legging it. It originally started with playful little slaps. But had now got a little more serious and physical. Her sore arse and bollocks kicking to my full on mammary bruising fornication's.

ELEVEN

"**O**uch! You rough bugger. That hurt! I'll have your balls for that."

Not a happy bunny, Linda rubbed her breasts, and showered my head in guilt, then started running after me.

"I mean it, I'll fuckin kill you!" She probably will? I thought. She rarely swears. She's bloody fast too? She'd ejected herself from her heels to pursue me. I very soon decided, I couldn't keep up the beer-swishing pace, and holed up in a bus shelter, at the bus lay-by of the road. I cowered down, hands aloft.

"Don't. OUCH! Don't hit me with them things. They must be murder to walk in too?" I

exclaimed.

"Hit you, I'll batter you if you do that again. It's bloody sore that."

I'd managed to break free, and ran out of her striking distance, behind the bus shelter litter bin.

We chased each other cat and mouse, around the shelter, five or six times. All the while, being watched by an elderly couple waiting inside. As we stopped, to get our battle breath back, she dropped her shoes to the floor, and slid back into them. She didn't carry an audience well. Being glared at by the elders, ended the conflict. Probably noting 'to be continued' in her head.

I slowly re-convened, the side of her. Hoping to gain some kind of mutual solace. Nothing but silence ensued.

"Excuse me, Is there a due mate?" The oap couple compared their watches.

"Ten minutes lad. Be no seats though? Bloody school kid's you know? No shame kids these days, they just.............."

"No mate, that's ok. Really, it's fine." I'd narrowly just avoided, a concise ear-bending sermon, on the why's and where-be fore's of how public transport could be Improved. Only to get one more readily gain one from Linda. "I'm not waiting here any longer. Besides, I thought we were getting a taxi you cheapskate? You'd better change your skin-flint ways quick. If you think I........"

"Right! Fine." I grabbed her hand-bagged arm. Adopting a frog-marching patter.

"Come on then, let's go down for a cab your highness." I looked over at the tweed-

coated couple.

"It's ok, she's always like this, I just do as I'm told." I was thankfully understood by the man, by his agreeing nod.

"Aye lad so do I and look where it's got me?" He smiled.

His wife looked straight through him. I held Linda's hand.

"It's only there," I pointed out. "Pretty regular Crusader cabs. We won't be in long." I

decided a loving side was what was needed. Bring the nice Stephen back. Give the usual one a rest.

"Here Linda, change from the money you gave me before."

"Oh, keep it Stephen, I've plenty more'. She was being so caring and honestly nice, I felt guilty again. We carried on regardless.

Walking, talking and holding hands. "Linda listen, can I get serious for a minute. I get paid and I'm off soon. Then it's my turn to treat you. Fancy a night out somewhere? Pictures and a club? Maybe even a weekend away to Blackpool? We can both chip in like a proper couple. What do you think?" The funny thing about it

was, I didn't even expect myself to think such things, let alone come out with it, in an undying love kind of speech.

"Really? That would be really nic......" She stopped mid-sentence. "Oh, I remember the last time you were like this though. All lovey-dovey and that. Then I didn't see you again, for two weeks! Remember? You pissed off to Ibiza with Eric, Ian and the rest of them from the Tippings.

"That was an offer I couldn't refuse Linda. A spare place goin beggin, cos Wayne Reddy broke his leg. You'd have done the same? Come on admit it? She quietly pondered.

"Umm maybe, but at least I'm with you now, not meeting you up town! She suddenly

found a partly dusty memory. Mr Sheened it and carried on.

"That was another one. Outside the John Bull again! Eight o'clock you said? Then you turned up at a quarter to nine bladdered."

"Suppose so, hold my hands up to that one." Shit? she can see right through me? I bet she's got a book full of these.

"If it wasn't for you pesky kids, I'd have carried out my ruthless scheme, and got away with Haggard's millions." She totally ignored my 'Scooby Doo', psycho-babble sabbatical.

"I got propositioned twice too, bloody sweaty hogs and Goths go in there." She gave it a minute or so, to take my giggling reaction in. Before she re-launched on me.

"Funny is it, I thought so too. I thought your excuse was hilarious, hahaha."

She feigned laughter, "Sowwy, wuv, I wuz workin winda......"

Linda did an impression of me, slurring and staggering. Not a bad one either. Giving my brain another-buck up your ideas jab.

"Ok then, right listen" I said grabbing her shoulders, in a; this has gone far enough mode. Even though she wasn't the guilty party.

"Number One; it won't happen again, I really promise.

Number Two; Your driving the forklift tomorrow night when we off-load at the market.

Number Three; Peter's sorted my holidays, and I'm off fri for a whole 7 days. Oh, and lastly:

Number Four; Get your smackers round me neck!" I kissed her cheek, disconnected my arms, and ran down the pavement, leaving her standing.

"I'll bloody shag you, when I get hold of you." She shouted, grinning wildly. Clearly now upbeat now about the whole scheme of things. She finally caught me at the taxi rank office door.

As we walked in, she straightened her short-tight, black skirt and pushed it down, into her above average tanned legs, and bounced down on her shapely, gym crafted arse beside me. Slammed the door and began multiple questioning.

"What you on about, work tomorrow night?"

"Exactly what I said Linda. That's what I was doing, the night I met you late. Unloading stuff at the market for the next day. Me and Paul."

"Oh, I see. No problem. We'll be able to do something nice together, when you're on holiday this Friday too. We've something to look forward to now." She smiled.

"Can we have a taxi please?"

"Yes love, where you goin too?"

"Wigan love, town centre."

"Can I have one at the office please, over? One at the office for....... What's your name love?"

"Whittle, it's Whittle" Linda reliably informed the chain smoking woman.

"Taxi at the office for Whittle over?" She paused and took a long drag. "Town centre. Joe, where are you love? Your nearest I think...? Call back here after that one at Jackson street will you." She turned back to face Linda.

"It's on't way, alright love." All the time she was talking, I was quietly having a childish, open feel of Linda's chest area.

"Get off Stephen........ stop acting stupid?" Her playful defence, soon erupted into an all out, embarrassing pushing match. Then a fatal, smack across my head.

"Ooow.... you bitch!"

"I said ... pack it in!" The radio woman watched on like a fire-breathing dragon, minus the fire. Puffing out her smoke in a long plume. A Tinny sounding voice emanated from her ancient wireless box.

"Roger that Kath, on me way back now love, over, ohumm."

"That's it. Keep him in his bloody place love. Bloody men! They're all the same. They only want us for one thing? Oops, Sorry Joe, wasn't talkin to you love, over."

Women's lib I thought, Thatcher, fuckin suffragettes. Not a clue. I decided to shut up, and playfully sulk, like the naughty boy in class.

"Stuff it, I'm nipping outside for a smoke." I stood up and walked out of the pre-fabricated office, Leaving

Linda with her new friend. Outside, I caught a cig in my teeth, at the exact same time as lighting It. Very James Dean, Happy now. I'll leave the females gabbing, what they do best. Linda joined me not two minutes later. Then, the driver, in a typically knackered Crusader cab. A red Sierra, emitting black smoke, in much the same way, as Kath the Crusader wireless woman.

"Afternoon, hop in, ohumm. Town I was told? Whittle in't it? I'm Joe."

Mmm, very obliging bloke, I thought. That was, until he set off the wrong way. Now he became like the rest of them. Out for what he could get. Taxi driving scum, I thought, sneering in his direction.

"Had a row then have you?' ohumm." Linda and I looked at each other. He's bloody nosey as well I thought.

"Sorry, something Kath said on the radio. I'm Joe by the way?"

"We know!" We said in unison smiling. Well at least we can agree on some things, I concurred to my good tempter.

"Never mind, it'll all come out in't wash, thanoes." Joe said.

"Dust kno ohumm, why we argue and row? Couples that is? Oi... ohumm. Watch wer't goin to pal? They think you've got ohumm, eye's int back o thi yed some folk thanoes? Hello little chick a dee. Ohumm! By heck, bloody buses ohumm."

He can talk to three things at the same time this fella? I thought. A bus, a car and a baby in a pram. And all from the comfort of his cab seat. He could cough for medals, at the same time too.

"I'll tell thee why we fall out, For the fun o' making it up that's wot, oohhuumm."

"Is that right erm Joe? No shit pal' I concurred. Linda smiled. So, did I. His world changing statement, lost a lot of Its impact on us, due to the constant oohhumms.

Once he got started going the right direction, after an unscheduled home visit, to pick up his tea flask, the journey took no time at all. I took in, some of my old stomping grounds, on route. The three sisters. An old BMX haunt, where many a happy day was spent jumping gravity challenging ramps, or riding over obstacles, in pursuit of the total rad-ride. But mostly underage drinking, breaking of limbs and wrecking of good clothes. Much to the pooring effect of emptying my mum's already 'it's that empty its floating' purse.

Closer to the town centre, was the Poolstock lane pub run. The high school days of

learning the craft. Bottom of the league boozers, with easy access for us minors. The Bold Hotel, The Grapes. Even one with playing cards glued to the ceiling! 'The New Cricket Club', Allegedly done up with a much-needed brewery grant. But looking at the committee members. It wasn't hard to figure where the money had gone. Along a bit further, Worsley Mesnes Labour club, which at one time coincidentally, had my uncle Colin, as It's steward. Not what you know, but who. I remember spouting to friends at the time. Ah happy days. The spluttering Sierra pulled onto King Street, and into the mess of Wigan's new-fangled one-way system.

Another mini M25 if you like. All the way around the outskirts, to get to the centre. Where the main core of drinking houses where situated. So close to each other, it was a wonder they made any money. Library street was exactly what it said. A street with a library and pretty much, nothing else. Apart from a die-hard greasy spoon, and Twiss's bakery. Still standing on the same spot it had when my Nan was a nipper. Remarkably unchanged by the years. The only noticeable, technological change being the white new registration Twiss vans. Constantly darting in and out, of the cobbled side-street. Carrying the popular pies and cakes, all over the district, and further afield. They even had the contract for Haydock racecourse. A shipping order in itself.

King Street ran almost parallel to library street. This is here Joe had decided was the quietest and closest drop off point.

"Right you two, this alright for you?" The handbrake was rasped into place, and Joe spun round in his seat, to eye the flashing fare meter, in-between the oil dirty front seats.

"Here's just fine Joe. Are you getting this one sweetheart?" I was out the door before she could reason a reply. Raring to go again, despite my slight hint of a wobble.

"How much do we owe you Joe? I gather I'm paying." Linda unwillingly eased her purse from her bag as I looked on. Feeling for my crushed, packet of Benson and Hedges.

"Well my love, oohhuumm'. Joe coughed another tune from his chest. Here we go, I thought.

Linda, assume shock position.

"Seeing as we.... I, went daft way round, furt flask like, and thee ne'er even moaned about it, we can call it a straight fiver? Cheep at arf'rt price." Linda crouched at me through the open passenger door, for approval to pay. I however, was too busy looking for our next port of call. it didn't matter either way. She wasn't about to start haggling like a Spanish market stall holder. Money gratefully changed hands, and the strength of the wind showed, when the cars choking fumes, blew it's the way into Linda's nostrils. The fumes only other exit being Joe's, slightly ajar, flick ash window.

Joes continued coughing, and the smog gave Linda the urgency to get out. Promptly slamming the door behind her and immediately looking for ash stains on her coat. In her fuming panic, she'd trapped her coat in the cabs rusty door. She hastily opened it, to free it. As she did, a chunk of Loctite 'plastic-padding' car body- filler left its intended place, and dropped to the floor at Linda's feet,

"Shit, my coat! What a bloody wreck."

Joe looked down at the filler, and tended, if a little half-heartedly to agree.

'Aye love, last legs, last legs, this bloody heap. They're on about getting us some new one's soon? I've heard it all

before though. Just shuts us driver's up Forah bit suppose. Never change this lot. Not as long as that tight bugger's in charge, ohhumm! Right, I'll be on me way then. Have a nice afternoon. Be nice and look after each other. Come in Kath? Joe here, I'm free in't town centre? over ohumm."

Mmmm, indeed I thought. Who d'you think you are mate, Derek Batey from 'Mr and Mr's'? Bet your fairly bothered too pal. Just keep on smoking and drinking your shitty tea. I lifted my two fingers and waved him off.

"Cheers Joe, thanks a lot. Oh, and get something for the fuckin cough."

TWELVE

"**S**tephen, look at my bloody coat with that damn taxi." I turned back to look.

Linda was knelt down and bent over, trying to brush away the rubber door seal mark, now adorning her smart, but wounded red coat. I looked down, like the look out in the crow's nest, I now had a rather exceptional blimp of Linda's finer points.

"Swine, it's ruined." she concluded. I moved toward her.

"So where shall we start this wonderful afternoon beer-fest?" I offered, looking around rubbing my hands heartily together, then, nicely cupping on her shapely skirt covered behind.

"It'd better bloody come out, or I'm gonna hit Crusader cabs with a dry-cleaning bill."

She hardly flinched. It actually seemed to me, as if she was in her element, with me man handling her selective parts in full view of Joe public.

I've always thought she was probably, a closet naturist. Whenever I stayed over at her parents, it was guaranteed, the heating would be on full bore, and she was parading around with just her pyjama top on or simply starker's. Always a plus point for me.

"Oh, I don't know? My bloody coat! How long d'you think Karen & Paul will be?"

"Not a Scooby Linda." I replied. Swiftly grabbing her hand.

Wigan, was its typical, afternoon self. Dull, overcast and rush hour raining. Not usual rain. That other stuff, that gets you sodden-soaked, and piss-wet through in seconds. Wigan rain. The Wigan flat-cap folk were frantically rushing about their normal, everyday business, at a pace that led you to believe, the world was going to end tomorrow.

"No matter fair maiden! I shouted. "Let us sojourn to this, (pointing) world renowned watering hole where you, my prettious

Miss Whittle, can conflab to your heart's desire, and I, as your master, can partake in some of the finest beer swilling, this liverish little town, has had the noble fortune to witness!"

At this point, I'd also turned, unbeknown to me, nor anyone else, into a cross between some local town crier, and a happy sea captain, who thought he was treading the boards, at Drury lane. Or maybe just Brian Blessed?

"Come forth my merry wench, let us begin."

Linda looked on smiling, as we quickly ran out of the rain, into the town's most prestigious bar. The Bees Knees. Or to its older patrons, the Dog and Partridge. Only prestigious in its title. It was a veritable shit hole, in dire need of either a complete makeover, or more readily, a match. The first pub I can ever remember, sampling the delights of merry-down cider In.

"Lind's babe, over here!" No sooner had we crossed the threshold than Linda's barmaid pal Julie had clocked us.

"How does she always see you so fast?" I asked. Linda just looked up, and smiled as she collapsed her sodden telescopic umbrella, playfully soaking me in the process.

Mmm, I mused... there a pair of swingers... a pair of closet AC/DC lesbians. Just like her closet naturism carry on. Bet you can't swing a cat in her closet I thought. Bet George Michael's in there somewhere too.

I was possibly not far from the truth? Linda arched herself over the bar, and exchanged a friendly peck-cheek, as Julie leant forward and offered one swiftly back. As Linda eased back from her tip toes, I could see Julie, feistily about to load all cannon, to commence a catch-up banter battle, on Linda's eardrums. She picked up an empty pint pot, and pulled forward on the Carling pump, as she began wittering.

Julie could probably bag countless orating awards, or local recognition, as the world's fastest talker. Shame most of it was utter bollocks.

I slowly sidled up, cloth-close behind Linda, putting my hands on the bar, either side of her and nudging myself between her butt cheeks.

This, un-surprisingly, had no effect whatsoever to the current, blah, blah, yappy situation at all. Except a slight, but nice, nuance knowing riposte, Linda returned into my crotch.

"I'll have a pint of Lager, Linda thanks. Back in a sec."

I retreated to the gents, planting a kiss into Linda's hair as I left.

Walking the length of the 'Bees' from the cider bar, to the tiny 'cabin fever' gent's toilets, I glanced around. Madonna was happily warbling another of her tunes on the jukebox. Some familiar faces, in their usual places, dotted up and down the dimly lit 'meeting place', made some small kind of tip-hat, 'I know you' acknowledgement my way, as I pushed open the gent's door.

The toilet stank to high heaven of bleach. Doing a pretty bad job, of masking over the main, underlying problem, of bad aim. Drunken punters missing the urinals completely. It was much more in terrible need of a complete re-vamp. The wallpaper was peeling off the walls, as if it wanted to escape, and get the hell out of the piss-stinking, glorified cupboard. It wasn't so bad, on a rainy, Tuesday afternoon, with minimal customers, in a reasonably sober state of mind. I'd normally use the Ladies, on a typical bog-standard (no pun intended) Friday or weekend night, to avoid even entering the shoulder to shoulder, squalid mess of a room, with free urine as a carpet.

Despite this, and on the upside, just like the main pub, it's adorned with countless pictures, and enlarged photographs, of Wigan rugby stars. Both past & present. Signed rugby shirts, in glass frames, littered over every wall. The ladies loo is just more of the same.

The reverence, honour and worship, Wigan folk have for its 'team' goes before it, beyond it, & then some. It really is something to behold. The glorious prize, always being the Challenge Cup. The holy grail.

You can almost feel it, in the beating of the town's heart. If I ever found myself fighting in the trenches, I would hope it was Wiganers down there with me. They have the bull-dog spirit, bred deep into them. A working class, Lancashire mining town, that isn't afraid to get their hands dirty.

I wash and shake my hands on the Wigan Warriors hand towel, hanging just below a snap of Billy Boston, holding the challenge cup, high in the air. Flanked by his team mates, and thousands of black & white idolising fans. Shaun Edwards is just to the side of Billy, giving me the ok to leave. I exit the latrine, to hear the last few bars of 'Like a prayer,' fading from the juke box. I'll be needing one of those, if Julie's not slowed her machine-gun yapping down any. As I approach my girl and my pint, a very familiar, female voice shouts my name. Oh, Oh.... Mmm, this isn't going to go down well at all.

"Stevie here! up here" I look up. From the top of the stairs, of the middle snug, stands a jumping Debbie, with a pal in tow, and her a big smile. The best smile. My platonic pal.

Debbie is a regular at the Pier nightclub, on a Wednesday. Alternative night or Weirdo night as it's nicknamed. I hadn't been for a while, and it was showing, by the size of the doc martin jumps she was doing. Debbie is, as they stereotype, a 'weirdo'. Dressed always, in Stranglers black, with her customary, and individually named, 18-hole doc martin boots. She actually gave names to them! Tipex-ing it boldly on the back. Sid and Nancy. Amazingly, rather apt names considering her favourite leisure time activity is getting shit-faced on Newky brown, and po-go-ing madly, out of her head, to the sounds of, amongst others, the Clash's 'Should I stay or should I go'. Incredible!

She has short cropped, natural black hair, with a never-ending curling front quiff. To the type of standard, even Elvis would be proud of, peeping out from a black 'Motorhead' baseball cap. She's also sporting a new edition to her look. A full sized, multi-coloured. golfing umbrella, emblazoned with the words 'Legal & General'. Clearly striking, against her stranglers black.

But Debbie's not a weirdo at all. Just likes different things than ordinary people. A different taste and different music. She enjoyed creating an entrance too. A showstopper, and natural show-boater. She liked to turn a few heads. With her incredible assets she did that. Nothing wrong with that in my book. She was a breath of fresh air, or a break from the norm. To me, a perfectly normal, human being with a heart, of pure gold. She was a people carer. A fully qualified home-help. Not the type you'd take to meet your mother, in her usual guise granted. But if your mother could see beyond Debbie's exterior. She would quickly realise, never to judge the book by the cover. The most unassuming, yet naturally friendly person, I've been lucky enough, to walk through my life, and call me her friend. It's at this point reader, I feel I need to point out, that from your point of view, I know, I always get myself into sexual connotations, but that's how men are.

From my point of view, I also have to point out that there is an awful lot of points here. On a sexual scale of one to ten, Debbie has a body that ticks all the boxes, in any and every configuration, you could throw at any red-blooded male. Or female for that matter. Moreover, I feel I have to also point out, and ram home (forgive the sexual connotation) the fact that, whilst her body is pushing up in the high echelons, of a perfect ten, it lags strenuously well behind, what I can only describe, as the best personality, I have ever met. Debbie is fantastically loveable, in every way. This said, even though my mind would love to get her between the sheets, my heart knows that, just my friend, is all she can ever be, so there's no reason, I should try. Though stunningly beautiful inside and out, that is the line, that would never be crossed by me, ever. She's my lovely pal end of. She still knocks the spots off Ian's love interest, Julia. Hands down!

Sadly, for me, my dilemma isn't going to be seen like that by 'her indoors'. Who at this juncture, is probably already sharpening her claws, swords and knives, and possibly growing shamus teeth, to slay either Debbie, me or the pair of us!

"Where the hell have you been hiding Stevie?" Debbie continued.

"I haven't seen you at the Pier, in like, forever!"

"Well erm, no erm, I haven't been in, quite a while." I evasively replied, glancing in Linda's direction as I did.

Debbie quickly interjected, finishing off my sentence for me.

"Must be what, wow, over a month at least?" Debbie continued doc martin-skipping down the stairs at the same time. Strangely reminding me of Fred Astaire, in Top Hat, and tapping her full size legal & general umbrella, step-ward in one hand, with a bottle of Newcastle brown, sidled precariously in the other. As she reached the bottom step, she quickly placed her brolly to the side, and beer down, so she could flick the now long, hanging, 'Dot cotton' style ash, from her cigarette. That was perched between her lips, throughout the whole Broadway performance. Talk about west end performance! I even thought she was going to ask me to dance?

I looked sheepishly over at Linda. As I did, a still 'excited to see you,' Debbie kissed me on the cheek.

This wasn't boding well for me at all? Worse still, was that fact that, by now Julie, was obviously speedily and systematically, poisoning Linda's mind against me, and there wasn't a thing I could do about it.

I was firmly stuck between a rock, and a Debbie place. Much favouring the latter.

"Stephen... your pint!" Linda sternly and visibly offered. Lifting the inviting looking lager up, from the bar, in my direction. Making my mouth water as she did. "Yep... I know, won't be a sec" I replied.

Although I was unaware of it, Debbie had already clicked to my unabridged, unavoidable situation. But because she simply didn't possess a malicious bone in her body, she'd automatically decided to diffuse events, before they were blown totally out of the water by any all involved, innocent bystanders, viewers or any green-eyed intolerant individuals, whether thrown in indirectly, directly or completely by accident, by simply offering herself up on a plate, as a human sacrifice to Linda.

"He's coming love, he's coming!" next thing I knew, Debbie smiled, and put her hand on top of my head, forcefully swivelling it through 180' degrees.

I found myself being pushed along, being indubitably frog-marched back towards Linda, as my weirdo platonic pal, blatantly swigged from her biker's beverage bottle, and copiously giggled behind me.

"There you go love, he's here. All back in one piece, without so much of a hair on his head out of place. Well, maybe just one or two? Almost untouched by human hands, ha-ha. Or mine at least. I'm Debbie by the way?"

Debbie outstretched her hand toward Linda. "Call me 'Hopper,' Most people do, except him. But then Stevie's a gentleman. You're lucky to have him."

Linda just looked on gobsmacked. I expected the 10-30 from London Euston to appear ahead of schedule, out of her mouth at any moment. She was still probably deciding at that point forward, to forthwith dispense with Debbie's olive branch, hand by either, promptly chopping it off at source or instead, embrace it willingly, and constantly hit me on the head with it, whilst also then, crushing it, sinew by sinew, as she pleased.

Nope? Nothing? None of the above. Zilch?

"Oh hi, Hello there! Erm Hopper. I'm Linda, tut? I can't call you that? Sounds silly? I even feel silly saying it." Linda retorted laughing and pushing me, like it was my fault at the same time. "I'll call you Debbie. That's ok isn't it?"

"Are you calling my name silly?" Debbie feigned a fist fight, lifting up both her arms, whilst smiling and laughing.

"Just kidding. Yep Linda, Debbie will do just fine."

To my amazement, they were getting on famously within minutes. Either Linda was listening to too much of Michael Jacksons, 'I'm a lover not a fighter' ramblings, or she'd just bottled it. Or maybe she'd simply warmed to Debbie's black stranglers glow. She hadn't even seen Debbie as a threat. Not even a question as to how Debbie knew me. No Creeping jealousy at all. Whatever had come to pass, because Linda was a nurse, and Debbie was a carer, a common ground was found between them instantly. Before I could say, 'In the red corner' Mutual NHS guidelines and statistics and were being compared, negated, and dismissed or approved. New 'care in the home' policies, politics, or strategic new health models, were being launched. I was probably supposed to be taking minutes by now? Instead, I just smiled into my pint looking on at the pair of them, and thanking my lucky stars and Debbie's wonderful, warm charm.

Time had gotten on a bit. Three pints and lots of, Linda - Julie chatting later, it was a quarter to seven. The evening shift drinkers, had slowly begun to arrive. Filtering in from a wet underfoot, but slightly sunny Wigan. Debbie and her pal had also left. Sighting a surprise 21st party as the reason she was even up-town at all. Linda had also relaxed a lot more, thanks to the lip loosening, libations imbibing. Her pupil dilation was well in effect. This normally happens when you see something you want or desire. Or are getting tuned in. In Linda's case, when three halves of lager and lime have taken effect, on a normally drink free system. Rarely have I seen her this relaxed, or easy to be with. I always used to sing Spandau Ballets 'Highly Strung' at her, in an attempt to either wind her, up or convince her to chill out.

I'd even managed to get through a hit and miss, one-way conversation with Julie, after her afternoon giro shift. She was now at the opposite side of the bar with us. Regaling us with stories of Mike, her new fella and his new 'kit' car.

Time and alcohol had also made me almost forget that we were to rendezvous, at the John Bull chophouse, not the Bees knees.

"Come on Linda, time for us to make tracks or were gonna miss them."

"What?"

"Karen and Paul remember? Meeting them at the John Bull!"

She paused talking to think. "Oh yes, bugger? I'll just leave this then. It's getting a bit sickly now, anyway. Apart from that, I'm well bloated. I feel like a beached whale, full of wind too. Ooh God! I'm gonna explode." She put her half empty glass down on the table, covered her mouth, and rifted at the same time.

"Burp! Oh God, excuse me. I sound like Paul."

"Better out than in Linda." I assuaged

She picked up her coat, and stood up, to put it on.

"Ooof, I can't move?

Ooof, Stephen, I need the toilet quick?

Ooof oh my God, everything's gone south! I'm gonna burst!

Oh, this is not right? I feel like I'm going to have a baby? Look at my stomach Julie? Linda put her hands on her slightly obtuse belly, forcing it out, making it look like she was expecting. Making it look worse than It really was and laughing loudly at the same time. I was almost in hysterics. Then she started again.

"God, this skirt is cutting in to me? Ooof! I'll have to stay off that stuff in future *'burp'!* oops! pardon me again! Why didn't you say you it was so gassy Stephen?"

"Typical! I knew it would be my fault? Oh, stop moaning. Just have a big fart instead of holding it in until you get to the toilet. You'll be ok then."

"Ooof, God! You, cheeky swine! Don't be disgusting."

I received another two of her hand slaps, in quick succession. Which had no effect whatsoever, but to further push me into laughter melt down? Tears were running down my cheeks. She had even joined in. Julie too. I was leant over onto the table, with my hands in my head, pissing myself with laughter, because she was still standing up in front of me, Ooofing and holding a hand to her tummy. She was also in so much agony, from both the lager and Ooofing, she quickly sat back down on her chair, laughing and taking small breaths in-between, as if she really was having a baby.

"That's it, calm, small deep breaths, it'll be here soon." I joked, still laughing and putting my arm over her shoulder, and giving her a quick kiss on the cheek as I did.

Our laughter slowly calmed down to an acceptable, audible level, as we smiled at each other. At the height of all the hysterics, Julie's fella Mike had arrived. But because we were in such out-of-control laughter, that we couldn't even speak to explain things to him Which made things ten times worse and made him think we were actually laughing at him. Julie, had to put him in the picture, filling him in with all the Ooofing details, as he slowly began to see the funny side. He moved on from the subject, he felt was no part of, and immediately changed the conversation to his new car. Which was more than enough reason, for me and Linda to depart. At which point, my slightly worse for wear, Brian blessed character decided to make a reappearance.

"Come on, hold my hand, dearest creature. I will guide you on, as you are follied with wind, and are with my child." Which mental behaviour only confounded to confuse and alienate Mike from us even more. I slid my arm through Linda's, and necked the last of my drink, and tabled the glass, burping as I did.

"Come forth, my dear!"

Mike looked on, seemingly even more stressed with the situation. Julie and Linda kissed their goodbyes. I even went to plant one on Julie, just for the fun of it. Receiving instant daggers from Mike, and a laugh from Julie.

We walked out of the 'Bee's' arm in arm, into the Tuesday night watery sun. Its power fading in the west... To the right of the Bees was a small alleyway, leading to the towns bus terminal. The town church stood to the right and was chiming out a quarter to nine. I turned to look behind me, to see the moon slowly rising, to replace the sun, for its evening shift. Instantly reminding me, that I would have to be up again, at an un-godly hour for work, whilst all around me, Linda included, would still be happily tucked up in bed. Whether she stayed over at me mams, taking our Johns bed, who would be over at his Karen's, or retreated back to her mum and dad's.

THIRTEEN

In the evening sun, another thing soon formulated in my grey matter. In her present cosi-cosa relaxed state, she would more than definitely want a full sexual service, probably with a complete oil change later? Possibly filters, and a timing belt check too? I suppose that would help her bloated state immensely; I mused. Forcing the wind out of her, in regular stoic bursts. Or maybe it will release itself naturally, dependent on secret-farting, and also, how long it takes her system, fully to process. Or how much walking, or even dancing she gets up to tonight? If she even dances that at all? Mmm, I think I'm really over analysing this a little. More to the point why am I even bothering? Mind you, a full sexual service, was never really achieved at me mams. Noise being the major factor. Especially considering me mam would be in her kip. Even Shamus blowing one off downstairs, was enough to stir my Mam from her touch-paper slumber.

Once, when we'd first met, I brought her back to the house. We'd messed about on the couch a while. Until we started hearing pronounced erroneous coughs from upstairs. Faked out, to let us know, that she, Poirot-mother was on the case, and nothing untoward would be allowed to conjugate, under her nose, roof, or in her four walls.

In spite of this, and with a further few small tweaks, with my spanner I'd actually got Linda's engines purring so well, and just the way she liked it, our half naked fornicating fun, was hastily ended, by the stomping footsteps from mam's room, to the top of the stairs. As we heard the stern, solemn, and authoritarian words;

"You two... bed! You're not at Linda's house now."

All things considered. I'm feeling an early retreat home, to replenish both sleep and sustenance, might be in order. Having only eaten a packet of pork scratchings since my afternoon pies.

As we cross Wallgate, I'm hit by the smell of pizza, from Tolono's. We continue up wallgate as the sun fades, and an uncontrollable rumble from my stomach, makes us stop in our tracks.

"Was that your or mine?" Linda asks.

"Mine."

I was feeling some-what similar to Linda. Although she's on full to bursting mode. I feel like I'm running on empty. Empty of fodder, Clempt, and starving. My belly thinks my throats been cut? A situation I think I must alleviate very quickly. To also help soak up all the lager, I can feel swishing about in my mid-riff. Also, to minimize the need to cook if I decide to depart sooner rather than later. Which is currently at the latest odds?

"Come on I need something to eat. Let's get something to eat. Are you hungry Linda?"

"Oh God no, perish the thought of anything at the moment. I'm stuffed with the lager. Wouldn't have anywhere to put it." She fervently replied.

"Well I'll have to get something pronto. I'll nip into Tolono and get a nine inch of something? Eat it on the way. They don't take long, you can have some garlic bread with me, while we wait. That's usually free on the counter." I explain willing her on.

"No really I'm fine. You get what you want. I know it won't take you long to demolish it on the way you gannet. Probably take longer for them to cook it than for it to disappear?"

We walk a little further up Wallgate and cross the road near 'Oobidoo'. The weirdest name for a cheap shop I've ever known. I look at its bold red and white facia and start humming the catchy advert tune at Linda.

"Oobidoo the store for you... cut's the price of shopping...!"

She smiles back contently. "Shut up, you nutter!"

Tolono pizza and kebab is empty. Only just firing up cylinders for the night. The usual balding, grow it on one side, and comb it over the other, Greek charmer, Kostas is at the counter, kneading away at some pizza dough, and making light work of it too. He's a smooth talking, ladies man. His two underling, identical brothers are to the rear of him. probably his twins, but with a little more hair. They are also prepping the night's tomatoes, lettuce, cucumbers, cabbage, salads and various meats.

Mmm, I looked on. Kosta's lives on the premises with his lovely greek family. Usually, if one of them fades, or needs a sleep from all the relentless cooking, slicing, chopping and pizza and kebab selling, he would be instantly replaced, 'conveyer belt' style by another, family member, woken from slumber upstairs. That seemed to be how they usually kept going. Long hours and a forever open shop. A very hard working, and busy shop Indeed. They are like robots, automaton's or machmen, constantly dipping and chopping various bits of limbs. Chicken and pork, or kebab meat. Drowning them in fire-red sauces, for consumption by later-legless customers, through into the wee small hours. Probably, just before I have to, regrettably vacate my pit. Kostas throws an onion into the air, then masterfully picks up his huge knife, and slices away at it, without even looking down. Making full eye contact with me as he does. Mmm, funny I've never seen him on the fruit market? Bet he gets his stuff from Jimmy Highams, or Conroy's, I conclude as I'm being hypnotised, by his speedy knife action.

"Good evening sir, good evening, madam! What can I get you lovely people?" He throws a magnetic smile out at Linda. It's almost as if his, unnaturally white teeth, audibly ping, making both the noise, and emanating a sparkle at the same time. Just like Roger Moore's seventies playboy character does, in 'The Saint'.

No chance pal, I muse. She's definitely mine.

I scan the pizza menu, above his balding head, and opt for a 9-inch feta and mozzarella, gyro meat special, with extra mushrooms and no tomatoes.

I turn to Linda, resting both my arms on her shoulders, and clasping my hands together, behind her. Pulling her towards me in an embrace, whilst putting my head, cheek to cheek with hers.

"Are you ok, sweetheart? Won't be long with this, then we can meet them, if they've showed? Have a couple more, and head home. What d'you think?"

"You're tired Stephen. I can always tell. I'm fine really. On the top of the world."

She kisses me on the neck, making a big popping noise in my ear, and sending a shiver down my spine. She continues her sweet nothing, shit-job whisper.

"Tonight's been brilliant. Still is. I've not done a day's like you. I'm only part time, remember? You really do wear yourself out with at that market. So un-sociable, and long hours too. It's scandalous. He's scandalous. I wouldn't do it. We never get any decent us time together cos of it too? He has you doing far too much. And you let him take advantage too? You really will burn yourself out with that job."

She was right. I hated getting up so early. Not a morning person at all.

I didn't have a trade like joinery, plumbing or an electrician. I should have, but at the time, didn't see the point. I had to earn a crust quickly in life, and this was all I knew. But yep, she was completely right. I should find something else. Something I could pick up quickly.

"Gyro special! Black pepper? Sir, Gyro special, black pepper?" Kostas repeated louder, possibly thinking I had dropped off, with my head on Linda's shoulder. Either that, or he really needed a good sale, to clothe the 50 something, friends and family, he had squatting above the pizza shop.

"Stephen!" Linda shook me.

"Oh, sorry pal. Oi you?" I said to Linda "I was enjoying that snooze. Erm sorry pal, yes please." I continued to Kostas. "But not too much. What's the damage?"

"Three ninety-five, Sir."

"Here Kostas, Keep the change." Opening my wallet, I handed him a crumpled fiver. Take the pizza box in my left hand, whilst grabbing Linda's hand with my other.

"Thank you both very much! Enjoy the rest of your evening." Two more dazzling Roger Moore, teeth pings later, we're outside.

Walking up wallgate. As we walk through the now-bustling Tuesday night crowd. Some of the Maxims-massives, rock night, long haired punters, are blended in. Complete with signature devil's horns, Ronnie James Dio, hand gestures. As I wolf down my spicy pizza, Linda continues in the same vein.

"What about going working for your Dad? You said he'd already asked your John? Is his business taken off as well as your John says?"

"I dunno Linda, I haven't heard anything from him in ages?" I swallowed the last piece of pizza. Quickly licked my fingers, and wiped my hands, on the Tolono napkin. Made a quick about-turn, and walked back down the hill, I'd just walked up. Crumpled up pizza box, and firmly deposited it, into the large plastic bin, we'd just walked past. Then, Rush back up the hill, to tickle Linda's waist, just before we hit the Wiend. Wigan's oldest and narrowest street.

This led us, to the 500-year-old, second oldest building, in the town. The 'grade two' listed John Bull Chophouse, and hopefully, Karen and Paul. Named so, as it is reputedly, an old 1800's slaughter house, converted by some clever or skint soul. Now making it one of Wigan's most intriguing, real ale drinking haunts. Haunts being the operative word.

Regularly frequented by a myriad of strange and interesting folk. Ageing hippies, rockers and on Wednesdays, the stranglers black Pier bound Goths, punks and strange. Of which Hopper was one.

Similar to Scotland's Rosslyn chapel, but not on half as grand a scale. Just a pub in basic brick. But even so, still an architectural curiosity, with its sloping floors, wooden beams and five coursed, bonded brickwork. Hooks where the slaughtered carcasses used to hang, still visibly jutting off the walls. There's even an archetypal ghost, associated with it. A horse travelling stranger called at the pub, to drown his sorrows after a secret and failed love tryst and fell drunk from the upstairs balcony.

"Hope we haven't missed them?" Linda asserts, tripping on the mangy door mat, with the words 'Nice normal Family', weaved into it.

"Ha-ha, steady Linda, you numpty."

The place is jam-packed and already buzzing with atmosphere. The huge 70's antique jukebox, playing one of the most grooved out records in it. Patti Smiths, 'Because the Night'

"I wonder which alcoholic route to take in here." I ponder.

"Try the slowing down route Stephen." Linda unhelpfully but helpfully advises.

There were probably a handful of CAMRA buffs standing around me, who could give me some sound, tried and tested advice on that score. Whilst also boring me to tears, with personally sampled, ale tips and trips. Recently attended festivals prices, and tell me of, new strange named, beer additions and then go on to introduce me to their family of 'panurus biarmicus' birds, individually and by name, presently nesting in their long grey 'Hamlet' looking beards.

"Get me half a still orange Stephen. I'm nipping upstairs to the toilet."

"Yes love, what can I get you?" shouted the small, demure, unsurprisingly Goth clad, trainee bar girl.

"A Newky, and some still orange thanks."

"I'll have to give you a pint glass with that. They're stopping us selling it just in the bottles now? Bureaucratic, Brussels bastards!"

She bent underneath the optics, to fashion a cold orange from the cooler. As I waited puzzled. I telescoped the room behind me, to see umpteen bottles of Newcastle brown, being cordially necked by bottle, and a corner table, of stacked and clean empty pint glasses.

Linda was quickly back, after her fated goth and rocker clamour, to get to the loo.

Totally unimpressed by her fight to pee and going on to explain how the balsa-wood looking quality of the balcony, at the side of the toilets, hadn't impressed or filled her, with any courage to stand anywhere near it. Nor even attempt to hike her way back upstairs, as there were no tables or seats spare, and Karen and Paul, were its balcony rails only brave, or clueless leaner's.

"Oh, they're up there, with the Gods, are they?"

"Yes, they are, and it's bad enough down here. They didn't see me either. Too packed. I'll be damned if I'm fighting through them lot again."

"Look, we may as well Linda? Let's just go and show our faces, for half an hour, then let's go. By the time we get a taxi down the road, it'll be getting on a bit, and I much as I'd like too, I don't want to stop out all bloody night either? You're working tomorrow too Linda."

Linda, unlike me, had a good part-time job, with decent hours. She was a trainee psychiatric nurse at Billinge hospital, and as far as I was concerned, a multitude of benefits. She was pretty career minded too. She was on her third year of a residency. A residency, that sadly for me, didn't include the benefits of sleeping over. Strictly banning all, or any kind of bunk over activity, of their precious trainees, on the nurse's quarters, in the grounds of the hospital. When we first started courting, and I first found out about her job, and how she lived on the Hospital grounds, my over imaginative brain, rather happily envisaged myself, in some kind of 'Carry on Doctor' scenario, possibly as the Jim Dale character, and Barbara Windsor as Linda's flatmate Jill.

I'd lost count, and finally given up, on the amount times I'd tried to twist Linda's arm, into letting me stay over with her, at her butlins-ish, chalet style quarters, instead of at me mams, or over at her parents. It would probably have been, a virtually impossible goal to achieve, anyway. I'd already tried and failed. And as far as I was concerned, never again. Linda went nuts when she found out.

When I attempted it, Billinge seemed like it was run like Colditz, but like breaking into Fort Knox. I wouldn't go as far as guns, Goons, Gestapo and barbed wire, on stalag luft 1. More like CCTV, security and Alcatraz. With me as a drunken, Sean Connerys character, John Patrick Mason. After a rather heavy night up Wigan, on the piss. Only instead of breaking out, trying to break in.

Linda was in the final, and hardest year of her training. But at the end of her path, stood to be in an excellent position, career and dosh wise. But not content with that, she was also attending a part-time college course in social work, and hoped to combine the two, to end up in some shit hot, high end administration or management job.

I would hazard a guess, that after all her constant, continuous training malarkey, she'd much more realistically, end up sitting very pretty, and more than comfortably well off than most. Possibly not only swimming in money but also in some kind of government run, health management committee job. Driving a BMW, and living in some mega-posh house in standish, near Jimmy Beeches restaurant, and married to some high-faluting, NHS executive. With me an old man, having gone through a long and haggardly slow metamorphosis, through the countless decades of early morning market years work, into a Lancashire speaking equivalent my boss Peter. Smoking like a trooper, and still pedalling leeks, lettuce and the like. Still drinking, Klix-cup coffee, or the Oxo drink, laced with whiskey, from a silver hidden hip flask?

Linda now looked like she'd clearly had enough, and was forcefully pushing her way through the packed, and ever-increasing pub, of Jon Bon Jovi, and Joey Tempest lookalikes. Credence Clearwater grand dads, or rag tag, Lord of The Rings cast, and extras misfits in the room. She finally reached the bottom of the stairs, for the second time, and had almost worn her orange juice all over her red, now battle-weary coat, twice. The sardine-tin alcoholic, argy bargee had now really pissed her off. She finally ended up, being face to face, with a smiling, Kate Bush clone? Complete with flowing russet coloured locks, and huge red, wuthering heights dress, completely blocking the foot of the stairs.

"Excuse me love, but shouldn't you be in a farmer's field somewhere, looking for that fucking bastard Heathcliff?"

I nearly spat a mouthful of Newcastle brown, all over the back of Linda's coat.

"I beg your pardon!" Replied the shocked Miss Bushalike. Obviously taken back by Linda's sarcasm.

Ha-ha-ha fucking brilliant I thought! Well done Linda.

"Karen!" Linda shouted, now taking the first of the stair steps, with me happily bringing up her rear.

"Woooh, hiya!" Karen extended a waving hand in our direction, as Paul looked on, stony-faced as usual.

I look up, still following, and take a last swig of the brown stuff. Here we go, I muse. The final push toward the summit of Mount Doom-amon armath or Weather top-amon sul, In Lord of the Rings, I playfully imagine. At least this body-ridden, bloody stair case anyway.

Probably go through all this hassle, just so we can end dying a horrible and painful death, by being slowly, and eventually inched off the love tryst balcony, by the minute by minute ever expanding, assemblage of people, cramming our space. Finding our final resting place, on the York stone, flagged floor of the place, after being multiply mutilated, and impaled on the slaughter house carcass hooks, on our way down.

"Hey you two where've you been?" Karen asked.

"Bloody getting here! excuse me mate! I don't know how you can put up with this!" Linda groaned. "Be careful leaning on THAT! bloody, rickety thing too Karen." Linda the instant architectural engineer points out. Rigorously grabbing the balcony rail, and yanking it side-to-side safety, checking its rigidity.

"What time d'you fuckin call this Inge? We've been here fuckin ages waiting for you."

Paul wasn't too impressed with my time keeping.

"Oh, calm down Paul? You're in your favourite boozer, what more d'you want? We said we'd definitely be here. Just got a little held up, with people, pizzas and perms."

"Well, we're going to Maxims after this, anyway. Fancy it Linda?" Karen asked.

"Yeah. You should both come, it's a fuckin great night." Paul added. "It's a heavy rock fuckin-frenzy ha-ha!" Paul shook his head, heavy-metal fashion, fully completing his homage, by turning his lager bottle into a miniature air guitar.

"Not for us" Linda replied. Looking at me for agreement.

"Nah," I added. "Don't fancy it."

"Oh, come on Linda? You told me you'd try anything once?"

"I know I did, but to be honest, I've just about had enough of it in here? Let alone going through it all again in Maxims. I don't think my eardrums would take it, and I'll probably end up with a headache. So, thanks, but no thanks."

"What about you then Inge? Think you could handle it?'

"I'm with Linda on this Paul."

"Shitter..."

"Oh, here we go? Christ! it's not about being a shitter. It's not about anything, other than I'll be wasted in the morning. If I come along to some place, I might not even like, so; no! Thanks, but no thanks," I repeated.

"Shitter.... ha-ha."

"Paul! Shut it."

As Paul was winding me, Karen was also trying her British, welter weight, level best, arm twisting Linda. Who I knew, wasn't going to move an Inch.

Paul smiled and cranked it up a notch.

"Shitter... come out to play!"

"Paul, enough."

"Shitter... come out to play."

"Shitter... come out to plaeeeeaaaay!"

He lifted his voice, a full octave higher, and turned it into an improvised version, of the bottle-chinking scene, out of 'The Warriors'.

"Shitter... come out to plaeeeeaaay!"

This continued randomly, for another two minutes. I went through various motions, of putting my fingers in my ears, pretending to leave, by taking the stairs. Pretending he wasn't even bothering me and finally sticking my head under Linda's coat.

"Oh, for fucks sake."

I grinned and started laughing. Realising my utter defeat. Soon joined smiling, by Karen then Paul, and finally Linda.

"Ok, ok. But it can't be for long though? And the sooner we get there, the sooner we can leave. You and Karen can stay all bloody night. But we're pissing off home. We'll give you an hour max. No ifs or buts either! Non-negotiable, an hour ok."

"I'll hold you to that Stephen." Linda announced. "I'll bloody skull-drag you out of there!"

"Good. Hold me to it! That'll do for me. Come on, let's sup-up, and get the hell out of here."

FOURTEEN

Queuing up outside Maxims at 10pm, I felt, and probably looked strangely out of place. Un-rock-like? Going into a nightclub, to listen to a completely different type of music than I would normally allow to take assault on my senses, and ears. But was quite looking forward to experiencing something different. I didn't even any preconceived idea, of what to expect either. Apart from knowing the inside of Maxims, like the back of my hand. I'd been in the place, literally dozens of times. At the under 18's disco, and more than enough, after I'd eclipsed that age too. Oh, its maybe just loads of young and old blokes, in dark corners swapping biker talk, tips and probably swapping girlfriends too? Wife swapping rockers.

Mmm? Maybe it's just a slightly bigger version of the John Bull, except with a dance floor, and more room. There wasn't really much of a queue either. People were being let in to pay, almost immediately. Just a quick up and down glance from the two bouncers, who were hardly even paying attention, and through the door we went.

"Alright Paul? Your Marks in." said the shaved headed, 'world's strongest man' one, as Paul gave him a knowing nod.

"Tell him I'll come see him later."

"Ok, Ripper, thanks."

What the fuck? I thought. I quickly put my head down, and hand over my mouth, as fast as I could, just managing get the door between me, the bouncer, and just out of his earshot, and burst out laughing. I couldn't help it? I was doubled over instantly. Almost, physically imploding on the spot. I was in pleats of laughter. I'd probably be needing some stitches too, if I didn't shut up? Oh my God that was fucking great? I grinned.

"What the fuck Paul?" I asked, still working his name out in my head.

"Ha-ha-ha, did I hear you right? Did you call him Ripper? Or was it Rapper ha-ha?" He does look like a fat, white version of Grandmaster Flash, ha-ha. Ripper, Rapper? oh my God! *There's not a problem I can't fix... cos I can do it... in the mix. White lines!*

"Shut the fuck up Inge, Come on, your turn. Paul grabbed my shoulders and shoved me forward.

The ageing till woman, wasn't amused with me either? Giving me more of a once-over look, than the bouncers.

"It is rock night you know? four fifty please." She snarled.

"There you go love," I replied.

Mmm, I should calm down a bit. I bet that's Rippers fucking Mother, I thought. *Or his wanna-be bitch Stephen?* my baddie tempter added. I was still internally laughing, but the rest of them were solemn as hell. It was as if they were attending a funeral? Looking at me as if I was the naughty child. I was half expecting to be crowned with the 'Dunce' hat. Even as we climbed the two long sets of stairs, up to the club, they were still silent.

"What the hell's up with you lot? Aren't we supposed to be enjoying ourselves? What have I done now? Why so sombre?"

"I'll go get the round in" Paul said, giving Karen a moody glance, and headed quickly away. Straight for the long bar, behind the DJ booth, where he'd immediately spotted his older brother, Mark. Karen and Linda quickly found a small round table, and parked their arses, as Karen spoke. "Nothing Ste, you've done nothing wrong at all." She said. "Unlike some jealous bastards." She looked over in Paul's direction.

"That's him, the bouncer. Paul and he had a fight, last time we were here. Remember he told you earlier in the Freemasons."

"Oh right." Linda said.

"Paul thinks he was trying to tap me up, when I went the loo." Karen continued.

"I went for a pee, and when I came out, Ripper stopped me, asking how I was. Only because he hadn't seen me for ages and ages. Then Paul started his usual jealous crap. Christ! I've known Nigel for years? We were in the same class in primary school."

"But Paul said he launched him through a window Karen? Doesn't look much like much glass damage on him to me." I retorted. "Anyway, hang on a minute." I said, turning to Linda. "How did you know?'.

"Karen filled me in, when we were walking here."

"Oh right. All becomes clear now." I nodded.

"One more thing?" I said. "Why do they call him Ripper? and is it Ripper, or Rapper?" I smiled, bursting out laughing again.

"It's Ripper!" Karen said, quickly looking around, and bursting into a long overdue smile.

"It's actually Nigel."

"What! Nigel, bloody hell! I don't know which is worse, Nigel or Ripper? Come on then, what's the story?" I asked.

"There's nothing to it really Ste. He works on a farm. Actually, lives there. Generations of his family are farmers. I would probably be better off going with him than that arrogant, ignorant sod," she said glancing in Paul's direction.

"He's absolutely loaded! He's next in line to get his Dad's farm. Only has a sister, and she's training to be a lawyer. She's not interested in the farming life, so it'll all be down to him."

"I still don't follow Karen."

"Oh sorry, the nickname? It's because he drives a massive combine harvester. Something called a Massey Ferguson he said? Oh, I dunno what it is? His Dad was the first in the country to get one. It has special extending arms. Anyway, all the farmers in the country, went over to watch him take delivery of it. Even the national press was there, taking pictures. The long and short of it is, it has the strongest, grass ripping percentage power out there. So, cos he had it first, and drove it first, they just started calling him Ripper, as a joke and it stuck.

"Don't tell Paul his name's Nigel, or even mention him, or he'll only start his jealousy shit all over again. Or just start taking the piss out of Nigel's name, and I really don't think I can go through all that bullshit again. I just can't be arsed with it all. You know how jealous he gets Ste. I just can't do anything anymore." Karen continued, as if she'd finally found a release at long last. My Mum told me to get rid of him? But she just doesn't like Paul. Never has. I can't talk to me Mum at all. I get more sense out of Dad, and he's not much better. Even the girls at work have told me to dump him. He found that out from Mark too. Doesn't like me talking to them now either. That's why me and your Linda have been getting pallier and talking more. D'you know, even if I'm going swimming, or keep-fit, with some girls from work, he pulls a childish tantrum. All he wants us to do is sit in his front room, watching telly with his mum and dad. We hardly do anything anymore, and it's all because of his jealousy. He's turning into a right boring bastard."

"Shush! Karen." Linda reached over the table, grabbing Karen's hand. "He's coming back."

Paul plonked a beer tray down on the table and passed me a bottle of Newcastle Brown.

"Here Inge, get that down you". Paul, as un-charming as ever, left the girls drinks, on the tray and proceeded gulping his bottle. Linda eyed her alcohol absent orange as Paul, yanked out a chair, whilst gulping. Wobbled the table and spilled Karen and Linda's drinks in the process.

"Paul! You, clumsy git!" Karen said, picking up a beer mat, and chasing all the liquid onto the floor.

"Stephen, d'you mind if I have a cocktail next time?"

"You can have anything you want sweetheart. Do they do cocktails?" I dumbly added.

"Course they do." Karen smiled.

"There's a big list, at the side of the bar. They do specials too. Quite reasonable."

Compared to a 'typical' Friday night's crowd rock-night, still looked quite empty? I looked at my watch. It was only just past 10-30.

"Does it get packed later Paul?"

He looked around. "About the same amount again. its early doors though yet Inge. Some really hot bitches get in here. It's our Marks bitches, Birthday party here tonight. She's not in yet? She's coming with a load of other bitches from work. She'd better get a fuckin move on. He's got a fuckin stripper for her. Gonna get his fuckin big, fireman's hose out ha-ha."

I looked over at Karen, beginning to favour her corner, when it came to Paul.

I was quite caustic and could be blatantly foul-mouthed if need be. But there's a time and a place for it. You don't have to be rough as sandpaper and swearing all the time. Especially with your woman on your arm.

Paul was on the money, regarding the women though. As I look around the room, there are some rather tasty specimens, throwing some weird shapes, on the dance floor. The music was good too? I even knew the last three songs, both title and artist. The dance floor swelled with bodies, or swiftly emptied, like a bad smell. Dependent on what track the bald-headed DJ put on next.

As the incessant screaming of drums, and guitars from a particularly heavyweight track faded, the place went quiet.

In the absence of any kind of music whatsoever, the rock crowd's voices instantly became louder. Everyone looked in unison, over at the DJ booth, to form some kind of conclusion, as to where the hell, the music had disappeared too.

He picked up the microphone "Sorry good people. Do we have a Sharon Spencer in?"

The room fell even more silent. People whispered and blankly looked around at each other.

"Sharon Spencer? Any advance on Sharon Spencer? Final call for Miss Spencer?" the bald DJ added smiling, as if he was some kind of airport announcer.

Silence, Nothing?

Pauls brother Mark, appeared at the side of the Dj's stand. Leaning over the decks, he pointed in the direction of the exit, and was flailing his arms, for the Dj's benefit. Doing the universal ad-libbed, sign language equivalent for, I'm skint or I don't know.

"She's not fuckin turned up yet? Marks gonna go apeshit."

Paul said, swigging his bottle.

Everyone was still looking as confused, as everyone else, as to who the mysterious woman was. Meanwhile, Pauls Brother, was still madly flailing his arms, at anyone who was the slightest bit interested.

Just then, an opening music crescendo, familiar to me smashed the silence to pieces. The 'no show' birthday-bitch situation was instantly forgotten. 'Whitesnakes' rock ballad 'Here I go again' came thrashing through the speakers, like a juggernaut. Within seconds, the dance floor was full. Even I'd fashioned the table as my drums, and somehow accrued, a handbag air guitar.

"Oh wow! What a brilliant song! I wish I was, David Coverdale? I shouted over the music.

"David who?" Paul asked.

"The Demi-God, David Coverdale, you dip-shit! 'Whitesnakes' singer! Oh, never mind, go back to sleep Paul." I said, drumming into the table.

The women on the dance floor, were going bonkers. Some of them had amazingly, un-humanly tight-fitting red, blue and gold skirts. There were long, jet black and blond hair, writhing and swinging everywhere. Some women, looked like they'd just stepped out of a high-class hair salon. Some with Lycra pants, leaving nothing to the imagination at all. A couple of them, were only short of a pole.

There was bouncing cleavage everywhere. Some stunningly fit women, with incredibly outstanding figures, and some with absolutely no figures at all, fat, with bingo wings, saggy tits and flesh popping out all over the place. Possibly the last figures they'd watched the pounds on correctly, was giving the right admission fee, to the other female, ageing rock, let it all hang out women, on the entrance door till.

Karen and Linda had joined the dance floor too. Linda had left her handbag on my lap. Judging by the packed dance floor. I don't suppose it would've lasted long on the parquet floor, with them dancing around it.

I was feeling really glad I came. The music was very positive and uplifting. Acknowledging my approval, I gave Paul an 'Oh no! it's 'Selwyn Froggitt' thumbs up across the table. He didn't even hear me singing over the banging Coverdale track either. He hadn't even see my thumbs up. He was too busy watching Karen and Linda, on the dance floor. "Hey Paul! it's alright in here, mate!" I shouted across the table.

"Mmm, good isn't it."

The song came to an end, and was instantly replaced by another, just as lively tune, which didn't ring any bells on my music antenna. Probably hadn't rung any bells, with the girls either. Looking doubly confused, 'I dunno this one' and head shaking mode, as they came back and quickly took their seats.

Linda flicked her wrist, keeping a keen eye on the time.

"How long have we got I asked?"

"You're alright just yet. I'll come with you to the bar though. Not leaving here without a cocktail."

"You can have one of them, when we get home if you like? Without the tail." I grinned.

"Same again Paul? Karen?"

Paul tilted his bottle, like a nodding dog, in acquiesce.

"Get me one of what Linda's having." Karen said as we stood up.

"I don't know what I'm having yet Karen?"

"Oh, it doesn't matter. It'll be a surprise then." Karen offered.

"Oh, come on, come with us Karen, and you can pick one yourself." Linda grabbed Karen's hand, in an affectionate 'were in this together' way.

"No, it's ok, I'll stay here with Paul. Just get me the same as you."

Linda looked over at me. "Oh, ok then, we won't be long."

When we were a safe distance from the table, Linda looked back at Karen.

"She wanted to come with us then, didn't she?"

"Yep, I know she did."

"He's an arrogant bastard! Ooh, I wouldn't put up with him at all."

"I know you wouldn't."

"Oi, don't you bloody patronise me Stephen." Linda said "I'll have your bollocks for ice cubes!"

"I wasn't, and yes, I know you will."

FIFTEEN

W e walked along the edge of the circular dance floor. Through a hive of tables, and up three steps, to the smaller cocktail bar, just to the side of the long one. It was now, almost three deep with sweaty, thirsty punters, who'd probably just been getting their rocks, air guitars, hair, tits, crotches, and every other sexual part of their anatomy off, to the 'Whitesnake' track.

Paul's brother Mark, was still aimlessly talking to the DJ. Looking even more confused than he had before. Probably sucking up, to get his fav rock bands, track played I thought.

I dallied myself through the ever present, Maxims circular walkers. Mmm, I thought. That never changes. The anti clockwise walkers. That was something that always puzzled and made me scratch my head, about this place. Ever since I'd started frequenting it, years ago and no matter what night, or what type of disco. Under 18's, over 18's, alternative night, or even on one of the rare punk nights. People have walked around and around, the dance-floor and place for no apparent reason. Constantly, in circles, and all in the same, anti-clockwise direction, for no logical reason at all. There's more than ample, ass parking space, tables and chairs, bar stools, high stools.

Even a hot food bar, adorned with extra seating, you could to use, if the place was really splitting at the seams. But still, the anti clockwise walkers, walked. They were like a stream of zombies, following something, and each other, but not knowing what the hell, it was they were to follow. Visually, all they were short of, was putting their hands up, in front of themselves. Akin to the zombies, in Michael Jacksons 'Thriller'.

Oh, and God forbid, if you tried to walk in the opposite direction to them. In fact, it was virtually impossible. I'd tried it one night, just for the fun of it. You would be completely bumped out of the way. Pushed around, like a pinball, until you gave up. Shunned, and looked at, as if you were the unclean, or had the plague. Ultimately, forced by the continuous human vortex, to concede, turn through 180' degrees, and become like the others. The anti clockwise walkers. Mmm, that actually sounds like a rock band.

I was sidled between the end of the bar, and the back of a very dishy, twenty something, rock chick. With a short gold skirt, and amazingly long black hair. Her hair was quite a feat. Being so long, it stopped, just above, her asses tail bone. The best thing about it though, was she had a red fringe too?

Linda was eyeing the cocktail board. I tapped her on the shoulder, to grab her attention. Clenched my fist, pretending to tug on the rock woman's, long black mane, as if it was going to ring a bell somewhere.

"Stop it Stephen!" Linda whispered, turning quickly, back to the board, and pointing, waiting for cocktail ideas from me?

"Ooh, I don't know what I fancy? Ooh, that's good? buy two, get a vermouth red taster free. What's vermouth?"

I was still marvelling, at the cool rock chick's hair. Still astounded, by its length and now, after many careful, 'Nicky Clarke-ish' glances, I'd now also noticed, it's amazing straightness.

"Stephen, are you listening to me?"

"First here?" Asked the bar man. The long-haired girl frowned at me, with her perfectly straight red fringe, then turned to the bar man, and gave him her order, turning back to me when she'd finished, and smiled, as if to confirm that I could order next.

Her cool fringe reminded me of Elizabeth Taylors in 'Cleopatra'. I bet you could draw a line with that perfectly, aligned, horizontal fringe. Just hemmed over her, come to bed eyes, I thought? She's like the equilateral triangle girl, or 'pi' girl? Or something from my technical drawing class at school? Both sides of her lovely, highpotanuse arse, equalled the sum of the other bits. Mmm, haha?

Or she could be Heineken girl? Refreshing the arses other hair can't reach. God knows, her hair could reach it, even encompass it, if she spun around? Meanwhile, Linda was still perusing the board, looking even more deeply cocktail confused.

"What shall I try? I'll get something with Vodka I think? Maybe I should get a Rock Lobster, seeing as its rock night haha. Oooh, yeuch, I bet that Pochin cocktail will kill your guts? That's potatoes isn't it? Does Karen like gin Stephen?"

"Erm, I have no idea, Linda."

'Fringe girl' was now deep in conversation, with her leather-clad boyfriend, who looked to be sipping something, that looked like frothy engine oil, from a tall over-sized glass. He sported a huge, black mop of hair, not dis-similar to Andrew Eldritch, from the 'Sisters of Mercy'. Probably his brother I thought.

I bet she loses a good few lengths of her hair, when he's grabbing hold of it, yanking on it when he's stuck up to the chunks, giving her all he's got. That's probably why it's so straight? Countless hours of hair grooming, after a particularly extensive night's, sex-session, between the sheets. I thought.

"Have you made your mind up yet Linda? I think we're next."

"I'm more confused now, than I was before? Erm, go on, I'll have a 'Rock Lobster' and you can get Karen 'A Bloody Good Time'. We can compare, taste or swop."

The order of beer service, seemed it might take longer than I'd first anticipated. The bar man had started with fringe girl, and gone along the bar line, person to person, and was currently on the sixth rocker. I hope he wasn't some kind of robot server, who was going to continue right on through the other five people, until he reached the other end, bounced off the wall and landed in front of me? I should really stop, constantly day dreaming? He'll be here shortly.

"That's the Lager barrel changed Sam."

"Ok, thanks Gerry. Start over that side, I'll stick over here." said the busier barman, to the Irish one.

"Next down here please!"

I was in like a rash.

"Two bottles of Newcastle Brown, and erm, a couple of cocktails please mate."

"Tell him what cocktails you want Linda?" Rather than sounding like a complete twerp, I'd quickly opted to let her shout over, the daft sounding, cocktail names.

"A 'Rock Lobster' and 'A Bloody Good Time please."

The barrel changing bar man, looked over at Linda, and smiled. She smiled back concurring. I felt myself, slightly turning into Paul. Almost green with envy. This fella's right down Linda's street I thought? She was liking his attention too. Taller, and stockier than me. Short, gelled hair, with two large gold sleepers. Quite rugged, unshaven and gypsy looking.

"Coming right up darling! Is it all right if I give you an extra Rock Lobster? we've no red vermouth left?"

"Erm, that's ok, anything at all, is fine thanks." Linda replied to her new beau. Inching herself tightly, between fringe girl, the bar, and me. So tightly in fact that I was forced further in to the corner. Fringe girl had already looked around twice, and further fidgeted, when she heard Linda's voice. Now seemingly to have adopted, a rather more rigid, 'I'm not fucking moving bitch' stance.

I decided to concede my corner, and moved away from the bar, then I could easily access my wallet. "Here Linda, It's my turn."

"I'll get you a tray for that lot." The 'drop dead gorgeous' gypsy smiled.

"Thanks." Linda puppy dogged.

Linda was now so close to him, she was possibly, melded to the bar.

Since I'd moved, she'd managed to galvanise her elbows, either side of her, with both hands covering her purse in the middle, thus creating a gypsy swoon space. The elbow previously in my chest, now tight to the wall, and the other elbow promising to seriously impale, or damage, fringe girl's middle-back, or flowing locks. Linda was being mesmerised by his cocktail shaking credentials. He cracked the tops of two bottles of Newky, consecutively with one hand, whilst also lacing two cocktail glasses, with various unnamed liquids, from unmarked bottles, further adding cherries and umbrellas, with his now finished, Newky hand.

Mmm, neat bloody council pop, he's putting in there thought. I was secretly seething, at his innate ability, to adorn Linda's attention. Fringe girl also looked, continually more restless, and agitated with Linda. Maybe she fancied a piece of him too?

My head now imagined, a Linda, fringe girl, cat-fight. With Linda clawing out strips, lengths, and locks of perfectly, coiffured fringe girl's mane, as her Andrew Eldritch boyfriend, sang his rendition of 'The Sisters of Mercy's', 'This Corrosion' for the whole wrestling bouts theme tune. Watched irreverently, by the clapping gypsy bar man, who at this point in my head, was quoting realistically cheap prices, to concrete or tarmac Linda's driveway?

Mmm, I know which driveway he's after laying.

"Alright Inge! how's it going?"

Mark woke me from my daydream.

"Alright Mark, how you doing pal?"

Mark looked seemingly, as agitated as fringe girl, but for totally different reasons. At least he wasn't madly flailing his arms like a human bird anymore.

"I'm alright Inge. I saw you come in with our Paul and Karen. I'm friggin sick of watching that bloody door! And she's still not here the fuckin cow!"

"Oh, the girlfriend?"

"Yeah her. She's not gonna be the girlfriend for much longer, if she doesn't get her fuckin arse here. Fifty fuckin quid I paid for a stripper, and he's just said he's gonna leave, if she's not here by eleven.

"Oh, not good? What time is it now Mark?" I ask.

"Nearly five too."

"Bloody hell is it? Shit! I should think about getting out of here soon too? Work in the morning. I'll be knackered again, if I don't get a rush on. It would help, if that bastard served us the drinks a bit quicker, instead of trying to get into Linda's knickers?"

"She's fuckin here! Thank fuck for that!" Mark said, looking relieved.

"I wouldn't worry too much about him Inge. He's gay. Right, gonna go tell that stripper guy. Another fuckin gay boy! before he finally decides to fuck off. Make sure he gives her the show of his life. Talk to you later Inge."

Bloody hell, I ponder, he's gay? Little does Linda know, haha. Little did I know? Amazing. He looked so much the ladies man? Oh well, looks can be deceptive. Mark seems to know a lot about gay spotting. Maybe he's gay? They do say a gay can spot a gay a mile off? Mmm.

Mark was gone in a flash. Just as soon as he'd appeared. He's like 'Mr Ben' I thought. Without the suit and hat.

I could just make out Marks blond bald patch, bobbing through the anti-clockwise human vortex, as he made his way towards his rather obese, cowboy hat, wearing girlfriend and her band of fat-jeaned, duplicately, attired posse, now milling around the entrance door. You couldn't miss her. She seemed to be glowing. Standing out at the front of them, like a human Christmas tree? Not shape but also in glow. She seemed to have been kitted out with some human form of Christmas tree lights? Finished off, with a red-flashing crown, around the brim of her mock, ten-gallon hat. Probably some battery-operated lights, they pinched off a Christmas tree too? I thought. Hope the batteries go bloody flat? Mmm, bet she's got them concealed in her knickers too I thought?

Her eight-strong female party, were closely followed by none other than, Nigel. Possibly deciding that now was a good time to show all and sundry, but particularly Karen, his bouncer presence and prowess. Escorting the all-female, cowboy throng to a suitably, large hussy, butt parking area. Then he'd also be able to suss out, where Karen was sitting, in the bigger scheme of things.

Rather, you than me Mark, I thought, as he scurried up to the fairer sex desperados.

"Stephen Stephen! here!................ grab this tray off Gerry. Thanks Gerry, and good luck with Sebastian."

Mmm, first-name terms now, I thought.

"Alright, alright, calm your jets Linda."

Linda moved out of the way, as I scooped the full drink and change laden, steel tray up from the bar. Nudging fringe girl in the back, with the tray as I do.

"Ooops, sorry love."

"Thanks again Gerry." Linda smiles.

"No problem at all Linda. You go on now! have a lovely night. First here please!"

"Oh, he's really nice. Lovely fella. He's gay you know?"

I look back, at a somewhat relieved looking fringe girl, as we leave the bar.

"Is he really Linda?" I inquire, "You'd never know."

"Yes, Gerry's got a new boyfriend, Sebastian. Posh Londoner, with plenty money. He's moving in with Gerry, at the weekend. I hope it works out for him. He's a lovely fella."

"I know Linda you just said."

Linda was prattling on regardless. I was using all my balancing skill, to avoid a serious, beer spilling accident, on the three steps down, from the bar to the dance floor level. All major junctions, trunk roads tabled areas, in and around the full and rocking dance floor, could draw me to a slippery halt, if I wasn't careful. It would be a liquid-spillage, equal to an overturned, rock music tanker, as I felt the tray getting heavier and heavier.

"Paul, quick, lose that empty tray, let me put this bloody thing down."

"You, fuckin weakling!" Paul said grabbing the empty tray, just in time. Reaching behind him, and sliding it in-between the legs of the chairs, on an empty table.

"Fuckin hell that was heavy."

"You're a fuckin weedy bastard Inge. I see our Marks bitch finally turned up. Couldn't put up with her. She'd do my friggin head in."

Karen looked up at me as I sat down. I inquisitively glanced back. *Yes, I know Karen. I know exactly what you're thinking. I'm with you*, I thought.

"Ooh, what have you got me? Cool, which one's mine? They look good. What they called?

Karen smiled at a Linda.

"Take your pick? I don't mind. Have a taste of both and have whichever you like Karen?

"That's a Rock Lobster, and that one's 'A Bloody Good Time' I think? Oh, I'm not sure which is which now haha. Can you remember, which was which Stephen?"

"I have absolutely no idea? Didn't even see what he put in em either."

"Oh, just have a taste and see which you like Karen."

"Have a taste quick Karen. We really need to be leaving soon. It's great and all that, but we've been here too long now? It's nearly eleven Linda," I say, recoiling in a rushed over-indulgent mouthful of beer.

"Oh, is it? I'd better drink up too, Karen." Linda says, picking up her cocktail of choice.

It's at this point, that my ears are pricked up to the music. Followed rapidly, by another, but more fierce, human surge of bodies, to the dance floor.

"Who's this Paul?"

"No good askin me Inge, I don't know."

"Karen who's singing? Any ideas? What's the group or song?" I Impatiently ask. Karen was partaking in cocktail, small talk with Linda. Probably about a cock, of the Gerry and Nigel kind.

"What? oh, I don't know what the music is? But them lot seem too, don't they?" Karen points her straw, at the packed dance-floor, sipping and tapping along at the same time.

"Bloody hell, four of us at a rock night, and not a one of us knows who we're bloody listening to?"

"Go and ask our Marks mate, Tony the DJ." Paul interjects. "But go around the back of the booth. You'll need an 'Uzi 9mm' to get through them lot, haha." He says, nodding at the dancing multitude, currently amassing every inch of the parquet, wooden dance floor.

I look around Maxims. There's virtually no anti-clockwise walkers to be seen at all? Mmm, they're all on the bloody dance-floor that's why.

Astounding! No zombie walkers. Now that is a first! I should take a picture I thought. Maybe if I had a camera.

"I bloody will Paul. Tony? Which one's he? There's two blokes in there Paul? I ask, putting down my bottle, and rising to my feet.

"But I thought we were going Stephen?"

"We are. But this is Important Linda, won't be a minute."

"Phil's the permed dude. Tony's the baldy." Paul swigged.

I make my way quickly, toward the DJ booth, through the empty seating area, and up the three steps. Because I was such a major pain in the arse music lover, and with an almost un-humanly keen ear for a good tune. And also, the type of person, never wanting to be kept out of the music loop, or ever look in any way un-informed. If it was anything remotely or heavily music driven, I wanted to know. I quickly arrived, at the side of the banging rock booth.

SIXTEEN

At home, Mam was always having a go at me at the amount of money, in her eyes, I frivolously wasted, week to week on magazines, records and cassettes. My room was stacked with it. In every possible form. Even my bedroom wall, was covered corner to corner, with album artwork and covers of my favourite bands 12'-inch record sleeves. It was a constant nagging and bain of mams life, for her to try, to make me agree take them all down. An argument she continuously gave in too. Bowing down, to a myriad of interesting, but clinically boring facts of how brilliant Scritti Politti's 'Wood beez pray like Aretha Franklin' artwork was. Or how it would be criminal to take down 'The Clashes' 'London Calling' album cover. Or indeed, touch any of my coolly devised, and personally designed, new wallpaper. Proceeding to further annoy and bombard her, with how long it took me, to arrange the album covers, in a specially, chronologically, and alphabetically ordered format. Also regaling her, with how much money, the legendary and masterful singer and lyricist, Green Gartside had spent on making their albums. With Arif Mardin, at the producing helm, in various mega-posh recording studios, all over the world.

Music was my life. My necessity. Everything revolved around it. "It's your fault anyway", I would say. You got me the organ lessons. To which she would retort "You bloody wanted them."

I was once, the proud owner of a very loved, Farfisa B44 organ, on which I'd received years of countless lessons, that she'd footed the bill for.

Although the B44 and me had parted company, it had been not forgotten, but replaced and superseded with two synthesizers. A 'Roland Juno 106' and a smaller, Casio CZ101' respectively.

The latter bought for me by my Dad, as a tokenistic, equalling gesture, to the £385 quid he'd forked out on fines, to keep our John from heading to one of our Majesty's finest, Strangeways.

Along with the synths, a brilliant Boss 110 Dr Rhythm drum machine. A TEAC 144 multi-track cassette recorder. Various microphones, headphones, tape splicer's, sound effect records and countless other music making accoutrements, I'd accrued, to make my assault on the UK pop charts.

Something which although very dear to me, had slowly, and sadly become a backseat dream, nestling somewhere in-between, I'll do it tomorrow, and it'll never see the light of day, this side of never.

SEVENTEEN

As I neared the DJ stand, I could see 'Tony' carefully sliding another record, out of its sleeve. He looked over at me, smiled and continued with his task. Being careful to keep his fingers to the edges and centre of the record, and out of the grooves. Mmm, fingerprints, dust or a hair in the gate, can play havoc with a songs continuity, I thought. Tony smiled and gave a 'With you in a minute gesture' at me, as he carefully laid the vinyl down on to the deck, as importantly, as if he was doing some kind of life-saving surgery to it.

He turned toward me, whilst also lifting up one 'can' of his headphones, to his left ear, allowing the other can to dangle, and wobble aimlessly, at the side of his head. His other hand, and index finger, cued up the record firmly, but delicately, on the vinyl's printed centre label.

"Yes, mate what can I do for you? There's a pen and paper on that table, for requests?"

"Erm, no erm, Tony, I don't want a tune. I just want the name of the artist?" Can I call him Tony? I thought.

"A piss? The toilets are just over there," he explained. Plainly offering more of his concentration, to the pending rock, track than my inquiry.

"No, I want the artist, not a piss? Who's the artist? Who's the band? What's the song called?"

"Oh right, sorry pal, hahaha. I thought you said I want a piss hahaha, cracker!" He was clearly enjoying the scenario. A totally green, unknowledgeable, naïve rock music interloper, asking him where the best place to take a slash was.

"It's 'Sugarland'. The groups 'Sugarland', Jennifer Nettles sings, and the songs called 'Gotta be something more'" he shouted over the music. "Cracker innit?"

"Erm, yes, it is, Tony, erm, yes cracker? Very catchy. Jennifer Nettles you say? What album's it off? I further quiz. Trying to prise my question between him, and his vinyl needling.

"What albums that one off again Phil?" Tony shouts across to his 'Joey Tempest' lookalike buddy.

"Twice the speed of life." Tony's Dj mate, gives the Ronnie James Dio, two fingered hand gesture toward me, with an even bigger smile than Tony.

"Twice the speed of life. Cracker!'. Tony echoes further, just to be convincingly sure, I heard what smiling Phil said.

"Oh, ok erm, thanks. Thanks for that, cheers.

Mmm, I turned around and gave Tony a thumbed, agreeable nod. I'll have to investigate this Sugarland lot further?

They're very smiley. A kind of happy folk, this rock lot? That Tony fella really enjoys the word cracker too? Probably eat a lot of Jacobs and cheese, I muse, grinning my way back to the others, as the dance floor slowly empties, after the song.

"Did you get it Ste?" asks Karen.

"I did Karen, Sugarland," I reply.

"Never fuckin heard of them?" Paul negatively adds.

"Neither have I" Karen concurs.

"Me neither. But I'm going too. Right, I think we're about done, aren't we Linda?"

"Yes, we're really going to have to go now Karen." Linda states, putting her arms into her coat. "That cocktail was lovely. It's a quarter to twelve? He's going to be a bag of angry this morning, when he gets to work."

"Here Paul, you can finish that off, I slide my three-quarter full bottle, across the table.

"Nice one Inge thanks. Think we'll go after I've necked that to?" Paul says across to Karen.

"Night night, you two." I give them the thumbs up as Linda hugs Karen.

"I enjoyed that Linda, did you?"

"Yes Stephen, a nice change."

"Mmm, Very different. Very interesting bunch, and the music was great Linda. We'll definitely have to do it again sometime. Thanks for thinking of me and dragging me out too."

We walk down the stairs, heading hopefully, for the fastest space-shuttle taxi, I can hope for, in an attempt to get to my bed, and throw out the Zzzz's, ASAP. If Linda wants any conjugal favour, I'll probably have to oblige, in a vein not less similar, to a space shuttle too? I'd imagine she's possibly gagging for it? We hadn't seen each other in over a week. What with all the In-house nurse training, and the French cauliflower offloading I'd been doing recently.

EIGHTEEN

Taxis were in their usual pecking order. You get what your given. The one at the front of the queue, low and behold, was Joe. Wigan's answer to chronically kept cabs, or the English equivalent to the American Marlboro man. He spotted us and appeared from behind a freshly, exhaled plume of smoke. The coughing splutterer, lent on the side of what I thought was his red sierra. He was puffing intently on his park drive, and was obliviously talking away, to and another smaller, flat capped driver, who seemed to be avoiding Joe's smoke rings, as if his life depended on it. Quickly moving out of Joe's way, around his identically, sign-painted 'crusader cabs' sierra, with a cloth in his hand. Cleaning the wing mirrors. The silver radiator grill and even rear spoiler to evade him.

Although identical in age, make and model. The two cars were in two, completely different states of repair. One totally buggered, with the other sparkly clean but getting there.

The smaller moustachioed cap wearing driver, had clocked us quick smart too, and being at the front of the queue, had quickly seen his chance to escape Joe. Which was more than good enough for me? I just hoped he'd be as fast on the accelerator, winging me home. quick smart, and not a lingering driver, like Joe had proved to be earlier.

"Alrrighty! Looking for a rride?" The smaller cabbie inquired, in a Liverpool accent, with added lisp, sounding rather like a scouse, Jonathan Ross. He looked at us, and motioned to his car, as if to imply, we were going to bloody get one, whether we wanted it or not. Mmm, I bet he'd do well selling on the market, I thought.

"Yes pal, erm, we do," I agreed.

"Norley Hall please." Linda announced.

"Come on then jump in. Therre you go love."

He opened the rear door for Linda, losing his chamois cloth, to his pocket at the same time. Leaving me to follow suit, around the road side of the car. Joe was still smoking, muttering, and coughing away to himself, on the pavement. Realising, now would be a good time to get into his car, to move it forward one car length, after our impending departure, to allow another waiting cab, over the road, with hazards on, into the back of the now, ten-strong cab waiting queue.

"Bloody hell. Thanks. Oh, am I glad you happened along when you did?" He explained.

"I can't stand that bloody fella. The obnoxious, fuckin twat! Lanky strreak of fuckin piss! Sorry love.

"Linda unashamedly burst out laughing. Continuing to giggle profusely, into her hand. The cocktail had seemingly worked its magic. All her defences were clearly down. She was having fun with swear words, as the lisping scouser, loaded his lisp word gun.

"Fuckin stinking bastarrd! He's like death warmed up yer kno! Shat himself in the cab last week, he did! The dirty fuckin scumbag! Am not jokin........! The bag of dirty, fuckin scum. I'm Garry by the way." He paused, to take a well earned, lisp breath.

"Ooh, the rrancid, dirrty fuckin bastarrd! We got a complaint off a punter. Am not shittin yer? Sorrry love. Envirronmental health! we got thrreatened with, the dirty bastarrd! I'm rreally sorrry love, but he ooh, gets my goat! All the other drrivers fuckin hate him too! The rregular punters won't get in his cab! Sick to bloody death, of the sight of him I am! The unkempt, fuckin stinking, bastarrd. Sorry love."

Linda was looking at me and still laughing into her hand.

"His cabs bad enough, but with his own shit on the uphollsterry too. Yeuch!

"Dirrty bastarrd! Sorry love. He makes me curse, the bastard." He smiled, looking over his shoulder.

"Well there was clearly a smell of something, in his car on the way up here? wasn't there Stephen?" Linda funly added, making pretend conversation, and dryly attempting to start him off again.

"Did he brring you up here did he? The fag ash bastarrd!"

He looked over at Linda, who was still clearly in knots. There were tears running down her face, and I wasn't far behind. What a rant I thought.

Scousers are renowned for talking fast. But this fella was pulling no punches in that department at all. Quick draw McGraw, I thought looking over at Linda. He actually reminded me of Peter. What with the scouse accent and being pretty similar in height.

H could tell a fine scouse tale when he got going too. He could be pretty mesmerising, when he started talking about his own, 'barrow boy' youth, down the dock road in Liverpool. Most of the stuff, he'd told me, of the bad-black 'edge lane' days, had been respectfully confirmed by Brillo. Who'd also served his market apprenticeship, in and around Peter, paying his dues back then. He'd watched many a market big mouth, being brought down to size, with Peter's small, but rapid fighting fists. Told me never to cross H, and pointed out, in no uncertain terms, that H was made of iron and rock.

As our laughter and Garry's ranting eased. I looked around the cab to realise how clean it was, compared to stinky Joes. Even the engine sounded cleaner? as he whisked us quietly past Wigan north western train station, and soon, swiftly past the new Asda, on robin park, heading towards Linda's Mum & Dads house, on norley hall estate. Garry's innate, over acute, hatred of Joe, had wonderfully put a nice end, on a pretty 'cracker' night. And big smiles, on both our faces. He pulled up, in no time at all, outside Linda's.

"Get to you bed pronto Stephen! I'll ring you tomorrow night. Linda planted a kiss on me, just before, she shut the door of the cab.

"I'll get this bloody coat dry-cleaned too." She rubbed her hand across her stained coat, tucked her brolly under her arm, and lifted her coat over her head, to save her from the rain.

"Don't worry, I will. Night sweetheart, sleep well. Concorde avenue pal. Hawkley hall next erm Garry. Thanks mate."

"No prroblem squire. Bye love." Garry added. Linda waved her brolly up at the cab, as her coat slipped, and she dropped her keys.

"Good night out pal?" Garry asked.

"Yes Garry, very good mate." I went on to regale him of the nights events, as he parped his horn at another red sierra, heading in the direction of town.

"Never any trrouble in the cab with them lot. Manners of the Queen some of em."

"I noticed that about them tonight too Garry."

"Concorde you said."

"Yes mate, number eight. Where in Liverpool are you from?"

"I'm a Bootle boy. Then I moved to Huyton, wherre I met the wwife. Now we'rre in Skem. The Liverpool overspill. Not over keen on it though. Trrying to convince the wife to move too? Rrougher than the blloody pool was, back in the day."

"I'm in Liverpool fruit market all the time. For work like." I add.

"Are yeh lad? We're good people. Salt of the earth folk. Our generration are anyway. Not the bloody youth coming thrrough now. Bloody scumbags! Give us lot a bad name. Robbing cars and thieving and drugs all."

"There's good and bad everywhere, I suppose. Wigan's much the same." I add, doing a somewhat, poor impression of a slightly inebriated, Wigan Aristotle.

I look out the window and notice that, Garry the space rocket cab driver, has got me In-explicably to Carr lane, in no time at all. We pass the Hawk pub, halfway down on the left. Sensing I will have less than a little time, to strike up any meaningful or, a world changing conversation with Garry, I decide to end our tete ta tete, by asking the age old, taxi driver question, when you're all clean out of things to say;

"Have you been busy Garry?"

"Not bad Stevie, prretty slow, but steady. I've got an Airport rrun at 3am, so that'll help a bit. It's hard making your money, if you don't get at least, one of them durring the week though? Hardly worrth botherring goin in at all? Crrusader have the cheapest prices In Wigan, so you can make your money on fares, using the 'B' rroads to get there. Shouldn't be telling you that though hahaha. Sometimes, if you're lucky though, you can pick up a farre on the way back too. What number Concorde was it again?"

"Number eight."

Garry eased his red rocket, around the corner of Carr lane, and Concorde, coming to a steady stop outside the house. A couple of muffled 'woofs' came through Garry's, slightly open window.

"What do I owe you pal?"

"Erm, that's £5-60 squire."

I slid my back up the seat, stretched both legs under the passenger seat, and bent my head, to avoid the cab ceiling, to get my wallet, from my left front pocket. As I wriggled, and yanked it upward, a gamut of loose change came with it, depositing itself, between my legs, either side of me, on the seat, and a couple of coins could be heard, dropping on to the black mats, under my legs.

One rather daring, escapee nugget, found itself in the drink holder, in the centre console.

"Shit sorry."

He leaned over the driver seat, picked out the console coin, and turned on the cab, centre light as he did.

"There's a pound down herre."

I opened my wallet and grabbed a tenner from the middle sleeve.

"Here Garry, there's a tenner. I'll need all the change I can get, for the coffee machine at work this morning."

I picked up all the escaped coins, dotted around me, as he opened what I could only describe, as a market-traders, money apron. I gave It a strange look.

"It's the wife's. She was gonna thrrow it away until I got me hands on it. Ideal for all the silver you end up with in this job." He slid the tenner into his front pouch and grabbed a handful of coins.

"Just make it seven Garry."

"Rright you arre, and thrree makes ten. Did you get all the others?"

"I think so. If you find any when you're cleaning, you can have them on me. Thanks again Garry, hope your airport run goes ok?"

"Aye, I'll get there. I think I'll call it a day after I've done that though? Been on the go since two this afternoon. Takes its toll on the old eyes."

"Ok thanks again."

"Toodeloo pal."

Garry glided off into the night.

NINETEEN

I quietly open the back gate, to hear a couple of barks. Being careful to properly click shut the gate as silently as possible.

My 'troop on silent night manoeuvres', scenario would make absolutely no difference whatsoever. There was nothing surer than when I pulled on the kitchen window, it would be followed by a tirade of barks and soon after, the creaking footsteps of me mam upstairs. That's if I hadn't already been lucky enough to made it to the safe confines of my bedroom?

'Woof woo.... aooow.' Once into the kitchen my usual way, I quickly calm him down. 'Wo....of' a half-hearted bark later, he lifts his still slumbering legs, from the patio door rug. Stretches his legs backwards, then shakes his whole torso, as if he's just been given a bath. I turn on the kitchen light. He bends his head, as if to say 'I didn't need the bloody light on at this time'?

His head joins in, with the full body shake. As he shakes, his jowels flap a few hours' worth of sleeping dog saliva, on to all unsuspecting parts of the kitchen floor, cabinets, chairs and the glass of the patio door. The last smidgin of which, lands itself firmly on the left leg of my jeans. *"You mingin bugger Shamus"* I whisper.

"Oh, never mind, they're due a wash anyway lad."

After his 'blow the cobwebs off' dog shake, his long fluffy starts to slowly wag. I run my hand along his mane, and into his back legs. Underneath his spit jowelled jaw, and across his snoozing half-flopped ears. He multiply sniffs me, at what I can only guess, is Linda's perfume. I move to the sink, grab a glass from the draining board, half filling it with cold water, as he continues his night-stretch workout. Lowering his head, to just above the floor, he pushes out his front legs, on to the lino floor in front of him. Rises up, shakes again, and looks up at me, as if to say *'Have you got another bowl of that stuff?'*

"Alright lad, yes I know. What time do I bloody call this? I know, I've no right stirring you from your slumber, have I? Bloody humans. No respect for you dogs, have we, eh?

Aye, you're a good boy, aren't you? He lets out a half-baked moan, confirming he's enjoying the unscheduled late-night petting. I bend down, and grab his water bowl, emptying and refilling it, under the strangely noisier than usual tap. And place it down at the side of his rug bed.

"Are you alright lad? Eh? Did she take you out for a walk eh? Bet she bloody didn't did she? Mothers eh? D'you want a piss lad? Bet you do, don't you?"

His wagging tail, gained instant momentum. Before I know it, my chest is embellished by two massive paws, creating enough front force, to almost push me backwards into the sink unit.

"Mmm, you do want a piss. Bet your friggin bursting aren't you, lad."

I click-slide the patio door lock down and turn the key anti-clockwise. Push the handle away from me with my right hand. It swishes almost silently open. Just like the Starship Enterprise lift doors. He's gone.

Now I'm no any kind of law, or reputable, acknowledged expert, on the strange and wonderful world of dog pissing. But watching Shamus, performing his unique toilet duties, for a number of years now, has always made me, quizzically wonder. I must point out, that I don't mean that, in any kind of perverted 'I love watching dogs' sort of way. But I've just always pondered? Does he opt for the correct, alpha male dog method, or is he just bone idle? Granted, you can see most everyday breeds, commonal garden dogs, Heinz 57's Shiatsu's to Akitas, quickly cock a leg up on a tree, and move on to the next tree forth-with. Marking out their 'this is my patch' ground.

In regard to dumping. Most take a dump in pretty much the same, standard vocational way. Adding optional, kick-dirt onto It, disguise and hide it movement, depending on the environmental circumstances afforded. I've come to the conclusion, after many years of dog walk viewing, that he just couldn't be bothered, nor even gave a shit (excuse the pun) what other, dogs thought, or cared. I shouldn't care either, apart from it being so, laughably comical to watch. He just spreads both his rear legs apart, lowers his hind quarters, and pisses for all he's worth. Sometimes for the whole of eternity, or at least a couple of minutes. I don't also consider myself, some kind of dog sexist either. But I always thought, that was the way she-dogs did it? Or at least, that's what they were taught, at dog school, and in the best selling re-issued, hard-backed version of; 'Dog pissing for puppies and beginners,' sixth edition. If there were such a publication? He also, always seems to opt for the same part of the back garden. At the top, where the sun shines the longest, and where mam plonks her small garden table, and deck chair, reading Catherine Cookson novel in the summer months. And bleaches the grass completely white, in her favourite sun spot.

He was back. Done, dusted drained and finished. The patio doors rattled, as he mis-judged his night re-entry, in to the confines of the kitchen. He spun round, firmly nestling himself into his bed-rug.

"Is that you? happy now lad?"

I rinsed out the empty glass and placed it on the drainer. Star Trek shut the patio door, up-clicked the lock, and turned the key.

"Right get to sleep, you big hairy monster. That's where I'm going."

I closed the kitchen door tight, to prevent any illegal, couch-mounting and dog-napping. Heading for the hall door, I hear the familiar ceiling creaked, thump of footstep. Followed by another, then another. The unmistakable slipper patter of me mam, getting out of bed. On route, to humanly copy shamus's last trick. Taking into account my upward stair velocity, divided by the darkness, and multiplied by my body-weight, and me Mams vigour to get back into bed, with minimal angry mother-son debacle.

I reckon, I should either stop dead, halfway up the stairs, or increase my optimum sneaking speed, now I know she's partially awake, into a full-on, stomping stair race, and get into my room quick smart, close the door ajar, and then when she's finished in the loo and flushed as she always does, I can also join the rest of the night, piss party and partake in a rapid, spent beer, relinquishing burst, before bed.

"That you Stephen?"

"Yes, Mam it's me." *Who else would it be Mother?* I questioned to myself.

"It's late. Get to bed."

"I know, I am. Night."

"Don't be late for work."

"Erm, I know, I won't nite."

Her door slides over the tight-fitting carpet and clicks shut.

That wasn't as bad as usual, I affirm, as I take the last half of the staircase in silent stride. Creaking as I go.

As I open the bathroom door, the cistern is still filling up. I'll leave the light off I think? There's enough morning light, coming through the blinds to make an accurate enough aim.

I finish quicker than anticipated. Mmm, there's plenty more used newky in there yet? It's probably not processed yet I giggle. I Close the bathroom door, and turn to go into my bedroom, the muffled but stern words, 'FLUSH IT!' echo across the landing.

"Ok sorry."

"You will be."

I quickly push down the cistern handle, whom at this point is feeling, it should at least, be getting paid double time, or extra shift allowance, as it's not yet finished its first cycle. Mmm, I wonder if we pay more than the rest of the street, in water rates? I ponder, as the handle catches itself coming back up, due to a half empty water reservoir.

You'd think so, the amount of times this handle gets pushed down?

Has she never heard of the phrase 'one flush is enough'? the leaky-pipe, water companies are peddling that out every hot summer. The time for pondering anything whatsoever, should be well and truly over, says my head, as I finally drop my clothes to the floor, and flop onto my bed. Covering myself quickly, to retain optimum body warmth. Positioning my pillows, my head at drawer-level with the bedside cabinet, where the clock is staring alarmingly back at me in stark red numbers. Edging close to one twenty-eight am, I Titanly compute, that if I fall asleep at this precise second, and stay in bed an extra thirty minutes than I normally allow, I should get a grand total, of four hours sleep. Bugger! It'll have to do.

TWENTY

It's Thursday, two nights later……. at around the same time. But I'm getting into a different bed. A strange bed. I'd nodded off when I'd first got in. It felt like I'd been sleeping hours when I opened my eyes again, but in fact was only two minutes. Funny how the mind can play tricks on your senses. The ceiling is different too. So are the sheets. But I knew that when I jumped in to it two minutes ago. I just hadn't paid any attention before. Even the bed posts have a lovely elegant gold shine. A much bigger, better bed. More rigid, un-creaking affair completely. Oh, I'll have to get a duvet like this one, I thought, rubbing it over my chin *"Yum yum."* God, it's so thick and plush. I wouldn't mind all this elegance at home. Mmm, the telly perched on the chest of drawers at the end of the bed, is another luxury bonus. Luxury upon luxury. There's also, a brand-new Ferguson Video star, sat on top of it. I bet that's top of the range too? Might have a go at that later. I guess that's one of the trappings of working at Heinz's baked bean factory, for donkey's years brings.

I stretch back in to the pillow. It swallows me up, into a knowing that I can enjoy this state of bliss, for at least a few more days. Even mid-week Maxims was good tonight too. But instead of the rock fraternity, it was the ordinary every day, run-of-the-mill disco lot, with their Budweiser, Becks and pop chart hits, with a bit of old school soul, and the last dance, slowly thrown in for good measure.

Now, I'm in a much more relaxed state of mind. After another night out on the tiles, and now in a luscious bed, except this time, I don't have to worry about rushing up, In four hours. Or even worry about waking up me mam up either. In fact, its absolute heaven, to know that tomorrow, I'm on holiday for seven whole days. Granted, I've agreed to unload a wagon of caulis Saturday afternoon, as a favour to Peter. But apart from that, I'm going to be able to lie, lozz, fart, sleep, chill out, snore, have sex and even watch telly in this place, for as long as I damn well please.

Linda's Mum and Dad have taken their yearly travel agent package deal to Spain for a week. A last-minute, sojourn to warmer climes, in an attempt to ease her aged, Dads arthritis-ridden legs. And satisfy her Mum's love of the sun. One thing for sure, is that I'm far from alone. In more senses than one.

Linda is in the bathroom, taking a shower, and her dog Denver, is staring right at me.

Probably a pretty plush bathroom affair, I expect too? That much I can only guess, due to the fact that, this is the first time, I've ever been allowed, thus far in to her parent's hallowed house. The downstairs toilet, living room and the kitchen, is only as far as I'd made It, or they deemed necessary before. Pity, they don't know who's head of the bed now? King of the castle, and master of their little palace, I affirm, stretching out my arms. I could definitely get used to this.

Mmm, I glance at the clock on 'her side'. How long's she was in there now? I hope she's not disappeared down the plug hole?

Thinking about it. Maybe I should go in and join her? She wouldn't mind the cramped space at all would she? In fact, she'd probably lap the attention up If I did. In more ways than one, I dirtily grin. I pull the duvet cover over my head, and feel the electric blankets, instant warmth. Nah, never mind. I'll give her, her space, and some personal pampering peace. After I've had my filthy hands all over her, she'll probably need another shower in the morning? Another interesting addition to the new sleeping scenario, is her parents dog, Denver. Currently curled up in an American style, Caddis dog bed, just along from the white, UPVC bay window. It completely matches the overall interior of the room. Carpet, curtains and bedding, with brown, bolstered corners, acting as his pillow.

Tailor made in my opinion, to correspond equally, with the decor, and also to cope, with his long floppy ears and elongated head.

Linda's Mum, loves anything Americana. From Elvis to Eisenhower, to New York to New England. She knows it all. A human encyclopaedia, all things stateside. Linda said she's off over the pond again, in about two months' time, to experience Broadway. A lifelong dream of hers. Explaining that the holidays just a cheapo, and as far as her mums concerned the downside. It's 'Liza Minnelli', her top hat, and her whip that's at the crux of the whole trip.

Bloody hell? she's been ages in that shower? Or was it a bath she said she was having? I've forgotten now? I've been to America and back, and she's still preening.

"Are you ok in there Linda? I need a pee."

"Yes, I'm Fine. Go ahead, help yourself. I'm just finishing off now. I won't be long."

Finishing off? Finishing off what? Am I suddenly, surplus to sex requirements or something? I ponder.

"Ok, if you don't mind then." I quickly throw back the duvet cover, making Denver and his neck, lift to attention. His head now bolt upright, but the rest of his long, sausage like body completely un-moved, and nestled down in his doggie quilt.

"Wow! look at the steam in here. It's like a bloody Turkish bath." I slightly, prise open the cubicle door to let the water run through my fingers. "Ouch! Jesus Christ! Is that on the hottest setting or what?"

"Haha, I like it hot as possible. It opens up all your pores and keeps your skin clean. Are you coming in or what?"

"Erm, I'd love to, but I wouldn't be able to stand it. Far too hot for me, I'd probably melt. Or at worst, end up with second degree skin burns. That bed of your Mum's is luxury personified."

"I know, she likes everything like that. Only the best for her. Dad lets her please herself. She spends an absolute fortune. And why not? he gets the best of it too."

"I'm done."

"Ok, just conditioning my hair again. Won't be long now. Are you going to have a beer?"

"You've got beer as well? Brilliant!"

"Haha. Yes, we've got beer. You know we've got beer Stephen. You had one with Dad, first time you met him."

"So, I did? Forgot about that."

"We're short of nothing we've got. I think there's lager and bitter. Might even be some cider down there somewhere? Dad keeps all his cans in the back porch. Will you get me a vodka smoothie from the cocktail bar in the living room? They're underneath on a shelf. That's if that Mother of mine hasn't polished them all off before she left. If you don't want to go rooting in the living room, just get me something else. There's plenty stuff there."

"Vodka smoothie. Ok. I'm going to have a smoke while I'm there too."

While you're going down, do me one more favour.

"What love?"

"Let Denver out the back porch, for a couple of minutes. But make sure you lock it when he's back in though. Dad has a lot of stuff in there. We've been robbed before. He forgot to lock it. You may as well use Dad's robe. It's on the back of the door in 'our' room."

"Right. won't be long then. I'll close this door, then you don't steam up the rest of the bloody house. See you shortly."

I head back into the bedroom, with a big smile, rubbing my hands and lifting Stan's robe off its hook at the back of the bedroom door.

"Well, this is bloody brilliant in't it Denver? It just gets better and better."

I walk over to his corner bed, and rub his head, and floppy elephant-like ears.

"D'you want a can of beer Denver? No? What's that? You're on the doggie wagon? Ok then, if you're sure? Not to worry, I'll have yours too! ha-ha."

Denver looks at me dolefully, completely un-phased, and unimpressed by me, as if to say;

'Fuck off imposter! You charlatan! You're not my master? Who do you think you are? the Scarlet Fucking Pimpernel? And get his fucking robe off too! you thief! The next thing I know, you'll be wearing his flat cap, his slippers, and smoking his fuckin pipe too? You phoney? Do you think I'm blind? You're nothing to me. Nothing at all. If I could use a phone, I'd ring Spain, and get you the fuck out of here you, trickster.'

"D'you want a piss lad? Eh want a slash?" It was just like being at home with Shamus, all over again?

He un-eagerly, wagged his tail.

"Come on then lad. You, lazy lump of sausage meat. I'm not gonna do it for you. Come on Denver. Down the stairs for a piss. I stood and watched him. Initially, he didn't move a muscle, and just vacantly looked at me.

Then, he reluctantly rose to his paws. Flapped his ears again as if to say;

"Ok just this once. I'm not putting up with any of your jiggery pokery though? I'll be bloody watching you? D'you here me? Watching everything you do. Every step you take pal? I do want a piss yes, but that's not the point. I won't be pushed. You can only push me so far?"

"This robe's alright innit lad eh? Come on then. Let's go get some beers. I'll see if there's summat in the fridge for you?"

I make my way on to the landing, and down the stairs expecting to hear him follow.

As I get to the bottom of the stairs I look up? Denver is still stood at the top, with a 'carry me' look on his face.

"You might get that treatment when they're here, but not off me. You're a bloody dog? Come on, down lad. Come on?" It wasn't working? I tried another tact:

"Yum, boiled ham, Mmm yum, boiled ham? Cheese, bread, food, yum yum. Come on Denver? You, lazy bastard! It's a doggie tread-mill for you? You'll be on the cover of slimming dog world, when I've fucking finished with you. Come on pal."

I watched, as he began his descent, almost feeling slightly sorry for him. Because his legs are so small. He has to take each step, in a sort of horizontal, front-first fashion, allowing his back end, to flop-follow afterward, thumping down onto each step, on his back paws. God help him if he gets a step wrong, I thought. Rollercoaster dog coming. I sit on the last step, and patiently watch, as he manages to stick it out, for only half the stairs then stops. Staring at me as if to say. *"I'm really not made for this?"*

"Ok, ok. I see your point. Come on then, you win."

He looks waggingly relieved, as I climb the last few stairs, and scoop him up in my arms. Stroking his head as I do.

"Bet you get this all the time, don't you? I know, I know, It's not your fault? Come on then, let's go see what midnight delights, the kitchen holds."

His tail batters the hell out of my forearm as if confirming our new relationship. A new doggy bonding, he'd finally granted, now that I'd humanly realised, his stumpy, afflicted legs were doggily designed to short.

"There you go." I place him down on the hallway carpet, and re-fasten Stans, flailing robe.

His small tail was now in full wagging mode. Incumbently slapping my leg as he made our way down the stair-lit hall.

He agitated open the unlocked kitchen door, with his nose in a: *'I very often creep down here, for a midnight feast, don't you know?'*

fashion. As I switched on the light, he'd already made his way over to his dry water bowl. Nosing it and looking at me at the same time.

I picked it up, half filling it under the tap, and placed it back down. No sooner was it down than his lapping began.

I looked around. The solid wooden door to the outside porch, consisted of three locks. Bolted top and bottom, and sturdier looking, mortice in the middle. The mortice key stuck out from the back of the door and was surprisingly longer than any I'd seen before.

I turned the key and opened the door. With the kitchen light on, I could just make out, a white, old cobweb covered 'pull chain' lamp cluster, at the top. The lapping continued.

I reached up and pulled the cord. Nothing? The things bloody pre-war? I thought.

I opened various kitchen drawers, and then finally, under the sink I happened across what looked like a huge shipping torch. Similar to one we have at the fruit market, but distinctly bigger and older. Mmm, Bet It's knackered? I thought. I pushed forward on the button. *"Let there be light, and there was light."* It was as if the saviour himself, had just appeared in a startling flash of light.

Behind me, the lapping had stopped.

"Bloody hell, you weren't half thirsty Denver?" I said, shining the torch into his tired eyes. "Bet you want that piss now, don't you?"

TWENTY-ONE

The external porch door, although similar had even more locks? A slightly more wormwood scrubs affair. Possibly so, because of their recent break in. I slid over, four individual, rusty black hand bolts, two mortice locks and two small black latches. Then finally a three foot, roped 3" by 2" home-made, wooden securing device. Which Instantly reminded me of my Dad's, home DIY. Until finally, I pushed open the door to the back garden, and Denver's playground.

"Off you go little feller? Off you go. You can go piss to high heaven out there."

Denver was stoically, sat in his kitchen basket, looking at me expressionless.

'Mmm. Ok. So, there're steps? I get it. Come here, you un-ergonomic little bastard' I thought.

I grabbed him, climbed down the concrete steps, and placed him down, on the mildew covered grass. He looked at me as if to say:

'This grass is damn cold? I should have a word with the RSPCA about your conduct?'

"Oh, go get a piss, you thick, mollycoddled, little sod?"

Inside the porch, is what can only be described as, a mini-nuclear-war, stash of alcohol.

On the either side of the porch wooden frame, was an inch thick, wooden shelf, on top of which, there was 24-pack cases, of beer stacked to within a foot, of the pre-war light. Not just all the same brand either. Maybe Stan went through brand phases, or possibly had different types of beer, for different months of the year? Whatever it was, I was spoilt for choice. Carling, carling light, becks. greenalls bitter. tetley mild. Coors, American smooth. Skol premium. Tennants super strong? Finally, at the bottom, making a strong Irish base for everything else, four dusty cases, of Guinness (the black cow's milk)

Bloody hell? is Stan some kind of alcoholic, beer taster, I thought? Some of the plastic, vacuum packs, had cans missing too, where he'd slid out a couple of tins, and left the corner ones in place, to cope with the weight of the ones stacked above. Below the inch-thick shelves, and again, at both sides, there were various sizes, and types of wines and shorts. Mmmm, I'm guessing this is her Mums bit? Lambrini peach, white and red. Liebfraumilch, Pinot grigio. Thunderbird, Smirnoff ice and something, I'd had before called 20/20. There was even one, jazzy packaged brand called; American screw-top vodka, and gathering dust, some last resort miniatures, huddled together in an empty plastic, ice-cream container at the bottom.

"Bloody hell Denver? where do I start in this lot haha"? I felt like a kid in a sweet shop, or a slim Augustus gloop, in Wonka's alcohol factory. Mmm, what did she want again Denver? I'll get It from here. Can't be bothered, rooting in the living room cocktail thingy?

I'll have some of these Carling for Moi, and she can have an American screw top, and a smirnoff Ice, just in case I get it wrong.

I put the mock carry-out, on top one of the kitchen tall stools, and headed down the hall, to get my cigs and lighter, from my coat.

He'll be alright outside. He's not fuckin going anywhere, anyway. The back gates locked, and he can't make it up the steps either, I thought.

When I returned to the porch, Denver was miraculously, sat back in his kitchen basket. Vacantly staring at me as if he hadn't moved. "Who d'you think you are, Paul doggie Daniels? How did you get up the steps? And you call me a bloody fraudster, you little swine!" I lit up my shit stick and sat down on the top porch step. Wrapping Stans robe in-between my legs to keep them warm.

"I'll be up in a minute Linda. Denver's still on the toilet."
A muffled *"Ssshhh!"* came back down.

"Oh wow, look at that, It's a full moon Denver." I said looking up at the clean, cloudless sky.

"The stars are on parade too. Bloody hell, that would take a brilliant picture lad. Wish I had a camera?" The moon was completely astounding. If you studied it long and hard enough, it would to put you in a trance. Breath-taking and completely hypnotising. Look at those stars? I bet heaven's a wonderful place Denver? It's no wonder those bloody werewolves and vampires go a bit bonkers," I informed him.

I finished my cig thinking, should I have another quickie? Nah, I can always come back down if I want another? But I'd have to unlock all that crap again? Stuff that, I can have it standing with the front door open. But Stan smokes a friggin pipe in here, anyway? what you arsing about, you dick? It's just good manners, I thought.

I closed the porch door. Pushed over the multitude of locks, and turned the mortice, and slotted the rope lashed wood, back into place, then turned back to a statuesque, Denver.

"Bloody hell I'm forgetting about you. Sorry Denver. Let's have a look in here. See what we've got." He moaned with affiliation as If he knew what I'd said.

As I opened the fridge, his tail instantly began to rap against the floor

"Mmmm, what have we got here? Yummy Yum. Look, some bacon, and some corned beef. No, I'm not putting the frying pan on? and ooh, will you look at that Denver, some gammoned ham too? Oh, you are in for a treat, aren't you? His tail was going double time!

What d'you want lad? Which one? Or a bit of both, eh? I pulled a piece of ham and corned beef out of their cellophane, wrapping and dropping it together, onto the kitchen floor. "You, greedy little fucker? Aren't ya, eh, you're a fat little fucker?"

He jumped out of his basket, scooping his treat into his mouth, just as quickly as it had appeared.

"Bloody hell, anyone would think you'd never seen food before? Has she not fed you since they left? Never mind, I'll be around for a while. I'll make sure you get your jack-bit. You can have some more after pal. Are you coming up? or are you staying down here?"

He looked up at me hamless.

"Well, if you're coming up, you can make your own way there. I've got the beer to carry. In fact, I'm carrying you no more, you little gangster."

I grabbed my alcohol cache, and headed down the hall, leaving him to ponder on my last question, for as long as he liked.

Mmmm, we'll see how long these last, I said sneakily to myself. I think I'll be hearing the birds tweeting this morning? I thought.

I climbed back up the stairs. At the top, steam was still coming out of the bathroom door. Is she going for some kind of record? She'll come out like a human prune. I've heard of exfoliating before, but that's just plain mental. I wouldn't like to be the one paying her electric bill. Mind you, she doesn't pay It either.

"Are you still in that bloody shower?" No reply. "Oi, Linda, are you ok in there, or what? Did you open the bathroom window? This steam's really getting out of hand?

I walked into the bedroom, and put the beer down on to the bed, and headed back to the bathroom. Expecting to see a large puddle, of melted human gunge, oozing out of the shower cubicle and onto the bathroom rugs. How am I going to explain this, to her grieving Mum and Dad? I thought. Let alone, the Police Investigation team.

"Linda?"

I fully opened the bathroom door, and a huge plume of steam engulfed me. I couldn't see a thing anywhere.

"Oi, you really should have opened a window in here?" I reached up over the sink, unlocked and pushed open the quarter window. Immediately, the steam found its hasty retreat. I slowly slid open both cubicle doors, and looked first in front, and then down. I never expected to see this either.

It wasn't exactly a puddle of human gunge that met my eyes. But was enough to give me a fright.

She was sat down in the shower? and curled up, in the corner of the cubicle. Both her legs folded, knee to knee in front of her, and under her chin, with her hands neatly placed on top of each other. Her head was leaning forward, rested neatly on top of her chin, as the steamy water from the shower head, pattered down regardlessly, in front of her.

The thing that made me do a double take, was the fact that her face, was completely green and she was also asleep? As the steam slowly dissipated, I could now, just make out, a cabbage green tube, lying in the soap tray. I put my arm in, and through the water spray and grabbed it. As I did, I also bent down, with my arms across my knees, almost mimicking her, for a closer investigation of both her and the odious article. *'Cool it Cucumber'*, nourishing and moisturising face mask, with avocado extract.

The green slime had also slowly and visibly been dripping off her face, onto her hands and making its way down her legs, feet, and onto the shower tray. Finally disappearing down the plug hole. And yes! she was snoring. Falling asleep in a shower? That's just like something I'd do. Bloody amazing, I thought. Oh, how I wish I had that camera again?

Mmm, it seems such a shame to wake her? She looks so relaxed. Oh Denver, if you could see her now lad. What a picture?

Mmmm, I could turn the water to cold? That would wake her haha? I could stick my finger in her ear? That would certainly do the trick. I could burp loudly? Clap, sing, shout or run around naked?

My mind raced through a myriad of possibilities. I secretly smiled and rose to my feet. I'll let the steam escape first. I crossed the landing and grabbed a can of Carling black label. I cracked it open and took a long gulping swig. With it still in my hand, I returned into the bathroom, and again, into my crouched position. I'd decided I was going to enjoy the moment a little longer. A little longer was, from crouched in to a sitting position. I dropped backwards onto my arse. I quietly sat and watched her. Half a can of carling gulps later, there seemed to be some movement.

"Linda, Linda are you ok?" I touched her arm and softly moved it for a response.

"Linda come on sweetheart wake up."

"Mmm what?"

"You sat down and fell asleep love. With all this green crap on your face." I pushed the tube toward her green head.

"Mmm oh. Ooh, that was strange. I was dreaming too, and I never dream."

"Here, come on, give me your hands, I'll help you up. Wash that cucumber gunk of your face. It's bloody everywhere."

"Ooh sorry, I must have dozed off, haha. How did I manage that? In the shower too? Don't you breathe a word of this to anyone Stephen? Especially them lot, down the pub or at work. I mean it, I'll be the laughing stock."

"Come on, don't worry, I won't. You need to wash that gloop off."

"Ooh, I know I do. It's only supposed to stay on for five to ten minutes tops? It can burn. I hope my skin's ok. It's very good stuff. You should try it sometime."

"Oh yeah? then I'll be the laughing stock too? No thanks. I'm fine, and I'm sure you'll be fine, just as soon as you rinse it off. I'll leave you to it. I got you one of those vodka-shot things. There's some amount of booze down there. I didn't know your Dad was a mega, closet drinker?

"I'm going to get back in bed Linda. Leave that small window open too. It'll get rid of the condensation. I'm surprised you haven't got a raving case of damp in here? You will have, any more of these Turkish, skin cleansing, shower sessions. See you in a minute."

I placed a kiss, on the nape of her neck. Closed over the cubicle doors, and headed toward the bedroom, as she lathered up the posh Imperial leather soap, for another time.

"I'll be with you in a sec, Put the telly on if you like Stephen? I don't think there'll be much on at this time though? There're videos in one of the drawers."

"You've got videos in your drawers, amazing haha?" I walked back into the bedroom grabbed the huge remote control off the top of the telly and pressed the standby button. Threw it in to the middle of the bed and opened the top drawer. Nope? just knickers in here. Rather huge knickers. The second drawer down, was much more of the same but bras. Third time lucky I thought? Pants, Y-fronts and more pants. Forth drawer? ah bingo! Half videos, half pants, underskirts and shorts. The randomly ordered, homemade videos had the titles scribbled in the boldest black marker, across the side, facing the top for an easier choice. How very novel I thought.

That only left the bottom drawer. May as well have a gander? Nothing ventured, I mused.

I bent down and slid open the drawer. It was stacked corner to corner with videos, but this time pre-recorded, and in more of an obvious order. A full, end to end row of war films.

Everything from; *'Bridge over the river Kwai'* to *'Escape to victory'* Then on to most, if not all the *'James Bond* series'. Then a classic romance, type selection *'Gone with the wind' 'Casablanca'.* Cary Grant and Deborah Kerr's; *'An Affair to Remember'* Patrick Swayze's' *'Dirty Dancing'* and finally, Ryan O'Neil's' *'Love Story'.* The end row was certainly something more of an unexpected shock, and contained some surprisingly funny, and interesting titles, that I had heard of before; *'Confessions of a window cleaner', 'Carry on Emmanuelle', 'Adventures of a taxi driver',* and *'Debbie does Dallas'.*

Mmm, Interesting viewing, I thought.

I slid open the top drawer again, deciding that it would be in the best possible taste, and fun to find the biggest, most unflattering pair of knickers, I could find. And randomly place them on my head, and sit back in bed, as If I didn't even know, they were there. For absolutely no other reason than to make her laugh when she finally came back into the room. Hearing the shower doors sliding, I quickly rifled through, left to right, looking for the stupidest possible pair. Frilly and pink, I thought. As I felt blindly around, through the many, and varied, Mum panties. At the side of the drawer, my hand felt something strangely long, and solid. The shower had stopped in the bathroom. I heard various, clicks, thuds and bangs. She'll be here soon, I thought.

Oh, oh? Is this what I think it is? I started to grin, and panic at the same time. From out of the tangled mass of lady pants, I pulled out, what must have been her Mum's, secret Crown Jewels toy. Oh, I grinned, how they are seldom seen, and often hidden, but go by a variety of great names. What an Interesting find? I giggled. Her Mum has a: BOB? A battery-operated boyfriend, a bayonet charge. A fuzz buzz, a crypton stick. A big John. It was vibrating too? I must have inadvertently caught the switch when I was pulling it out the mass of knickers? I'd better put it back, and stop it's mad buzzing, and bloody quick!

I twisted what must have been the speed control, at the bottom for what, in my moment of panic, seemed like ages, until at last, it fell silent. Phew!

I quickly pushed it back in to the drawer corner, and covered it up, with the granny lingerie. Rapidly slid the drawer shut, whilst quickly covering my tracks, by opening the video drawer, as Linda walked nakedly into the room. Naked, except for the Korean wrapped, sauna towel on her head, fashioned out of one of her Mum's, pink bathroom towels.

"How do I look? Linda had walked over to her Mums dressing table, with her back to me, and bent over, randomly looking in the mirror, with her head inches from it.

"Erm, you look exceptionally good to me? Great look Linda? I suggest you do it all the time? Good enough to eat in fact."

"Behave yourself you perv. I mean my face Idiot! How does my face look? Does it look burned to you? I sidled up to her and stood her up.

"Nope, it looks fine. You look fine? It's bound to be a bit red. Is It sore? It was bloody boiling in there? Even a camel would struggle not to sweat." I neatly placed my hand on her still warm and slightly glowing left bum cheek. "You've got no chaffing on your butt cheeks either haha. You look absolutely fine. Go on sleepyhead, get into your bed."

Mmmm? I just hope I turned that bloody vibrator off properly? and it doesn't randomly start buzzing against the wood in the drawer.

Linda pulled back the quilt where I'd been previously nestled and sat nakedly down on the bed. Lifted and slid her slender legs under the quilt. Released the wrapped pink towel from her head, and let it slowly unwind itself, from her hair.

"Oh, is that your side?"

"It's actually Dads side, but I always take his side when they're away. Don't ask me why." She continued talking, massaging the towel into her hair. "Probably cos I can't stand all Mum's clutter over there?"

I compared our sides. Whereas Stans or Linda's bedside cabinet was empty, unlike his over-flowing porch and apart from my can of Carling.

The top of Linda's Mum's, or my bedside cabinet, was taken up the usual standard everyday clock and lamp set up. But was also, more than fully furnished, with lots of extra, untidy added Mum paraphernalia.

A basket brimming, full of half squeezed beauty creams, and potions and lotions. Vaseline, nivea hand cream. Organic face cream, and Cherry lip balm. Nail varnish, pain killers, face wipes, and even a hay fever hydrating spray. Hair clips, grips and hair net. Tweezers, and a set of silver toenail clippers, slotted over a small cracked, hand mirror Three romance novels, were the coaster to an extra large, black and white ceramic tea mug, adorned with a picture of Lionel Ritchie, extolled with the words *'HELLO... Is it tea you're looking for?'* There was even an; in-flight 'British Airways', black silk eye mask.

The distinct lack of room, had unceremoniously afforded her mums still sealed and boxed, Goblins teas-made, pride of place on the floor, at the side of the bed. On top of which, sat her Mums pink slippers. My feet had crunched on the teas-made box and almost crushed it climbing from Linda's side earlier.

Mmm? that's probably why I subconsciously took Stan's side in the first place.

Linda was still lightly rubbing the towel into her hair. I continued to feign looking through the video drawer. I moved around to my 'new' side of the bed and picked up her vodka bottle off the cramped cabinet, and walked to Linda's bare cabinet, placing it on top, picked up my Carling, and moved back over to video draw.

"Can I tempt you with anything?"

"I usually blow-dry this before bed, but I really can't be bothered. Erm no, I'm not bothered about the telly either. Being In the shower so long, has knocked the stuffing out of me. I feel really shattered now? I can't even be bothered brushing this?"

Linda ran her fingers through damp, black hair.

"I don't even want that vodka now? I think I'm just going to go to sleep." Linda dropped the pink towel to the side of the bed.

"Talking of vodka, what's with all the beer down there? Is your Dad a raving alcoholic or what?"

"Is he hell, they like a drink in the house that's all. They have friends round a lot too. Usually on Fridays. Dad plays poker with his pals in the spare room, and Mum and her lot do their thing downstairs." Mmm? probably discussing dildo's, and sex films I thought.

"Oh right, but that amount of booze, on those small shelves is a bit dangerous. Why doesn't he put it all upstairs with him in the spare room?"

Linda had closed her eyes and leaned back into her pillow.

"Oh, I don't know. They come in, grab what they want, and take bring up with them. Then go back down when they want some more. Mum and her pals like it that way. Probably so they can keep an eye on the men."

Linda sounded as if she really couldn't be bothered talking.

I stopped looking through the videos and closed the drawer.

"I'm not going to have the telly blaring if you're going to sleep. That's not fair."

"I'm not bothered about the noise either? Just keep it low." Linda wiggled her bum down the bed, fluffed her pillows, and again ran her fingers across her forehead and into her hair, closing here eyes again, as she did.

"Stephen would you get me a glass of water from the bathroom while you're out of bed? Please? Forget the glass, just take Mum's cup."

"Ok, no problem'.

"Throw me that eye mask too. Ooh, I'm so tired now."

"There you go." I said, throwing the mask, and picking up her Mums tea stained mug. It landed neatly on her scarecrowesque damp hair.

"I'll give Lionel a rinse out."

Linda was oblivious, as she fashioned the eye mask over her ears, and pulled it down to best cover her tired and fading eyes. She neatly tucked the quilt under her arms, and over her breasts, sighing as she did.

I pulled open the bedroom door, to see Denver, having finally decided to join us, hay-making himself up and over on to the final stair and landing.

"Welcome back, bed's made lad."

The bathroom was still settling its dampness. I turned on the gold cold tap, rinsed the Lionel cup. Swilled, rubbed, then swilled again, until the mug was filled to the brim, with cold clean water, and made my way back to the bedroom. She was gone. Sleeping like a baby. No rumpy pumpy for me tonight, I thought. Not to worry. Linda's been known to have a penchant and partake, in the odd-spot of morning friskiness, before now. I quietly placed the Mum mug down atop the cabinet beside her head, picking up her vodka shot as I did. Denver rustled himself in his basket, also settling himself in, for the long haul.

Mmm, well it seems I'm all on my own again? I eyed her bottle, walking back to my side of the bed. 4.8 proof smooth vodka? I silently put the vodka bottle down, on the bedside cabinet book stack, in place of her mum's Lionel mug. I'll have that a little later. I wonder if sleeping beauty knows her Mum has a plastic pal, called Mr Jiggles?

Mmm, I bet you sit there, and openly watch, when she's deep in an open legged session, don't you Denver? You dirty dog? Mind you, she'd be totally oblivious to your canine voyeurism, anyway. She'd be orgasmically, floating, or rather buzzing around in sexstasy land?

I bet she tells Stan, she's coming upstairs to have a bath, do her hair and nails, and pamper herself? I took another swig of my can. Mmm, he's probably out in the back garden, mowing the lawn, or trimming the hedges? Or quietly pruning the roses. Maybe in the shed bedding down new tomatoes, for eventual planting into the greenhouse. While all the time, she's upstairs, getting G-spotted off, to high heaven, with her mechanical Spam Javelin?

Getting her wizards sleeve oscillated wildly, with Mr Pink? Biting a hole in her lip, as her battery powered cervix-crusader tingles her badly packed, meat kebab through, a self-induced beef curtain explosion, with her undulating, vagina-miner at the helm? As poor old Stan weeds the back lawn. I wish my over active brain would go to sleep? I smiled.

Nah, I bet he's as bad? Secretly holed up in his shed when she's upstairs. He's so-called composting, and all the time he's tucking in, to the latest delights of 'Fiesta' porn magazine, with a can of Lager in his hand, and happily smoking his pipe?

I looked at sleeping Linda and Denver. Mmm, I don't know if I should just swing this, and join them? What time is it anyway? 2-30am. It's not that late? I've still got another two cans of carling left yet. Mmm, suppose I could watch a bit of a film?

I think she's rubbed off on me a bit. I can't really be bothered either. Bollocks to it. I'm gonna nip downstairs again and have a fag out the front door instead. Can't really be arsed with all the back-door locks.

You can stay their sausage features I whispered to a peeping Denver. I quietly closed the door behind me, and once again just like at home, found myself creeping silently on stairs. The front door wasn't even fully locked. I pulled a cig and my lighter out from my jacket pocket and opened the door. No beautiful shining moon, this side of the house sadly. Only the stars, lit through its night glow, dotted randomly through the sky. Sirius shimmering the brightest, I pick out easily, leading the pack, in the faint constellation of canis major. Its Greek name meaning 'scorcher' or 'glowing'. But even without the Moon, still a wondrous spectacle, that's still enough to take your breath away. Yep, I conclude, our tiny little piece of the universe certainly looks lovely, quiet and peaceful tonight.

I look up and down Linda's street. Just the odd, other night-owls living room light on, daring to try to compete with the moon. It's eerily quiet too. A silence broken only every so often, by a night cabs engine in the distance, quietly whirring to its destination.

A neighbour's dog blatantly strolls down the middle of the street. He stops to look at me as if I shouldn't be there, and skips off, speeding up and crossed onto the pavement, down a garden path, and disappeared up an entry.

I suppose it's time, really. Can't put it off any longer. The rest of the world seems to be at peace and sleeping. So, if I can't beat em, I'd may as well join them. I quietly close the front door and lock the dead bolt. Climbing the stairs for a final time.

I hope Linda's got bread in. I'll have some of that bacon, out the fridge in the morning.

TWENTY-TWO

I'm wakened by the radio. Frankie's 'Two Tribes' and the whoosh of Linda's hairdryer blowing on the landing. Mmm, what bloody time is it? I sidle over to Linda's vacant, but still warm side, to see her Mum's clock almost shouting, ten thirty. Bloody hell! It's opening time in half an hour. The whooshing ceases, and Linda strolls into the room, still starker's but with a perfectly blow-dried, black bob of hair, that wouldn't look out of place in a hairdresser.

"Morning captain snooze. How does my hair look?"

"Morning sweetpea. Erm, your hair looks great. As smart as it usually is.

"Mmm does it really. What you after?"

"Aaah!" I pull do big stretch. "Nothing at all, oh light of my life. That was a good sleep, considering we only got to bed so late. Your Dad's orthopaedic mattress must agree with me? Come back in? feel the quality of this? What are you up to today darling?"

I pull back the duvet, and pat her side of the bed, beckoning her back in.

"Don't even go there Stephen? and don't darling me! I'm meeting Julie up-town. We're having some well earned, retail therapy today, so come on, get out of the bed. What about you?"

"I'll have to go home and get changed first. Then head to the Tippings to see the boys.

"We'll you'd better move your arse, mattress monkey. I'm out of here shortly. Maybe we can hook up later? I'll ring you."

"Aren't we having some breakfast first? Some nice bacon on toast? Bacon and egg? Have you got eggs?"

"Eggs! You're not having any eggs, or any breakfast, and your certainly not having me either! Get up, lazy arse, I don't have time. I'm late as it is. I don't usually stay in bed that long. I must have needed it. It's all these late nights, I'm having with you at the moment. You were snoring all night too. You're a liability to sleep with, and it's playing havoc with my usual routine."

Tut? I thought. Bang goes the fry up. I was looking forward to that? Bang goes the bang too? So much for the early morning sex session. She wasn't gonna be reeled in. No bacon and eggs in both senses of the word.

"Right! out of bed. Come on, move it!" She ripped the duvet off the bed, and onto the shag pile carpet, burying Denver with it in the process, and disappeared out of the room. Only to re-appear almost fully clothed, less than a minute later. Before I'd even had a chance to un-frock Denver, and re-duvet myself. She stood in front of her Mums full-length mirror, wriggling her dress into position, on her slim waist. Then she stopped, looked into the mirror a second time. Pushed it down and into her thighs, wriggled again, as I happily watched on. "Damn these nipping knickers!"

As I began rising from the bed, I decided to stop forthwith, and watch the unwinding entertaining spectacle.

She stormed out of the room yet again. Rapidly returning to the front of the mirror, with another pair of knickers between her teeth. Looking slightly more harassed. She gave me the look of an assassin, as I suitably continued watch, interested and perplexed.

She grabbed the dress at its knee-hem, and either side of her legs, pushed her legs tightly together, and began yanking and wriggling it upward, at the same time. Once she'd wriggled it to just above her hips, she thumbed the 'nippy knickers', pulling and writhing them down on both sides, until they were finally on the floor. Once there, she salaciously stepped out of them, with one leg whilst also hooking them up, between the toes of the other, with as much skill, zeal and speed that would lead you to believe, that this was a regular occurrence.

"Bloody cheap rubbish!" With the knickers, safely secured between her toes and stood on one leg, she looked over at me, and swung the knickered leg, as if she was about to throw a dart and launched the unforgiven, transgressing pants right at me. Whilst also shouting the final warning, muffled words, from her still knickered mouth

"GET.... UP!!"

Although I was happily grinning ear to ear. Something told me she meant it this time.

As the knickers landed at the side of me, I acknowledged her request and quickly stood up.

"I'm up, I'm up. Do you do naked ballet too?" I laughed.

She skillfully spat out the 'new' frillies onto the carpet in front of her, climbed into them, bent down, grabbed and replaced them to the top of her thighs. Wriggled once, which seemed to be enough to do the trick then, pushed the black skirt firmly back down, into its rightful place. A turn to the side, one quick glance and a side-shuftie, and she was good to go.

"I'm going down."

"I wish you was going down on ......"

"SHUT UP! I'm going down Stephen, so hurry up. I'll make some coffee, and I'll make you some toast. That's all your getting! With or without you, I want to be out of here by eleven."

It had to be noted; She was looking hot! in the shortest time possible. Already, immaculately smart and dressed to the nines.

She left the room. Denver followed her. The sound from the radio was extinguished as her giantess, sounding and bounding, footsteps made light work of the stairs, shortly followed by a faint doggy thudding, and the odd yelp, leaving me behind with nothing but the stench of her just applied hairspray, wafting through my nostrils.

I quickly pulled on my crumpled jeans, from the floor beside the bed. Gave them my typical *'I'll get another day out of you'* once over.

I threw my arms into sergio tacchini jumper and hurriedly headed for the bathroom. Mmm, that looks ok? I thought. At least I had the foresight to put you on a hanger? But before my head had cleanly popped out the neck hole to see where I was going, I promptly walked into the bedroom door. *'Ouch! fucking brilliant'.*

I bet I get a bruise now. No matter, I'll tell everyone she battered me.

"Come on you, get down here! I told you eleven o'clock."

"Jesus Christ, give me a minute?"

I turned on the cold tap, and cat-lick washed my face.

"Where's your gel? Have you got any gel!"

"I don't use gel. Use my hairspray if you want and be quick about it."

"Fuck your stinky hairspray Linda." I whispered.

Soap, the age old, poor man's substitute for gel, will suffice. I slightly rubbed it in my hands, ran my hands under the tap, and quickly pushed it through my hair. I can give her a run for her money getting ready sharpish? any time I thought, looking into the mirror

Mmm, bit too wet? I grabbed the towel again. Her Mum had a hair brush in that basket, didn't she?

I quickly ran back into the bedroom, picked the brush out of the mum-basket, and stood at the full-length mirror. Yep. That'll do, you'll pass.

"Coming!"

TWENTY-THREE

I made the Tippings Arms bar, for bang on twelve o'clock. The usual early doors, Saturday crowd, and bar staff were in. I glanced over at the boy's, as John the barman appeared. The boys were huddled in our customary corner, playing cards. Our usual drinking pastime, along with the channel 4 racing and catching up with each other's news, events and work gossip. Who was shagging who? Who wasn't getting any, and where we were going later on, and bound for tonight?

"Now Stephen, what you avin lad?"

"I'll have a pint of lager please John."

"How's our Marg?"

"She's alright. Not seen her today though? I didn't go home last night. Linda's Mum and Dad are away, and when the parents are away, Stephen will play'.

"Stey........! are you gettin em in?" Eric shouted across the room.

"Aye, what is it?"

"Three bitter, two Labatt's and two Carlings. Our Anthony's with us too. He's gone for a piss. He's on bitter.

Six pints and there's only four of them sat there? That doesn't compute I mused.

"Always seems to be my round when I walk in? Amazing that always happens, innit John."

"Aye lad, amazing."

John was the regular barman, for a Saturday afternoon session. His daughter Lucy was in tow and learning the ropes off Papa. She was sat at the far-right corner of the bar on a high stool relentlessly smiling, but not saying, or doing much at all. All she normally does is, preen her hair, and herself, like there was no tomorrow, and constantly nips off to the loo with her make-up bag. She's roughly the same, slim body size as Linda, but a head-height taller. Obviously not getting her height from her pint-sized father. Her mass of blond streaked hair, usually worn loosely, but was tied up today.

Today Lucy was looking particularly fetching indeed, with black leather pants on. She'd probably had to jump from the top of the stairs, to get in them? They were, second-skin tight, and leaving little to my imagination, whatsoever. Along with the circulation hindering pants, she had a loose, round neck, baggy, bright yellow waffle-knit jumper. Sadly, just hanging over her lovely, pert, tight, apple arse, hiding its tight cupped magnificence from view.

The oversized chunky jumper, must have been knitted with extra large knitting needles, or Cuban cigars, the holes between the stitches were that big? Leading me to think it was a damn good job, she was wearing a white bra, to conceal her fun-bags, or we might possibly be regaled, with her mosquito-bite nipples saying hello? Peeping through a couple of the over-large, knit-holes. As she pulled forward on the beer pump, the yellow jumper fell off her shoulder, hanging down on one side, revealing her slim and tanned collarbone, as she pulled a pint for old Martin. One of the other Tippings regulars.

I'd often thought it would be a good idea, to fashion the bar with a hidden button that activates a drop-down mirror, in front of her, solely for her use, when it got a little busy. If she couldn't get to the loo to re-make up, she would diversify with a Joshua Tetley *'the old-fashioned flavour'* hunting scene advertising mirror, she kept at the side of the beer pumps. You could see her head, incessantly bobbing, in-between the letters printed on the mirror, like a speed reader, constantly looking at herself, to get the optimum view of her days make-upping. Being resolute, to avoid the horse's arses in the fox hunting scene. With the constant looking, bobbing and weaving over at the mirror, she often got as much beer in the beer tray, and over her hand, as she did in your glass. Making her smell like a strange mix of Chanel No5, and Joshua Tetley's.

What with dad John, in the snug bar, watching his gee gee's forever falling at the last, and Lucy away, prettifying herself to high heaven in the loo, it was a wonder anybody got served at all.

John, me mam reliably informed me when I started frequenting the pub, was also her half-cousin, which made him my uncle of sorts.

Therefore, making Lucy, on the back foot, and somewhere down the line, my relative cousin too. Now, I'm not saying I wouldn't go there, cos she was pretty hot, and around my age to boot. But all the habitual preening, and ceaseless primping, would totally do my head in. Linda was bad enough, but bearable in that department.

John was more than an avid horse racing fanatic, and to hear him talk, was the pubs biggest, regular winner, more than he was a loser. But aren't they all? I tend to listen to what he tells me he's won, and then reverse it, to be closer to the truth.

"Did Eric say two carling Steve? I couldn't hear him over the telly. That's my first winner of the day in the bag!"

"Erm, aye John, two of each lager, and the three bitter. Anything good running, I should know about?"

"Aye lad, there's a couple later on. PocketRocket in the 2-15 and Dragonfly at 4-45 both on the flat at Lingfield."

"Oh right. Are the odds any good?"

"Not bad at all lad? Especially PocketRocket. You can get 5-1 on, down at coral's, if you're sharp. It's not gonna go out. Only down. Second here last time out, and they say the trainers been holding it back for this race? Plus, it's got Declan Moody on it this time, and he's in top form at the minute. It's running four pounds lighter. It wasn't blinkered last time either. I've got a tenner on it to win. Plus, I've got it, in each way, double odds, lucky-six accumulator."

Mmm, well I did ask I thought. He completely lost me at PocketRocket. After that, everything else he said paled into insignificance or just sounded complete gobbledegook.

All I had in my mind was Linda's Mum, contently smiling at me naked, and waving her battery-operated boyfriend in her hand. But what was worse was, Stan was also there, shuffling a pack of cards, and toasting me with a can of Lager, and blowing smoke rings with his pipe!

"Steve, STEVE! are you with us today or what lad? That's £7-85 pal?"

"Oh, sorry John, I was miles away then."

"You looked it! £7-85. I'll top up your bitter in a minute, when they've settled."

"Ok thanks. There's a tenner. Give us a tray please John? I'll take these over and come back for the bitters."

"It's there in front of your face? You're in cloud-cuckoo land today Steve? I bet you've forgotten the names of the horses I gave you?"

Lucy walked through the bars middle adjoining divider, and disappeared into the snug, behind her Dad. Waved her make-up bag at me and smiled.

I placed the boy's bevvies on the 'Marstons Pedigree 1952 4.8 ABV' beer tray, and walked over to the boys, in the corner. leaving John rifling through his umpteen betting slips.

"What's with all the beers?" I asked. "Who's the other one for?"

"Bloody hell Ste, I didn't think you were bothering? Have you been brewing it yourself or what?"

"Shut the fuck up Ian, you impatient bastard! You're bitter's still on the bar, anyway. He's topping them up."

"Haha, only kidding. Where've you been anyway Ste?" Ian asked.

"I had to nip to the bank, get some beer tokens. That's why I'm late."

I put the full beer tray down, onto the wobbly table. Being careful to avoid the pack of cards in the middle, but profusely spill them as I do.

"Shit! I'm always doing that! Put a beermat under that table leg, Chris for fucks sake!" I slowly placed the pints individually, in front of them, then quickly moved away the alcohol swimming tray.

Paul had already read my mind, he'd put his cards, face down on his seat, and was presently ripping a beermat it in half, whilst also disappearing under the table, to rectify the sloshing alcohol situation. Reappearing forthwith, and returning to his cards, as if someone was going to turn them over, for a secret peep. He'd returned a little redder in the face. Eric's younger brother Anthony appeared sighing, looking suitably piss-drained from the toilet. He patiently stood behind me.

"Alright Ant. Eric said get you bitter. It's just settling. Be out of your way in a sec."

"No problem, ste. Take your time."

"Come on Eric! you slow-coach! it's you to go." Paul fidgeted.

"Is it? oh bollocks I can't go.........? hang on, plastics, wait a minute." Eric re-scrutinized his hand.

"Yes, I can, yes I can! A lovely red jack hiding at the back there. Pick up three Paul, you plastics! haha."

"Tut, I wish you'd fuck off with that Eric. I don't even work for Glasdon anymore?" Paul looked downtroddenly, through his cards, then pawed one out smiling. "Pick up eight Ian."

"Plastics bastard!" Ian affirmed.

"Go get my bitter Ste and hurry up about it." Ian impatiently piped up

"I'm dying of thirst here. I was gonna stick to orange for a bit, but it's a hair of the dog I need. I'm dehydrating here. I had too many last night. That Cow...................!"

"Do I look like fuckin Sting Ian? Have I got bell boy written on me somewhere? No, I don't think so! I'm not your fuckin servant. I don't want your fuckin life story either! If you want it that much, go get it your fucking self, you cheeky bastard. John's probably not even topped it up yet, Impatient arse!!

"Haha, that was a bit cheeky Birdy?"

"Shut it Chris!" Ian growled, trawling through his hand, realising he's gonna have to pick up a handful of cards.

"JOHN! Is that fuckin bitter ready yet?" Ian angrily shouts over at the bar where John is nowhere to be seen, and Lucy smiles over. Already back from her make-up sojourn and topping up the two remaining Tetley's.

"You've not got 'bell-boy', but you've got 'sergio tacchini' written on you Ste, haha."

Chris looks around the table for acknowledgement, to his late, and pretty piss poor joke.

"And you can shut the fuck up too Chris! You fuckin dour bastard! Your timing's terrible too! Here's your fuckin Carling." I grunt, putting his lager down, without so much as a dribble.

"I was only joking."

"Well fucking don't!" I say silencing him, and feeling beer confused. "Have I got one too many here?" I do an ad-lib headcount. "Shit! Who's is the other labatt's?"

"Bandit boy's in the snug Ste."

Chris says, gerrymandering the balance.

"Oh, Is he now? Well he can come and get his and all? I don't fuckin work here on my days off."

Ian looks up from his hand and throws a card. Glances over at Eric and assuredly leans into his backrest. "Pick up eleven Chris, you mother-fucker!"

"Plastics! haha."

"Shut it, calling me that Eric! Shuffle the pack Chris!" Paul blurts out.

"I know I know. I'm not daft, you mong!"

"Back in a sec with your bitter."

I leave them to their card sharping devices, and head back to the bar.

"Is that them done Luce?"

"Yes Steve."

"Just nip through, and tell Carl his lager's, here will you? thanks. You look nice today, by the way. Not that you normally don't, but erm.... yes, quite eye catching, erm jumper? Your pants are quite tight too?" I was digging myself a big hole.

"Will do." She laughed. "I need the lavvy, anyway."

"Just leave your make-up in the piss stones.... sorry, toilet Lucy? I'm sure it would be quicker."

Lucy blushes. Almost to the same shade as Paul had under the table. I'm surprised I could even make it out, under that trowel board of concealer, I muse.

Lucy smiles and walks through into the snug bar.

As I picked up the two last bitters from the bar, I could plainly hear the bandit, chuggingly dropping its guts.

"Fucking hell, I don't believe truncheon pants? Not again? That's the third time today, already! How does he do It? The jammy fuckin bastard."

Paul jealously conceded.

"That's just Carl though, isn't it'?" Chris affirmed.

TWENTY-FOUR

When it came to gambling, betting, winning money, or anything remotely ingress with hooking the fairer sex, Carl was your man or rather, 'The Man'. The luckiest so and so in that realm, I'd ever come across. He was a born woman, meat-magnet. What was even more annoying was the fact that, he also seemed to take it all in his stride and was quite 'matter of fact' and overtly blasé, about his natural uncanny luck, around them as if it were always the expected result?

The rest of us as a whole, were un-admittedly totally jealous of him because of it. In more ways than one. He always had more money, and women than all of us put together.

Once, not long after he'd become the gang 'newbie', we met him uptown, for our usual Sunday, swimming sabbatical, or dive till you drop and 'turn into prunes' residence, of Wigan International pool. With Eric, as our star diving, the team leader in every respect, and Paul running a pretty close second, and attempting to show Carl the ropes. But sadly, they were let down by his distinct lack of interest. When I say diving team, they were the only members. I was piss poor. Ian was rubbish too. Carl was a complete fish out of water, when it came to leaping, somersaulting and spring boarding off diving platforms. He was more at home in the shallow end, flaunting his mega, smooth-operator tapping up talents, and even more mega looking manhood, to any, and all females that swam his way. It was amazing to watch him at work too. Granted, it did help he was hung like a horse, and because the bulge in his swimming shorts, could be picked up by radar from the mid Atlantic. I bet on a particularly aroused day, he could knock you over at ten paces.

It was all second nature to him. All this, was more than confirmed to me, after we'd finished jumping, bombing and swimming for the day, and were drying off in the changing rooms.

I was late getting out the pool, after failing miserably, to arrange a date with Christine Winterbottom. Now I did have my tail between my legs because she'd turned me down. But what Carl had swinging between his legs after he'd pulled off his shorts was immeasurable. Jake the snake had nothing on him. It was like a third leg. I know it's not pertinent, or the 'done-thing' and you're not supposed to look. But freaks of nature, don't count nor do you come across that often.

As a result of his hidden baby's arm, Carl had rightfully earned, and continued to regale in an endless, ever changing myriad of nicknames, for his humongous weapon. Which would almost possibly follow him through the rest of his life?

What was even more perplexing to me, was that no matter where we went, or what we were doing as a gang? Women always seemed to know, it was him that possessed, the heat seeking venomous throbbing python of love.

Although the countless women he continuously flirted with in nightclubs, couldn't even see his massive packet. They seemed to instantly or instinctively know, he was hugely endowed, and hiding a branchless oak. Or they had some kind of sixth sense cock antenna, or built-in female dick-finding device, and knew he was packing a dragon's jackhammer. Therefore, making his regular tapping up, as easy to him, as a walk in the park.

I used to stupidly, make a point of standing near him, just in case some of the hidden, Macready magic rubbed off on me, and resulted in me getting my leg over.

TWENTY-FIVE

I returned, bitter laden from the bar. "There you go Paul. There's yours too Ian, you whinging bastard," I said, pointedly placing his pint down firmly on the table.

"Thanks, slow coach. Come on Chris, are you shuffling or what? Throw Carl a hand in too."

"I'm shuffling, I'm shuffling boss? D'you want me to shine your fuckin shoes as well, you impatient twat! What's wrong with you today? Have you been given the cold shoulder from Julia again?"

Ian animatedly, swigged his bitter and turned to Chris.

"None of your fuckin business cunty!"

"Haha. That's a yes then." Paul delightedly added.

"You can shut your fuckin beak too, shithead!" Ian glared at Paul. He silenced himself and zipped it forth-with.

"She can take a fuckin hike, the bitch!" Ian elaborated, wiping the ample white head from his beer, and licking it off with his finger. Twirling his finger in his mouth as he did.

"Winding me up on the phone, pissed with her mates laughing like fuck, in the background. The fuckin slut!"

"Unbelievable." I say, taking a seat on the back rest, at the side of Paul.

"All that time you spent chasing her from pillar to post, and now she's on your arm, she's a bastard?" I grin at him. He repeated his anguish.

"She is a bastard, the prick teasing cow! Going out with them, instead of me, then ringing me to take the piss. I cancelled my fuckin football training, to meet up with her, and she goes and does that to me."

"They're all bastards." Eric calmly points out, picking up his shuffled hand off the table.

"The lot of em!"

"Fuck me, listen him? How butter wouldn't melt? He's shagging one, and leaving two on the side-lines, and they're all bastards? You really take the biscuit Eric. We should start calling you, mini truncheon pants." Paul resolutely added.

"Truncheon pants long-lost cousin, with the needle cut." Chris laughingly added.

Everyone on the table burst out laughing, bar Eric, who glanced up then, continued to survey his new cards, non-plussed.

"There's one the bench. Not two, where d'you get two Paul?" Eric quizzically looked up.

"Alison. What about her?"

"There is no Alison? That's done and dusted. You can have her If you want Carl? She's now surplus to my requirements."

"So, you're just with pan-face now then?" Chris inquired.

"Stop calling her that Chris!" Eric assuaged. "She hasn't got a pan, face you bastards. Especially you two." Eric looked over at me and Ian. "Putting pans over your faces, in my mum's kitchen, when I was on the phone to her. I was dying to laugh!"

"Listen to us lot." I chip in. "We sound like a bunch of women. A set of fuckin sweetie-wife's. We're terrible. Talking about them, as if they're a commodity of sexual playthings, solely put on the planet, for our own fuckin personal pleasure? She has got a frying-pan face though Eric."

"Yep you got that right Ste! For our own *fucking pleasure'* haha. Women are worse than us when they get together, anyway. That's a fact!" Carl Interjected.

He'd returned from the snug, with his pockets bulging with change, like elephant's ears. To go along rather perfectly, with his elephant's trunk.

"Oh, here we go. Don't you fuckin start Carl? Mr fuckin play-boy, extraordinaire?"

"Well, you've either got it, or you aint." He said smiling. He calmly pulled out his chair, twisted it around backwards, and sat down like he was sitting on a horse. He picked up his cards and lent his elbows on its back rest in front of him, to get optimum card view.

"There's no fuckin answer to that?" I sadly affirmed.

"How many times have you dropped the jackpot Carl?"

"All the time Paul, all the fuckin time haha." Carl added, reaching around the chair for his libation.

"I'm talking about on the bandit you shit! Not your fuckin love life!

"Is that all you ever think about?" Paul further inquires.

"Is there anything else?" Carl assures.

"Who's turn is it" Eric confusedly asks.

"Yours you dick! Keep up, for fucks sake!"

"Nothing really." Paul finally agrees.

"Pick up two plastics!"

"That's what she said last night hahaha." Carl grinned.

We all laugh in unison.

I left them to the game and headed for the wall-mounted jukebox. Unlike the John bull gigantean, this little beast and music feast's selection was changed every two weeks, by the brewery. Updated, to keep up with the ever-changing charts, in an attempt to draw a younger, Wigan-bound clientele, through the doors, to increase brewery profits. Which suited me completely, as I was also luckily able to suggest choices to be put on, to Alan the landlord who was a terribly, unknowledgeable and lack-lustre music fan. Who would probably be much happier, with a jukebox full of easy listening, or Doris Day? But who invariably, just 'went' with the regulars, and my suggestions. Some of the 'new' tunes, I'd managed to get put on weren't even in the charts, and only existed in my own home music collection. I imagine Alan's 'music changer man' often left the juke box, completely lost, gobsmacked, and perplexed with 65-year-old, Alan's alternative, punk and new wave selections. Imagining Alan as some kind of time-warped, pre-punk.

A lot can be gauged from a person, by their music choices? I always took my time, and picked my tunes well, and solely for my listening pleasure only. Today's three for 50p, was The Waterboys *'The whole of the moon'*. Swiftly followed by the excellent 'howling' mix of the Cult's *'She sells sanctuary'* that was currently high, to the tune of 15 in the pop charts. The rebel rousing, alternative night's, current foot-stomping favourite, at the Pier on Wednesdays. Last but not least, on my Saturday afternoon playlist, would have to be *'West End Girls'* by the 'Pet Shop Boys'. A strange, but interesting new, electronic pop chart duo, akin to a latter day soft cell, that have come to my ears interest. I gave Lucy a smile over as John came cursing through the snug. "One bloody horse let me down Lucy. One bastard horse! £280 smackers down the pan! Always the bloody way, innit!"

I punched in my last selection, turned and slowly started walking back to our table. I paused and stopped, to look at them. Watching them all intently as they raucously and rambitiously played cards. Laughing and joking, without a care in the world. The six amigos, I thought. They reminded me of the famous, C M Coolidge paintings, of the anthromorphised dogs. Smoking cigars, and playing cards, seated around a card table. Definitely some different dog breeds personified in that bloody lot? I thought to myself. Paul, the little chiwawa, with the quick temper. Chris, the ever-faithful lassie, rough collie. Then there's Eric, reminiscent of dougal, in the Magic Roundabout. Birdy was the abyssinian, wire haired Gnasher. Carl probably fitted in, as an over sexed Muttley, from wacky races. With me as the littlest hobo, or even Toto, from the wizard of oz? Or maybe even the cartoon gang of cats in Top-Cat, with Eric, as 'Topcat'. Paul as 'Benny the ball'. Ian as 'Choo Choe', Chris as 'Brain', Carl as 'Fancy Fancy' and Anthony as a very young, 'Spook'. With

John the barman, possibly doubling as 'Officer Charlie Dibble'. As brilliant a set of mates that anyone could ever wish for.

"Hearts last card? Did you hear that Eric? John's horse went down the pan haha." Announced Chris.

"Erm, Hearts, I can't go." Paul ambled.

"Well fuckin pick up then!... If you can't go? You dipshit!" Eric scorned.

"I'm not fuckin picking up, if he's gonna fuckin chip out! arsehole! Are you chipping or what Chris?"

"Yep that's me.........! Come to daddy haha!" Chris exclaimed, revealing his winning cards. He scooped the mass silver up off the table as I sat back down.

"Cunt!" Eric thumped down his cards.

"You jammy bastard!" Paul agreed.

"I'm sick of this game. Play on your own. I'm out!" Ian announced, also hastily throwing his cards onto the table. Shortly followed by everyone else, who'd decided to have a betting breather, and instead, have a customary catch up.

"So, come on then Eric? what's the scores on the doors, women-wise? Spill!"

Carl asked, showing suspiciously more than a vested interest.

"Nothing to tell Carl. Alison's toast. Donnas gone. Tracy's' great in bed. That's it?"

"Donnas a gonner. Donnas' a kebab. Kebab meat! pan-face hahaha." Ian irresistibly pecked in and proceeded to throw in the word 'kebab' quickly In, every time her name was mentioned. Which became increasingly, and irritatingly and funny, at the same time.

"Donna?"

"kebab!"

"What about Donna...?"

"kebab!"

"I thought Donna.... *"kebab!"* was on the scene again?" Chris asked, looking over strain-faced at Ian.

"Is it bloody hell Donna!"

"Kebab."

"I met her out last week, that's all? IAN! shut the fuck up saying that, you dickhead." Eric carried on......

"I was chatting to Donna and her mate for a bit in the 'Moon under the Water', that's all. Only thing I can think of is, someone seen us together, put two and two together, and got fuckin twelve!" Either that, or it was you Paul? Spreading fuckin gossip again, to make yourself look good?" Eric raised his voice up, in Pauls direction.

Paul was ignoringly, looking down. Burning a hole through his 'patience' playing cards.

"It wasn't me." Paul exclaimed, not even raising his head.

"It was you! You lying little bastard."

Paul looked slowly up.

"No, it wasn't. I've got better things to do tha.........!"

Eric had a revelation moment, as he watched Paul, secretly squirming, yet trying to channel out, nonchalant emotion.

"I know it was you! I can fuckin tell! I can always fuckin tell when you're lying, you sly bastard. I can see It a mile off! You skulk like, fuck! You skulky, little bastard!

"He knows, I know it was him." Eric said looking around the table.

"Cos he was fuckin with me, the sly little cunt! Eric was slowly seeing red and continued.

"He's always wanted in Tracy's knickers, haven't ya? you creeping asshole! You were all over her in ours last week, you suck-hole bastard! Ever since I first went out with her, at the baths years ago, you've been after her. You're an underhand little shit! You've always wanted what I had, you little fuck-wit. If this gets back to Tracy, I'll fuck you, skulking cunt!"

"If it gets back to Tracy, she'll fuck him first, never mind you Eric!" I interjected, to try calm the situation. "She's always been a fuckin crazy bitch!"

Paul had nothing in defence and remained completely silent. Not even daring to make eye contact with Eric.

The table was silent. I looked over at Ian, who was halfway down his pint, and looking at me through his glass, with a grin in his eyes. He whisper-chanted *plastics* into his glass over and over as it slowly became louder until;

"You're a plastics.... What are you?" Asked Ian.

"Plastics!" Chris reluctantly added. Joining in ad-hochly swigging his lager.

"Fuck off you two," Paul said.

The chant was now being individually sang, person-to-person style, from all our mouths around the table. In short, sharp grin-based bursts, as Paul continued to look down, at his playing cards.

"**Plastics!** *Plastics!* PLASTICS! **Plastics!** *Plastics...!*"

Paul sadly looked up from his deck to see us all smiling, and chanting until finally, giving in by default, and deciding to smile, and even more curiously, join in, with the mocking chanty chorus....... of his wind-up nickname, and liberally mock himself.

After a second Ian, and myself idiotically decided it would be a good idea, to join up the words, and exchanged them at each other, in a further attempt to destroy him. To the further annoyance of the whole table and possibly the pub.

"**Plastics!** Kebab! *Plastics!* *Kebab*, kebab **Plastics!** *Plastics!* **Plastics!** *kebab*! **Plastics...!**"

"Right, come on lads that's enough! Shut the fuck up! Give it a rest! You'll have the fuckin place empty if you carry on? Let's have some peace and quiet. John said reasonably, regaining order.

We all burst out laughing as if to say; *"Shut up John, you weren't invited"*

"Kebab!" Ian had the last word, ducking as John went to slap him across the head, and instead bent forward, picked up the empty glasses, between his fingers and left to the bar.

TWENTY-SIX

The mood had really lifted, and the conversation slowly carried on, and continued in the same vein with added, ever present Ian-*'plastics'* and *'kebab'* announcements, randomly, and occasionally parped out, emanating from his corner, at any given moment, throughout the chatting.

"What about you Ste. Are you still with Linda?" Carl asked.

"Yes, pal. Just left her. I stayed over at her Mum and Dad's last night. They're in Spain" I second guessed him. "Don't even think about it either Carl, you wouldn't get past her dog. Let alone throw a fuckin party in her house."

'Kebab'

"She fuckin hates me, anyway." He affirmed.

"Hate's a bit strong Carl. I'd have said despises, haha." Eric said laughing.

"Wasn't my fault, her sister wanted me!"

"Who hates you? Paul inquired. Linda, Linda's Mum, or her Sister?"

"All of them" Carl laughed.

"Wasn't up for it? she's engaged, you dickhead! What do you mean?" I asked.

"It's not my fault she's engaged either? What does she see in him, anyway? He's a tosser."

"She doesn't need to see anything, she's engaged."

"He's a doctor" Paul randomly added.

"Doctor kebab."

"He'll have plenty of moolais then." Chris said.

"She still wants me. Still fuckin does......! That's what all the song and dance was for. Cos, she knows she can't get It now, cos she's been found out. She wanted it regular too? Every week? It would have been ok. He'd have never found about the first time either, if it wasn't for her Mum, the interfering fucker. Jane was pissed off, cos we were almost sorted for again. Then her Mum caught her on the phone with me and stuck her fuckin oar in. Jane's still pissed off. That's what she told me last week, anyway."

"What! you're still talking to her?" Eric laughed.

"Yep. Talk all the time."

"Fuckin hell Carl. You're a marriage wrecker, and they're not even married yet?"

"Jesus Christ Carl!" Chris exclaimed.

"It was just a bit of adult fun, before she does get married. Before she finally gets welded to the fucking boring twat! I don't see what all the fuss was about. Have they set another date yet Ste?" Carl casually inquired looking at me and taking a mouthful of his lager.

"No idea pal. I dunno? But I do know Linda's Mum will chop your bollocks off, if it ever happens again?"

"It takes two to tango Ste. I'm not the only guilty party? People are so bloody quick to judge and point the finger. She came on to me. It was Jane who wanted to play away not me. It's not solely my fault, all the time. What an amazing super-power that would be?" He smiled.

"She wanted her bit on the side. I was just the unlucky, or lucky party, depending on your point of view. It's too late to teach her how to dance now?" Carl casually added, smiling.

"You really are a bloody Libertine sometimes Carl." I laughed, slurping my lager.

"However, it happened, it doesn't bode well for the rest of the marriage, when they finally do tie the knot. I've seen it all before with our Lynne." Chris confidently threw in, matter-of-factly, swigging his pint, as if he was some secret, Claire Rayner marital expert.

"Yep, your right Chris," Carl affirmed. "If it wasn't me this time, it'll definitely be somebody else next time." He paused for a moment.

"My sister said that should be my middle name." Carl further pointed out.

"Carl 'marriage wrecker' Macready. Haha. *'Home wrecker Macready', 'Killer Macready!'*" Carl was vocally trying the nickname out for size.

"Mmm," he chortled. *"Wrecker Macready, Killer Macready, Killer creed?* Like that. Definitely has a ring to it?" Carl put down his pint, clasped his hands together, with index fingers pointed and feigned blowing smoke away from the tips. Chris, who had intently been listening throughout, piped in; "He's a 'Killer creed! gunpowder, gelatine. Dynamite with his laser beam. Guaranteed to blow you mind! Anytime! haha."

"I like that one Chris haha," Carl laughed.

"To be honest." Ian said. "You know what I think?"

"No? Eric said bluntly, 'But I'm sure you're gonna fuckin tell us?" he resounded.

Talking stopped, and the table went quiet. Carl slowly put his hands back down. Paul silenced his shuffling cards. Eric's glass stopped, mid-swig and was held in anticipation. All eyes were on Ian.

"I think it's all down to. PLASTICS! hahaha."

"Oh, shut the fuck up you knobhead! Go and get the ale in?"

"Fuck off Ian," Paul exclaimed.

"Hahaha" Eric laughed.

"Sounds like a wrestler? Killer Kreed," Paul muttered.

"You're all fuckin nuts!" Eric laughed.

Ian reluctantly stood up. "Same again bastards?"

"Yep go for it." Eric answered for the table.

"Hang on a minute?" Ian hastily added. "What are we doing, anyway? Are we staying in here, or going somewhere else before we head up-town?"

"I really don't care. Carl interjected. I'm with the majority?"

"Don't worry about it, doesn't matter, anyway. Just get the ale in. We can decide as we go along. There's plenty fuckin time yet." Eric concluded.

"By the way Eric. I've got a job for you. Well, I haven't, Peter has. He want's you to start full- time at Churches, if you're Interested?"

"Full time Ste? Are you serious? Of course, I'm fuckin Interested! Bloody brilliant!"

"Oh good. I'll let him know then. I'm on holiday from this Friday, I'll give him your number, then he can talk to you about it himself, ok?"

"Yep, I know you're on hols Ste. But tell him to ring me anytime. Anytime at all. Day or night. Oh, great, you've made my day now!" He smiled.

"Lucy! is there anyone on the bandit?" Paul shouted toward the bar. She nodded her head.

"Billy."

"Good stuff. Filling it up for me." Carl rubbed his hands together, looking at Paul.

"Come on then Chris. Get some of your winnings in the jukebox? Put some decent tunes on?" I said to Chris, who was merrily still counting up his silver.

"Stick 'Thieves Like Us' by New Order on for me pal?"

"Oh ok, they're good them." He agreed, standing up and sliding his cash into his pocket.

"Not a bad mornings work. five-fifty in slummy. I'll put a couple of quid in. D'you want anything else on Ste? I'm not leaving credits on. Paul always checks it when he comes back from the toilet or bandit and puts his rubbish on?" I quickly rummaged my brain.

"Erm ye!" I shout over as he walks away from the table. "Go on then, put anything by The Smiths or the Cure on?"

"Who?" He asks strain faced and cupping his ear, as if he's lost his hearing. He beckons me over.

Mmm, He either can't hear me, or he just doesn't like them.

The Cure, 'the walk!' I shout. Or anything at all by the 'Smiths'.

"Gotcha!" Comes the nodding answer, and the thumbs up.

He'll probably forget, or put his own on, I affirm to myself, taking a sip of lager. I peer over at the bar clock, catching sight of Lucy bobbing in front of her makeshift Tetley mirror, applying more make up. Rubbing it in under her eyes, as Ian waits at the bar for John, to re-appear, beer laden from the snug. He taps his foot and hands on the brass bar rails, to Chris's music selection as he does. One o'clock.

Mmm? I'll have to take my time on the old motion lotion today? I don't want to end up as pissed as I was, walking home from the Pier last night. I'm bloody lucky I'm still here. Mind you? If truth be told, I'm convinced I was 'spiked' sometime during the night. I'm going to make damn sure, my drink doesn't leave my side in the future. That was a night to end all nights. Let alone the rest of my life!

I haven't breathed a word of it, to the rest of the lads. Except Chris. I'd get the piss ripped right out of me and attain some new nickname for the rest of my days if I did.

Chris looks over and smiles. "Found the Smiths!"

They probably wouldn't believe me if I told them, anyway. Now I wish I could tell you, that my life flashed before my eyes, or that I saw the true meaning of life. Or the real reason we're here. Or some other such, astounding prophecy or wisdom. Or even next week's lottery numbers? But I'm sorry, I can't. All I can say is, I'm just happy, I'm still here.

TWENTY-SEVEN

Alternative night at the Pier with Neil Wilson. Neil's a nice lad, but quite a strange character too? I've not really been able to suss him out yet. Which is strange in itself for me? He probably says the same things about me? I can usually suss people out, within a couple of meetings or nights out. I probably don't really know him, well enough yet. We originally met up on the dance floor, at alternative night, in the Pier. I was minding my own business, bopping along to the sounds, with two female friends, more than similar to Hopper. 'Cool' weirdo and 'pit' weirdo, and with the rest of the bursting at the seams, dance-floor to a great new tune. 'Cool' and 'Pit' had earned their nicknames, from Birdy and me, just cos they did what it says on the tin. Jill was blond, really fit, and had an ultra cool dancing style, and the other black-haired girl 'Pit' or Grace, couldn't put one foot in front of the other, without looking totally naff, and was far from blessed in the beauty area. Neil just danced his way into our company, and we've been pals ever since.

The song was the jazzesque, state of the nation, thought provoking, 'Heartland' by Matt Johnsons The-The. The ever-important music connection was made. Tapes and records were borrowed and swopped and we've randomly met up there ever since. Tonight, it was a little different to say the least. We were meeting up first, at his house by his request, and then heading to the Honeysuckle pub, around the corner from his house, but within walking distance of the pier.

Roughly nine o'clock, I'd finished my first pint. Said my goodbyes, to Esther in the bar, and left the newly built but scaringly punterless 'Hawk Inn' on foot. Opting on the wet, but nippy night, to walk from home, and have a bevy in each watering hole, on the way down to give Neil a knock. Next on the solo pub-crawl list was The Bold Hotel, on Poolstock lane. I'd walked past this place on my way to the Tippings, on numerous occasions. Not specifically a Hotel as such. Just your typical, old grimy looking, Lancashire street corner pub, in a terrible state of disrepair. Probably full of flat caps, and woodbines inside? Dodgy Derek from the fruit market, had once told me of his affection for its vaults. Due to it being his Fathers, final resting place, and local before him. Externally, it was dog-rough, weathered. But as I walked through its doors, It's Internal demeanour, was surprisingly, quite regal looking. At least, it would have been, back in the 60's. Probably the last time it had had a decent lick of paint. Mmm, I mused looking around, I bet Derek's shares a pint with the ghost of his Dad in here quite a lot? The place was completely empty.

As I walked to the bar, there was an old, small, silver transistor radio, near the till, squeaking out a slow waltz. What I can only describe as, something akin to, Vera Lynn. The dumpy, grey haired, decrepit looking bar woman, looked pleasant enough, she was hard to spot though? Perched on a standard size chair, or less than high stool, behind the much higher bar. She was furiously knitting too. Mmm? I thought. She looks like a coffin dodger, but judging by the speed of the knitting needles, she's possibly sprightlier than myself, or a woman half her age. Maybe a black belt in kung fu with ten Dan's? with those speedy arms. She put me in mind of an over-inflated version of 'granny' from the beverley hillbillies. Or all I needed to do was to give her a lick of green paint, give her a broom and a hat, and she'd be a pure dopple-ganger double, of 'Witchy-poo,' from 'Emu's world.' I bet she's probably Derek's auntie, sister or wife? I presumed, as she looked up, and took to her feet. Feigning, a smile and placing down the large green, knitting bundle on the top of the bar. Then she opened her mouth.

"Aye lad. Wit cannae git yer big man?" She pushed her long floppy grey fringe away from her forehead, and to the side of her head. Twirling it together, with her stubby finger, and deposited it neatly, over the back of her ear.

She was definitely not from these parts either. Mmm? maybe Billy Connolly's Mum then?

As I watched, she tipped her head, and yanked apart the lapels, of her visually, home-made pink cardigan. Revealing her long chained, large rimmed glasses, that were hiding underneath it in the process. She grabbed them, by what I could make out what was, the only ear arm and promptly skewed them, onto the bridge of her nose. Balancing them precariously, yet somehow precisely, and effectively between chain, and arm as she did. As she looked up at me, the glasses wobbled slightly. Threatening to slide off her bulbous red nose. She again, pushed the ear-arm down firmly, to the back of her grizzled left ear.

"Fekin thangs."

"Erm?" I looked end to end, across the bar. 'Marstons,' 'Greenalls Bitter,' 'Greenalls Mild,' 'Flowers IPA.' "Do you have any Lager?" I asked, fidgeting with my ear.

"Nae lad. Wae dinnae heve any o' thit shite in ere. Oh, aye wee dae, In bottles. But it's shite, al thi same."

"Oh, erm ok. I've heard Flowers is good?"

"Aye lad. Tekes a while tae settle, bit it's a greate dranke."

"Go on then. You've twisted my arm." I laughed. She looked through me, stayed silent and continued to fight with her grey mass of hair. I wouldn't like her to twist my arm. She's got arms like Popeye. She'd probably break it?

"I'll try one." I smiled.

"Okeye lad, helde on. I aftae dee thas."

With that, she turned to her small chair. Bent over and put her fingers and thumbs firmly on the seat part and dragged it towards her. Making an almighty 'screeching' sound with the legs, across the tiled bar floor, as she did. Then, she literally, kicked it underneath the beer pump spill trays. Lifted up her bandaged, Nora batty, left leg with her arm, and kicked off the thin cushion as she did, and proceeded to put her left foot, shoe heel on the seat edge.

I watched on mesmerised. "It'll be reet, in a minute. I af tae... dae thas." She repeated. She slowly stretched her arm up, grabbing on to one of the beer pump arms. I heard an awful bone click from somewhere. "Ouch! aye, that's ate lad, am up!" She smiled.

With the aid of the bar pump, she'd wholly managed, to make herself twice as tall, as she originally was, when I'd first walked into the bar. She was now proudly, looking down at me. Mmm, should be quite Interesting to watch her get back down, I thought? Shame she hasn't got some kind of, crash mat affair, or mini bouncy castle, for when she base jumps back down?

She smiled down at me, clearly looking happy with herself, and her new-found height, now being, some two feet taller than me, standing aloft the chair. I now had, an unenviable bird's-eye view, of her grey, chinny bristles, dotted about her heavy, hanging, double chin area.

Not a pretty sight. By now, I'd parked myself on a tall stool, at the bar and was leaning, on my elbows, with my chin on my hands waiting for my pint.

She bent down, to reach one of the empty pint glasses, tucked under the bar. Holding on to the beer pump for stability. She grunted, unnervingly, as she put it up to the light.

"Aye, thit's a cleaen wan. Nae dist err spiders oan at fer a chenge ay lad, heehee."

She must be just about ready now, I thought. I looked at my watch.

"I weant bae a' tic lad." As she said this, the vault door was pulled open. Dodgy Derek, the wise old owl, from the fruit market rushed inside.

"Bloody hell! it's pissin daen agen out theere Margareet! I left t'owd van at hame. Wish I hadn't a bothered nae, am bloody soaked to't skin! Alreet lad? Ow't doin? Wot doin in ere Inge? Tha goe's in't Tippin's dun't thee?' He quizzically looked up at tall, granny hillbilly.

"Get bloody daen from theere, sharpish Margareet! Eh thi off thi trolley? Al get lad's pint."

"Erm alright Derek? I'm off to the Tippings. Just thought I'd try one in here, on my way past, for a change. As you do like?"

Derek had already lifted the wooden bar divider and seen himself into the back of the bar.

"Carry on lad, am listenin. Al Just gettin this daft ow'd bugger darn off ere. Come here thee?"

"Well erm, as I say. I was on my way to the Tipp ..."

I stopped mid sentence. Watching Derek grapple his arms around what I now know as Scottish Margaret.

I smiled to myself intently, as the oap, granny, pub rescue unfolded, in front of my eyes.

"Come hither, yer daft owd bat! Grab ow'd o' me? Put thi arms...! Ooof, Gis thi bloody arms ere wilt? Alreet lad, carry on. Jesus! your heeavy Margareet! Wil' aft put theee, ona carrot diet! Grab owd'......! That's it! Watch me bloody toes! Av only got me slippers on! Ouch! a sed watche fuukin toes!

Derek had wanted to lift her down, with his hands clasped on her chubby, waist in one fell swoop. Margaret on the other hand, had opted for other ideas, and had started to step off the chair seat. Ending up, virtually slumped on to his shoulder, and pushing him backwards, almost into the shorts optics, in the process. Two cordial bottles, and a bowl of lemons, almost ended up on the floor, in the debacle. It was like being ringside 'Giant Haystacks' and bryl-creamed, 'Cat Weasel' on Saturday afternoons, 'World of Sport'.

By now, I'd found myself stood up with my arms, outstretched, willing him to get her back down, to the solid safety of the floor. As he staggered slightly backward, he wheezed and coughed, sounding like an out of breath heavy smoking concertina. Just like Joe the taxi driver. Margaret, resolutely and copiously continued to smile, both animatedly, and embarrassedly in my direction, throughout the whole process. Her glasses finally slipped off her nose, and dangled innately, swinging in front of her. She even waved at me on the way down?

As wheezing Derek slid her gently down, two porky ankles appeared, and wiggled, slowly down, to feel the ground. Her flowery dress, had decided to remain arrogantly and firmly stuck In Its place. Statically charged, to his browny-green, black elbowed, hunting coat. Also snagging itself on his belt. Revealing more than a hefty eyeful, of her stubby wrestler's legs, ageing under-carriage and under-skirt.

"I'm just erm, off to the little boy's room." I quickly said before I burst out laughing.

It would be far more noble, that I make myself scarce, and less embarrassing for them at this juncture. Allow them to regroup, and get themselves back to some kind of, acceptable clothed normality in their own time. Derek can get his breath back and also prevent myself from pissing my pants. Let them and save a little face. Particularly Margaret, whose dress hem, was inextricably attached, to Elvis's smiling silver face, on Derek's massive belt buckle.

I randomly pushed the toilet door open. Inside was pink as Margaret's cardigan, and clearly the ladies. I hadn't even taken the trouble to read the sign. Didn't have the time. Didn't even matter. The wee was almost trickling down my leg, I was laughing that much. They could obviously hear me although I was trying in vain to stop. I looked at my reflection in the mirror. Randomly shaking my head. Through the mirror, I caught sight of the oldest tampon and rubber jonny dispenser, I'd ever seen. What made me laugh even more, was the blue and white embossed, bold and striking slogan, across the front; '*Never Get Caught Short Again!*' and a picture of a man, on one side of the letters, and a woman on the other, animatedly smiling, and showing off their product of choice.

I was laughing so hard, my legs were crossed, and my hand was now holding onto the radiator, for balance, in a fateful attempt to keep vertical. I unzipped my pants at the same time, with the other. Just managing to turn away from the mirror, and pull them down before the optimum moment, but still laughing uncontrollably. "Oh, dear lord" I said to myself, as my banks bust. I didn't even have to hold it, it was releasing its cache so furiously. Because I'm not circumcised, this was akin to a piss releasing, Gatling gun firing a full round of water cannon. Or a fireman's hose, without the fireman to keep it steady.

I just put both my hands up on to the pink tiles above the urinals and let nature take its course.

Mmm, never get caught short? haha, bit hard not to pee yourself either, when faced with scotch Margaret's bloomers, and Derek half-nelson wrestling her.

Looking again into the mirror, I calmed and composed myself. Glanced down at my jeans for tell-tale signs of wee and urine stainage? All clear. Mmm, that was more than lucky. I took a further few, deep breaths before returning to the scene of the crime.

"Alright lad? there's thi pint, it was 'Flowers' want it?"

"Erm yes Derek. Thanks."

"Margareet's gone up the stair, for a little lie down. I think she's a bit tired now, thanoes?"

"Erm yes Derek, I imagine she might be."

"Bar girl's due in dust see. Me wee Grandoughter, but she's bloody late agen? Thi can't telt time these yung uns these days. How's Peter up market?"

"Oh Peter... he's alright. Peter's peter, I suppose."

"I get mi stuf outta Conroy's, dost see. Off owd Charlie. He does me sum gud deels. Av only a little round in't van dust see? All thowd pensioners on't thestate. Thi can't get owt somer um? So, a' tek frut an't veg to um like. It keeps em goin. Keeps me gooin too. Am retired now, dost see? Dust want a rollee lad? Ave plenty bacca here?"

"Erm I'm alright thanks Derek. I've got Bensons here. You can have one of these if you like?"

"Go on then lad. I don't as a rule. Prefer bacca, but al ave one allt' same."

Mmm? I bet you will, I thought. You thieving old bastard. All you buy off the fruit and vegetable market is pure crap, on the verge of going off? Vegetables way past their sell buy date, and turning to mange, or mush. Now granted. You doe ferry it around to the old folks houses for them, which is on one hand, pretty commendable. But on the other hand, they run the risk of possibly paying a visit to the hospital for food poisoning. Or of constantly running to the toilet, with the wild shites, for days after on the other. I suppose if they ingest' it in a reasonable time, and not allow it to fester, any longer than it already has, in the larder they would be reasonably safe.

Oh, what am I thinking about? He's not a bad old skin? He looks after his own. This fella will probably be still peddling and selling his stuff, longer than I'll be at the market? God knows, I've seen him doing it on Worsley Mesnes estate, ever since I was almost knee-high to a grasshopper. So, it can't be any worse than B & R millionaire, Lenny Rimmer teaching me the most effective way to riddle through maggot ridden spuds.

"There you go Derek."

"Oh thanks. Reet you are lad. Al just finish rollin this, n' stick it back in't thowd pouch." As Derek's busies himself with his ciggies, the door opens again.

TWENTY-EIGHT

In walks a very tall and slim, black-haired, pretty girl. She has the longest legs, I've ever seen, even with flat soled pumps on. She has tight, black jeans, with purple pockets, and is approximately two, or three years younger than me. She had bold, cherry lipstick on, which stands out, from her pale complexion. Her top is white, and she has the shortest, black denim coat on. She's humming away to herself, as she tosses her blue lighter up into the air. She catches it, chewingly smiles, and looks me up and down. then throws her lighter up again. She reminds me of a young Morticia, from the Adams Family. Her hair's braided, into a long whip-like, ponytail at the back.

"Alright Grandad? where's Margaret? has she gone up? She picks her chewing gum out from her mouth and spins it around her index finger. Looks at me again, then puts it back in, with her finger. Then and spits it out, into the large blue, empty bottle-bin, jutting out from under the back of the bar.

"Aye lass. Gone for a lie down. She's had a hectic day, thanoes."

"What? hectic? in this morgue? Your kiddin me?"

"Aye. well let's just say she's been, erm busier, than she usually is. Eh lad."

Derek winks over at me. I politely smile at the tall girl, as she puts her red purse down, aside the till. And places her cigarettes, and lighter neatly on top.

"Darts & doms tonight isn't it Grandad? Is it home or away?"

"It's temorro, aner, a think they're ere, lass?"

The black-haired girl, looks at me again. Then casually walks over to a chart, hung at the end of the bar.

"Who is it then, lass?" Derek asks.

She yanks the chart down, from the wall. "I dunno? I can't bloody read this? Is this Margaret's scribble? Oh God! it's just scrawl?"

She looks at me again, and marches across the bar, to where Derek is still fumbling with his tobacco pouch and putting out the spent cigarette I gave him.

"Al stick tu't bacca in't future lad. Thi'd reely mek mi coff mi guts up, them fings. Wot thi wittering aboot naw lass?"

"What does that say Grandad?"

"I asn't got mi bins wi me? Am blind as a coot, wi owt um." He pushes away the chart. "Gerrit owt mi face lass! I caunt see it? A fink its Plough lot. Aye it is! a remember naw, lass. Plough n arrow mob, termoro nite it is. not the neet, So thers no panic."

Derek picks up his whiskey chaser off the bar and downs it in one. Splutters out a cough and clears his raspy throat. "Ooh, that bloody cigs got on mi chest already?

The tall girl swishes her ponytail back and walks toward me. Moves my pint to one side, and plops the chart down on the bar, right in front of me.

"Can you read that?"

I look down at the cardboard chart. Picking it up, to get a closer look. I lift my glasses out of the way. Then again, into the way. "Erm no. I can't?"

"Are you blind as well?" she asks.

"Leave him be lass, ave towd thi' it' team."

"Wait til I see Margaret, I'm gonna tell her get back to school.

Derek let out a knowing laugh. Then fished in his pocket, to reveal a crumpled, stained hanky and proceeded to blow his nose.

"PARP! Ooh! bloody hell! there's some shite fond its waay up theere today, haha. Ere lass av a look?" He laughed. She just Ignored him.

"It's ridiculous. It's scrawl pure scrawl!

"Giv her peace wilt, she neer went scool." He said, screwing his hanky back into a ball, and stuffing it back into his jacket pocket.

"WHAT!' The girl looked at me again. Yanked the chart from in front of me and stormed across to the other side of the bar. Replacing it back on the wall, then returning to Derek, at the far side of the bar instantly.

"Say that again Grandad?" Derek quietened.

"Naw keep thi marth shut! Dust heer mi? Dun't like folk nowin. She neer went school. Got up the duff wi thi Mam'.

"Oh Grandad? I never knew that?" She seemed deflated by the news. "That's just......? Aaw, It's just, not right? It's not fair either? It's terrible?" She seriously pondered, on the revelation for a minute.

"Naw think on, keep thi marth buttoned! Put anotha whiskey in theree, fo thi owd Granda lass?"

The girl genuinely looked shocked, whilst also giving me a look that almost said;

"You'll keep your gob shut too, if you know what's good for you? you nosey freak!"

"Get lad a top up too." Derek said to his tall granddaughter. She gave me another dark look, to sink a ship. Grabbed his short glass and held it beneath the optics.

After pushing on it twice. Squirted the smallest amount of lemonade known to man, into the glass, and put the whiskey chaser, back down at the side of him, and picked up my three parts empty pint.

"What is it...?" she said sternly. "Flowers?"

"Erm yes."

"Oh, ok...? she fumbled for a name.

"It's erm, Steve. I'm Steve. She remained silent, pulling down on the pump. Until the white beer froth reached the top of the glass and brimmed over.

"Top it up for you when it's settled Steve."

The ceiling creaked above my head. Rather like at home with me mam. Tending us all to be quieter and listen. The tall girl turned down the tinny radio.

"She's up Grandad" Shall I go up? make sure she's ok?"

"Towd thi, give her peace. She'll be reet."

The girl looked at my settling glass. Picked it up and did as she said she would. Then placed it back down, in front of me. "There you go Steve."

"Thanks, erm? cheers, Derek! I acknowledged him along the bar. I too, searched for a name?

"Tilly, I'm Tilly....pleased to meet you. It's Matilda really, but that's nothing but a mouthful of mad letters. German too. But then I am a little crazy! aren't I Grandad, woo! woo!" she smiled, and twisted her finger, on the side of her head. A much more pleasant, and real smile. As if she'd just bared her soul.

"Even Mum calls me Tilly."

"Well thanks, erm Tilly. Matildas a lovely name." I cheerfully said.

"Ah, it's ok, I suppose. Tilly's better. How do you know my Grandad? I know you know him. He doesn't get a drink for just, any passing stranger? Not that he even paid for it." She reached over the bar, grabbed a tall stool, from my side of the bar, and put it on her side. Then sat on it as she continued.

"Not that he ever pays for any of it in here? The tight old bugger, haha. Aren't you Grandad?"

I looked down the bar to see his reaction. But Derek seemed to be miles away and talking to himself as well.

Tilly picked up a beermat. "Oh, don't mind him. It's nearly his time." She turned and looked at the pub wall clock. "Nearly ten o'clock. It's actually way past his time. I'm very surprised. He doesn't usually last this long."

"Oh, really I offered. Why? is he some kind of vampire or something. I was just about smile when she suddenly slammed her beermat down on onto the bar. Turning more than rather stern faced as she did.

"Don't mock the dead, Infidel!" Then she came out with a mouthful of words, which sounded really quite scary. But much more logically as my brain worked out, just in another language. What the hell was that all that about, I thought.

"I'm teasing you Steve. I'm just playing with you. It's ok, really, haha. I was just speaking German. Look at you? Aaw, like a frightened, little rabbit without the ears, and teeth, haha. I love rabbits. They go very well in my teeth, haha."

"You don't know what to do...? you don't know what to say? You think I'm crazy, don't you?" She gripped the beermat between her teeth, and ripped it in half with her hand, feigning the roar of a lion, as she did. Then burst out laughing.

Now, my psycho sensors were slowly, creeping up the scale.

She picked up a new beermat, and again put it in her mouth, and started to hum again. I picked up my settled full pint, put it to my lips, to take a mouthful. When I'd finished, I put it back down, and looked to see Tillys back to me, across the bar, turning the radio volume back up, and tuning it. It buzzed, hummed, and squeaked through the various radio stations, until she'd found the one she wanted. She was still humming.

"Peelies due on in a minute."

"Who?" I swigged.

"Peelie idiot! The music messiah that is John Peel. That's if I can find him, on this damn piece of junk. I keep saying I'm gonna get Margaret a new one, but I always forget, when I'm Wigan shopping. Da dadadupdeda.... Do you like music Steve? Oh, come on bloody radio! Where are you Peelie? where are you? 'Da, dadupdumbumbumbum." She turned to face me again, just as I was about to answer.

"BUM!......... Hahaha."

She's highly playful? I'll give her that, I mused. Quite lovely, In fact. A tad different from when she first walked in. She certainly gets my attention. Or craves it? Keeps it too?

"Hooray! there he Is.............. got him! You've been hiding, haven't you John? You naughty boy! I love music." Tilly announced. She turned around from the radio, with a beaming smile on her face. She was exceptionally pretty. Took me a little while, to see how much.

"Do you Tilly?" She skipped across the bar in front of me. Spun around, with her eyes closed, then plonked herself back down, onto her high stool. Still infectiously humming. I looked down to a very quietened Derek, who was now leant on his hand, napping on the bar. His chin kept slipping out of his hand. He would then, repositioning his jaw, back into said place.

"Now prey tell?"

"I'm sorry Tilly?"

"Music Dumbo! Tell me about your music then. Who do you like? what do you like?"

"Oh, erm anything. Everything."

"Nah you can't just say that. You sound just like a lying politician! That's just not putting yourself on the line at all? haha. It's not even tennis. Do you like tennis? I hate politicians." She smiled. Then I smiled. "Give me a chance to answer then!" I said.

She wryly smiled and stood up.

"Stop changing the subject to Tilly!" I added. "You're almost as bad as me."

"Ok then, answer away. But choose your words carefully.... Or I'll eat you!"

"Chance would be a fine thing." I laughed, and took a swig of my ale, and hid behind the glass.

She stopped me in my tracks. Grabbed my glass, and slowly, pulled It away from my mouth. Then looked over It, at the same time. "I beg your pardon! Don't be rude Steve, haha." She smiled her beautiful smile, again.

She bent forward, put her finger across her bold red lips and *'Shushed me.'* Pointed over to Derek. "Give me a minute Steve, then you can have my full, undivided attention. I promise." She walked across to Derek.

"Grandad! come on now, wakey-wakey! It's time to go home! *Time to go home, time to go home. Grandad is waving goodbye, goodbye, goodbye.* Wake up, you old sod!"

One of Derek's eyes, slowly opened. He quickly looked at the bar, as if he was checking his whiskey was still there, or that he either, hadn't drunk it, or it hadn't been taken away.

"I kno, I kno it is lass. Am guin nar." He shook his head, and ran his fingers backward, through his jet black, Elvis-style, brylcreemed hair.

Tilly continued to serenade the Andy Pandy song as she walked back toward me.

"Andy is waving goodbye.... goodbye.... goodbye."

Derek took to his feet. "Am nippin for a quik pee, before I go!"

"Goodbye.... goodbye" Then she changed the words. *"Hello.... hello.... hello."* She folded her arms, leant on the bar, directly in front of me, and beautifully smiled again.

TWENTY-NINE

What a strange, and happy creature she is, I thought. With a soul-meltingly, beautiful voice too?

Derek was back out from the loo, in a trice. Still zipping up his fly. He walked towards us and briefly stopped. Put his hand on my shoulder, then straightened his arm-patched hunting jacket, as he walked past my stool. I looked down, at his knackered slippers, and sock-less feet.

"Ooh thit reminds me, al aft get some new steelies fo't work. Reet, al si thi on't market Inge. Tell thi Mother, al be over termorro, Tilly. Nite lass, nite Steve, Ama wayy!"

"Goodnight Derek!"

"Night Grandad!" She leant over the bar and planted a peck on his cheek.

"It sounds like the Waltons in here." She said, as her eyebrows lifted, and her forehead creased. She started playing with the elastic, in her plaited ponytail.

"Ok go ahead Steve. I'm all ears." She looked directly at me, put her hand under the bar. Grabbed a half glass, and reached across to the 7up, soda dispenser, and pushed her glass forward on the black tab. Then, she reached backwards, grabbed a straw from behind her left shoulder, and turned her body, back to face me. Slurping loudly, on the still frothing liquid, as she did. Throughout the whole motion, almost hardly breaking eye contact with me at all.

"I meant what I said. I know it does sound very vague? But I love anything, and everything. All sorts of music."

"Give me an example Steve? She slurpingly quizzed. Blowing bubbles into her drink

"Oh, talk about put me on the spot."

"You put yourself there, not me." She grinned.

"Ok, erm, right here goes. There're tons you know," I warn her:

"Scritti Politti, the Cure, Killing Joke, Otis Reading, TheThe, Clash, Suzy Vega, John Foxx, Aretha Franklin, Kraftwerk. Claudia Brucken and Propaganda, Erm, Joni Mitchell, Cult, Joy Division, now New Order, Northern Soul, ELO, Beatles. Oh God, Claudia Brucken has such a meltingly, melancholy voice. With such heartfelt meaning too. She's German too Tilly, Sorry Tilly. I got a bit side-tracked then."

"You gotta have the Beatles, keep going Stephen." She quickly bangs the bar, and interrupts. She seemed to be willing me on, as if it was some kind of race, or there was some, Imaginary or invisible, finish line? "Faster!" She smiled:

"The Rolling Stones, Scritti again! Oh, haha," I laughed. *"Green Gartside, that new fella? D... d... Dolby... Thomas Dolby, Talking Heads, Numan. The Jam, Magazine, the margarine,* the toast haha, just kidding. Oh God! Erm, *Pistols* just the early stuff though, *Siouxsie, Pil, Stranglers,* God how did I forget them? *Erm, Lou Reed....... Simone Nina Simone.................?*

Tilly was clapping.

"Bloody hell! *Bowie, Bunnyman, Jarre, Ska* I mean, *Specials, The Smiths, Sisters, Madness!* this is madness? Your madness Tilly!"

'Hooray' she shouted. 'Well done!

I felt like I was in some kind of therapy session. Or at least was in need of one.

"I like some of them to Steve. Especially, Siouxsie. Some, I've never even heard of though? That's why I like to listen to Peelie. He has some great new music and great new bands on. Who was that you said? Green Gartseey?"

"Gartside'. I said, reaching for my almost empty pint, and necking it in thirst

"Green..........? Ooh, that's a cool name. Who's that then? Is it a he or a she?" She asked, grabbing my empty glass. "Want more?"

"Erm it's a he, and yes, I'll have one more, before I go ta."

"Ooooh that sounds ominous," she frowned.

"No, it doesn't, you wind up merchant." She laughed out loud, as she filled the glass. "What are you like?"

"Big chauve. I'm a big chauve. Go on then, tell me who he is? Then you can tell me where you're going. It's Interesting. Your Interesting. It's nice to talk to someone, that has at least half a brain." She carried on talking before I even had a chance to reply. She looked down, and waited for the pint glass to fill, in her hand.

"Nobody ever comes in here. Nobody but no one? Except Grandad of course, and a few others on Fridays. Oh, and the darts team. Other than that, It's deathly boring. I'm always on my own. Reading or writing." She quietens, as the frothy head, drips onto the tray, and she straightens up the almost full pint.

"It is good for my college writing. I'll say that much for it. But that's about it? That's why John keeps me company." She looks up at my confused face. "Peelie!" I mean and puts the glass down.

"So are you.... Tilly, I reply.... Interesting!"

She settles back, onto her tall stool.

"Thanks. that's very nice of you to say so."

"I wasn't sure though." I smile.

"Oh, It's just my defence mechanism Steve. Nothing more than that."

"You have a lovely defence mechanism Tilly. Is it all your own?"

"Don't be a sexist pig!"

"I'm not."

"Yes, you are! and don't patronize me!" She smiles again. Pointing her beermat at me.

"Sorry. I apologise."

"So, you should be."

"I'll get you one of those for Christmas."

"Good. I'll need a new beermat by then."

"I'll get you two then." We both laugh.

"So, who is this Green feller?"

"He's the lead singer of Scritti Politti. Do you really speak German?"

"Now who's changing the subject."

"I am, so hush and listen Tilly! He's very tall, like you. They've just released a new album called Cupid & Psyche, which they spent a small fortune making, and it's bloody brilliant! He's got an amazing and weird singing voice. For a six-foot six bloke that is! And his real names Julian and he hails from Wales. Oh, and Arif Mardin produced it."

She *'shushes'* me again. "What is it.... Tilly? Margaret again?" I ask, taking my voice to a whisper.

"No" She shakes her head. "Oh, this one. God, I love this one. He's been playing this non-stop, the past two weeks. I still don't know who it is? Someone's always gabbing in the bar, or I have to go change a barrel, or something happens, and miss it. I can't even work out what she's singing at all? It's really lovely though. I'm turning it up."

Tilly runs to the radio.

"Tut. Tilly? I've just educated you on the basic ins, and outs of Scritti's latest album, and you don't even know who Elizabeth Fraser Is? Dear, oh dear, Off with her head!" I shout, sipping my pint.

"*Shush* Steve, I'm trying to listen."

"Blasphemy."

"Shush! Steve. Oh, please, do be quiet, I want to hear who it......"

"The Cocteau Twins."

"No, I mean the sing....."

"Elizabeth Fraser. It's one, I missed off my list Tilly. It's 'Pearly Dewdrops drops'"

The record fades out as Tilly turns the volume to its loudest possible. She looked over at me silently. Putting her ear closer to the radio and creasing her forehead again like a washboard:

'Well, this is one of my favourite records of last year. Pearly Dewdrops drops and The Cocteau Twins. And they were one of those bands again, like when I first heard them I thought, "Great, I'm glad I lived long enough to hear this. And here's another good tune from last year. It's the...'

Tilly turns the radio back to mouse level.

"Well, it goes without saying, John Peel would like them. I've a couple of their albums at home. You can borrow them If you like?"

"Oh wow, excellent, thanks. I'm glad you came in here now, haha. Are they twins then?"

"Haha no, they're not twins. Their Scottish like Margaret though. From Grangemouth I think?"

"That explains the voice then. No wonder I can't tell a word she's singing. I can't understand Margaret at times either. Especially when she's had a belly full of whiskey."

"You're not on your own, no one can understand her. Elizabeth Fraser, I mean. It's been said she has her very own language. You can sometimes pick certain words up, or at least you think you can. It's better to just listen to it, for what it is, instead of over analysing it. She's just blessed with a beautiful voice. A little like you. I liked your humming and singing earlier. I'm no expert, but you're not bad at all. It was easy on the ear, let's just put it that way."

"Thank you very much, you can come in again. She smiled. I'll definitely take you up on the records though. No, wait a minute, give me two minutes, I'll be right back!"

She quickly takes what I assume is the same door Margaret did when she disappeared upstairs.

"Bloody hell? she's off again? She never sits still this one? She always has a bee in her bonnet, about something."

A few over-head creaks, and thuds later, she returns into the bar, panting with two, white cassette tapes.

"Here use these? take them with you and record the albums for me. Would you please?"

"You can borrow them Tilly, it's no problem?"

"No, take the tapes, if you take the tapes, you'll have a reason to come back. You might walk out that door tonight, and I'll never, ever see you again? At least if you take them, there's a possibility you'll come back with, proper music on them for me? Lovely music. What's her name again?" She asked.

She stood more than close to me. Almost nose to nose, and although I was on the high stool, she was the one looking down. I almost wanted to lift up and kiss her? She pushed the tapes into my top jacket pocket and closed the zip.

"Elizabeth Fraser."

"Yes her! Oh, thank you, thank you, thank you Steve."

"So, what are you studying at college Tilly?"

"A few things. Art, psychology, music and criminology. I'm leaning how to kill people. The best, un-detectable way, Is with an Ice-stake. Like a stalactite, or a stalagmite. It melts afterwards you see. No fingerprints or anything." As she gets to the end of her sentence, she totally cracks up laughing

"Are you being bloody serious Tilly? You're not bloody real girl. are you?"

She continues to laugh as she sips on her drink.

"I bet you're a pretty smart cookie then? learning all that stuff at college.

"I'm smart enough. It's not what I want to do at all though? Just what I enjoy. I'd much rather be famous. A famous singer, like Siouxie, or Dusty Springfield. I love singing. I play guitar too."

"Do you indeed. I play keyboards, well dabble. Maybe we should get together sometime and write a song? Do you write?"

"Yes Steve, but I keep it to myself. I'm not one of those, who prance around at college all day, with a guitar hanging off my back.

They just get on my nerves. Arty-farty, arseholes! Who can't even string a few decent chords and words together? Half of them, can't even string a sentence together either? They do my head in!"

"I've got a TEAC, four track recorder at home Tilly. Never get the chance to put anything down properly, cos I'm always working. Just can't seem to find enough time these days."

"Wow, that's cool," She beams. "Was it expensive?"

"Well erm, second-hand, out of Dawson's in the Royal arcade, off King street in town. They have a music-ads board up, downstairs."

"One of those would be cool, but I wouldn't know how to work it?"

"I'm still learning Tilly. It's not that hard."

"I just press record, on my little Alba cassette recorder, and start strumming. That's all I know Steve."

"I've a couple of keyboards too. The Roland, has a lovely, warm, analogue sound. Listen, we should really, get together. Seriously.........? Come over to mine, or I'll come to yours. I'll bring my CZ101, and you bring your guitar. Both bring what we have written down, music wise, and see what we can come up with? I'm sure we can do something, vaguely interesting? What do you think? Do you fancy It?"

Tilly quietly sat smiling, and chewing on her straw, mulling my proposition over.

"I think that's a lovely Idea. In fact, It's the nicest Idea. I'm a bit scared, you'll laugh at my stuff though. They're very personal to me, and no one's ever heard the songs before either."

"Well excuse me for being blunt, Tilly. But you're not going to get very far, in the music business, with a 'holier than though' music attitude. Let's just make a date, or pick a time, when we're both work free, and we can spend a couple of hours together, with our music."

I took a sip of my pint, and waited for a quiet, Tilly to answer.

"No laughing at my music!?' she pointedly asked.

"Of course not. Don't be daft Tilly, I wouldn't do that."

"No funny business either?"

"Oh, I don't know about that Tilly? You are very attractive. You and me, In a room, all alone.... Oh God, hands could wander......." I said, grinning into my drink.

"She burst out laughing and put her hand on the bottom of my glass again, this time, pushing It drink further up, into my lips, until it spilled out, either side of my mouth." I tried to pull back, and started laughing, with beer smeerage, running down my chin.

"Don't do that........... You, mad woman! don't spill the nectar! We can even have a wee drink if you like too?" I added.

"Oh yes......... Then the hands will definitely wander. She concluded.

"Ok, alright then Steve, It's a date. Well, not a date? You know what I mean though....... A meet, a music meet, that's what I mean. As long as you promise, not to laugh, at my songs and take it seriously."

"Not at all." I said, wiping my chin. "I'm looking forward to it Tilly."

"So am I," she affirmed, smiling. "It'll have to be upstairs in here though? In one of the empty function rooms. They're never used, and a little tatty. Actually, a lot tatty but that won't matter. One has a single bed in it, where I sleep, if I stay over on 'lock-in's, sometimes. I stay over quite a lot, cos our house is always mobbed. I've got two sisters and a brother. It's mental at home. I can get peace to play my guitar here. Auntie Margaret doesn't mind either. She enjoys the company. She's always on her own. It's quite echoey too. My guitar sounds nice."

"Good stuff, when are you free Tilly? I'm almost off work for 7 days, yippee. So, I'll definitely be free soon. Well up to now, anyway."

"Don't arrange to meet me, and then not show up Steve. That's not nice. If you do that, I'll never forgive you."

She had a very, valid point. I was terrible, for doing things like that to Linda. Linda? bloody hell, this is a bit mad, I thought. Arranging to meet Tilly, behind Linda's back? Ah, it's not like that though. It's as Tilly said, 'a music meet'. Mmm? Who am I trying to kid? I'd be in Tillys underwear, as quick as look at her, If I got the chance. I could feel my tempters stirring into life.

"Yes, Sunday night, after the boxing. I'll be free then. It'll be quite late though? If not then, anytime, Monday onwards? I've got a lot of college work to do at the moment. But I can work on that anytime at all before it's due. Do you want another drink Steve?"

I looked up at the bar clock. "We'll erm, I'm meeting my pal Neil, and I should really be getting going?" I looked at Tilly, and then the clock again. "Oh, what the hell. Stick me a half in there then Tilly, Your company's lovely." I smiled and passed her over my glass.

"Ok, no problem."

I'm no human, behavioural psychologist, and she didn't seem the jealous type. And heaven knows, I'd only just met her. But as soon a Neil's name was mentioned, and the fact that I, would soon be out the door, she instantly seemed a little colder toward me. But was also acting, somewhat more blasé, about the whole thing. As if she were pretending, she wasn't the slightest bit bothered, when all the time, she actually seemed, a little saddened, that I would have to, be going anywhere at all.

She hummed almost silently to herself, she looked down, and filled my glass.

"What time Saturday night then Tilly? I'll come in early, and have a couple of beers, before we retire upstairs?" I jokingly said. Tilly didn't respond, and the joke died a thousand deaths.

"I said, is it ok If I?................"

"Yes! whatever you like Steve. I really don't mind."

It went solemnly quiet again. So quiet, even the tinny radio seemed loud.

"Have I upset you, or something Tilly?"

"No, of course not. Now who's being silly. I'm fine? Just thinking about the college work I haven't done." She more than half filled my glass and forced a smile at me. I was pretty sure she'd taken the huff.

"Oh, erm ok... thanks Tilly." She sat back down, leaned on her arm and sighed.

"I wonder who's going to enthral me with their company, in here tonight?" She twisted the beermat again. "Bloody morgue."

"It's the first time I've ever been in here. Simply for that reason. I heard it was quiet. It's better like this, anyway. Just you and me, and the walls to talk too."

"She jumped up, smiled and turned around, grabbing a pen and paper from the bar.

"That's brilliant Steve." She was all aglow again. "We can use that, In a song. Just change it around a bit...................*Just me and you, and the walls to talk too.* Cool! our first line together, and you didn't even know you'd said it, haha.

"I didn't haha. I'm like you Tilly. I pick upon things people say, or I hear on the telly, and madly scribble them down, on bits of paper. One of my drawers, is literally full of paper at home."

"Bring some of them with you on Saturday then. And yes, we can have a drink. It might get our juices flowing. She looked at me grinning. as If she knew, what I was already thinking.

"Our creative juices, you rotten sod!"

She leaned over to the coke dispenser again, to fill up her empty glass.

I'd sadly come to the end of my drink, and the time to leave had already passed.

She looked at me, knowing I wasn't going to ask her to fill my glass again. But was happily smiling.

"Well Tilly, that's me then. Thanks for the top up."

"You're welcome, anytime Steve." She took the glass from my hand, and dropped it into the bubbly water, in the empty sink. Cleaning it, as she did.

"Ok then, so I'll see you then Tilly. Nice to have met you tonight. it's erm, Something, someone, I hadn't expected."

"You to Steve!" She continued with the pint glass and stood it on the drainer. Grabbed her cigarettes and lighter and returned to her stool and coke.

"Night then."

"Night Steve." I walked out of the pub door, and into the unwelcoming rain. *I felt empty when I left her. Everything felt a bit empty. Why did I have to leave? I didn't want too? Why didn't I kiss her when I left? I could have kissed her, and probably should have kissed her...... Damn! Why isn't she my girlfriend to start with? She bloody should be. I wish she was..........? What a delightful, naturally, funny and lovely girl!*

To say I was feeling melancholy, was an understatement. I just wanted to ring Neil up, cancel the pier, and go straight back to Tilly, for the rest of the night. It was too late now. The moment had past.

THIRTY

"**B**ugger.... bastard!" I cursed. Bloody rain! Wigan. The rainiest place in the ionosphere. Twinned with bloody Swansea I bet? The Tippings is only a cock-stride from the Bold. I hope none of the boys are in? I'll get held back even more, If I get locked in their company. Tilly was the unexpected bonus of the night, but I did say no-later than ten o'clock to Neil. Aah, sod it! A few minutes won't matter. If this rain keeps on, I'll just get a taxi to Neil's. Stuff having one in the 'Eckersley's Arms'. It's a total shit-hole anyway, according to me Mam. Mind you, everywhere is a shithole, according to her?

I got a shift on, down Poolstock lane. Speed-walking around the myriad, of pavement puddles and watching for rear-water splash-back, from cars on the road behind me.

The Tippings was already in sight, when I'd left the Bold, and less than three minutes after that, I was in the door. I took off my coat, and gave It a much needed, shake and pulled the inner door.

"Phew. Bloody hell! Shocking out there!" I said to anyone within distance of the door.

"Good weather fur fishing. Might take a trip up lakes the weekend if it keeps up like this? Put your coat on't t rad, lad. It'll soon be dry. Usual lad?" Alan said. I looked around the pub. "Erm, please Alan. It's dead in here too? where Is everybody?" Alan quietly pulled the pint. There was a middle-aged couple, in the corner seats, swapping chat. Ginger Martin, had already given me a nod, from his tall stool, in the juke box corner of the bar. In an attempt to create an atmosphere, the jukebox sang out its usual free, 'random' selection

"It's quiet everywhere at minute Steve. There's either no money around, or everyone's saving up fur Christmas?"

"Aye, but even so Alan? There's usually a handful in?"

"I know lad, not to worry eh? Thi' brother John, were in earlier, looking for thi though? Oh, and thi cocky pal's in't snug, fillin't bandit as usual. Is it Carl? A told thi brother, I hadn't seen thi? There yer go lad. That should be a good un. First owta pump, and I clean't lines today."

"Oh, is it? Thanks Alan, there's a fiver." Cleaned the lines again, have you Alan? your bloody obsessed, with cleaning the friggin lines! If this tastes of that acid, cleaning shit again, he's getting It straight back. I reasoned to myself. Carl's In? my 'cocky' pal? Mmm, in both senses of the word Alan, I thought. Now that isn't normal at all? Mid-week, and Carl's in the ale house? He has to travel from the other side of town to get here? Nah, maybe he was over visiting his Sisters? The till beeped and slammed. "There's thi change lad."

"Cheers Alan. I'll go, say hello, see what the crack is with Carlypoo's. Alan." I picked up my beer, and headed past 'tall stool' Martin, the toilets, and through into the snug.

As I walked into the snug, Carl was with his back to me, facing the bandit, obliviously mumbling, and multi-coin feeding the bandit. I stayed silent and quietly parked myself on a tall stool and watched. He had his usual, black leather coat and black flat cap on. Looking like an old, but young Wiganer, and also slightly reminiscent of Sylvester Stallone, in the 'Rocky' films. As I silently grinned to myself, and sipped my pint, he got a nudge feature, and was bending up and down, in an attempt to survey the bandit's 'reels', for possible multi-nudge opportunities.

I'd bumped into him once in King Street's 'Starburst' arcade, doing exactly the same thing. But hadn't recognised him under his flat cap, due to the mammothly long hair, he sported at the time.

"One, two, nine, three, sod!" He pointed at the cherries, lemons and bars, doing his best Carol Vorderman, countdown impression. Calculating his optimum chances. "Rip off bastard!" He kicked the machine. I feigned Alan's voice.

"Don't be kicking the machine lad." He slowly glanced around, as if to acknowledge, yet ignore the voice. Quickly turning back, to reload more ten pence's. He realised it was me, yet calmly continued, to face the bandit. Taking up a blind conversation as he continued.

"Alright Ste? where did you spring from?" The bandit started to flash wildly again. He bent down again.

"Just heading to the Pier Carl. Alternative night." He kicked it again and grabbed his Lager.

"Oh right" he sipped. Quickly replacing it, aloft the machine.

"What you doing in here, midweek then? you been over to your Sisters?"

"Erm, not exactly." He glanced around at me again. Affirmly nodded, smiled, and eyed over my shoulder. I heard a door bang, and felt a breeze, and a strong whiff of perfume. He coolly turned back to the bandit, to continue his money quest. Linda's sister, Jane walked past me, realised I was sitting there, and promptly stopped, and reddishly turned to face me.

"Erm Hi Steve?" She smiled, looked down, and ran her fingers across her face, and through her hair.

"Well hello there, Jane! Not seen you for, ooh, ages and ages? Ever since, erm.... well. Your hairs different? blonder. Have you got streaks in it or something?" She embarrassedly brushed through her locks again.

"Yes, well yes. Actually, Linda did it for me. They're fading a bit now though. Gonna get it done again soon. Listen.... this is erm.... it's, not what you think."

"Look Jane. It's nothing to do with me, what you get up too. If you want to play around, behind your stick in the mud's back, it's entirely up to you? Have you got a drink? do you want a drink?" I said, wrong footing her.

She frowned. "I just finished one thanks. I was going to get another after I'd been the loo. I'm not sure if we're going yet? Yes, go on then, thanks Steve. Don't bother getting him one," She looked toward the bandit. "That pint will last him all bloody night."

"Well" I said shouting Alan. "If there's one thing about Carl, he loves his sex, and his gambling. Never sure in which order though?" I grinned at her. She didn't know whether to hit me or agree with me.

"We're sorting things out, getting this big mess undone. Nothing more." She nervously added.

"Yes lad, same again?" Alan Inquired.

"Erm no Alan. Nothing for me mate. Just get this one erm...." Jane finished my question.

"Just half a lager and lime please." She pulled up a stool as Carl continued on the bandit.

"Look Steve. It really is that, I promise."

"Woah, hang on Jane, slow down a minute. You don't have to answer to me. It's not my... listen Jane. I think your biggest problem at the moment, is how you're going to suss out, how to prise him away from the bandit. Then you might be in with a chance of some love action haha. Do you like the Human League? Great group!" I grinned, purposely winding her up.

"Piss off Steve!"

Alan appeared from the other side of the bar, with a crisply poured lager.

"Thanks Alan, there you go pal." I crossed his palm as Jane continued.

"Linda's out on a Hen-Night this weekend. It'll be mine soon too. Once all this rubbish has all blown over. I'm ending thing's once and for all with him tonight. It can't... we can't... can't go on like this." I need security, and stability in my life. I'm never going to get that with Carl. Much as I wish I could."

"I know she's off out on the Hen-Night, Jane." I swigged my drink "And nope," I grinned "You're definitely not!" I agreed. "Carl's not ready for anything like that yet Jane? Bloody hell, neither am I! He's sowing his wild oats, and good luck to him. And why bloody not" I added. "He's got mountains of the stuff to sow! He's loving the relentless seed-sowing processes too. Ooh Aaah! Haha!'. I mimicked a farmer's voice, as she burst out laughing. Carl peered around, then turned back.

"What d'you mean relentless? who else is he seeing......?" She inquired, immediately ceasing her giggles.

"I'm not his keeper either Jane. None of my business. Just as it's none of yours."

"Are you headed uptown Steve?" She changed the subject.

You might bump into Linda? Jane said, gulping from her glass.

"Meeting a pal, then off to the pier. Which reminds me, I shouldn't even be here now. Bloody hell, Neil will head off without me. Right, I think it's time to vacate. Oh, my coat's in there, on the radiator. I'll leave you two it, then shall I?" I grinned. "Alan!" I shouted into the bar. "Ring me a taxi, will you? Carl, I might see you in here, over the weekend pal." His arm shot up into the air saluting, like a winning athlete, as the bandit began to chug loudly. "Just say tata to him for me will you Jane. He's a bit busy just now." I grabbed my pint, and stood up, and headed into the lounge.

"Ok Steve, will do."

"Five minutes for the taxi lad," Alan said as I walked toward the radiator. "Is it dry lad?"

"Erm yes Alan, warm as toast too!" I said, throwing my arm into a sleeve. Two 'beeps' came from outside. I decked the last few mouthfuls of my lager. "Thanks Alan."

"Have a good night Steve." He said, as I opened the door. "I will mate." I smiled, out into the street, zipping up my coat.

"Hi pal 'Smithy view' please. Number twelve I think" Quick as you can pal. The taxi was moving before I'd even closed the door.

THIRTY-ONE

Within five minutes of getting in the cab, I was closing the cab door to get out and knocking on his door. Neil's house had a wooden, alcove porch. I knocked and sheltered under it. "Alright Ste you took your time?" he said, opening and closing the front door behind me.

"Go straight up. I'll be there in a second, just get you a beer out the fridge. First on the right. You remember where my shrine is don't you?"

"Hi pal erm, I think so Neil? I'll just follow the music." As I walked upstairs, I heard a slightly vibrated, and muffled version of 'California uber alles' by the Dead Kennedys, coming through a door. As I pushed open the beating door, the music became, Inextricably louder. I went straight across to his stereo, and quickly turned down the volume, to escape perforated eardrums, or tinnitus, in the miniscule box room. Thirty seconds later, Neil's head and arm poked through the half-open door, throwing two cans of 'Harp' lager onto his unkempt bed. "Back in a minute. I'll just go get the tea. Put what you like on? His head left the room and me, to his savagely extensive record collection. I sat down on the floor, cross-legged, at the front of the records.

The vinyl was in two long rows, on the blue, ash ridden carpet. The room smelt of bad beer. At the back of the rows of vinyl, there were two plain brown 7'-inch record boxes, sat on top of two larger, multiply stickered LP boxes, which were the lean-to, for all the rest. The whole bedroom carpet, was littered with randomly opened, LP sleeves, and records. An empty glass. A half open, spilled box of matches. Some clothes and a tea mug. There was also a large, lava-lamp, fashioned like a rocket, sat on its three tail tips, in the corner. Lighting up the room, along with a huge column candle, dripping its white wax onto a white, tea cup saucer, sat precariously, on a smoke tainted chest of drawers.

The room decor was similar to mine, with some wall mounted LP covers, but also posters of his favourite punk bands.

The Dead Kennedy's slowly faded. I silently listened, as the needle arm clicked upwards, across, and returned to its plastic chair, on the stereo. I pulled out one of the 7' single cases, and rifled through it, settling on 'The Cutter' by Echo & the Bunnymen. I slid the single out of the sleeve and centred it onto the turntable. As I picked up the needle arm, the turntable began to spin. As I tried to mount it onto the start of the record it clicked, then jolted itself out of my hand. Going through its pre-programmed motions, and returned its needle arm, promptly back into its plastic, arched seat as if to say, *"Fuck off Hamill! I don't like Echo & the Bunnymen."*

Neil reappeared into the room, laden with two small china cups and saucers, as McCulloch & Co sang into action. I quizzically looked at the small bone china cups. "Only one's I could find Ste." He smiled, placing them down on the floor, at the side of me. Then sat down, on his bed and cracked open his harp can. Neil was lazily dressed in jeans, and a scraggy, white loose fitting and possibly 'home' printed, tie- dye t-shirt. Neil has multiple ear piercings, and even a ring through his eyebrow. His hair was gel spiked up, and he had half a cig in his hand. He took a long drag from the cig, then dropped it into one of a growing empty beer can nest, at the foot of his bed.

"They really are the only clean ones I could find? But we don't need gallons of tea for what's in them haha," He smiled. "I really should do some washing up? Before me Mum gets back home too." He leaned over to his chest of drawers, for a crushed packet of Lambert & Butler, offering me one at the same time. "Thanks Neil. What's in the tea? You've not been at it again have you..........?" I had a pretty good Idea what was afoot. "What is the point of a nice cup of good old rosy-lea in your mother's finest china cups, when we're gulping on cans of 4.8' proof lager.

"Yep Ste, I certainly have been at It again mate haha. Over at Waddickers flash, I got this lot from. I was out lamping the other night, and there they were hiding under a tree. Well you can't, not pick em, when they're there waving at you. Haha, that'd just be a complete waste. I left some there. I'll go back and get them next week."

He picked up a cup of 'tea' and animatedly, sniffed it. "Where Is your Mum anyway Neil?"

"It'll be a pretty good brew this, I reckon?" He took a tiny sip of the tea. Ouch! Bastard!

That last cig got stuck to my lip going down stairs. It's ripped some of my lip off. Look? It's bleeding. He pushed his index finger into his lip. Taking another longer tea sip forthwith.

"She's looking after her sister in Salford. She broke her leg and is on crutches."

"Haha, burned your lip. You, daft sod! I sometimes do that at work, when I'm filling out the sales book, and I aint got a hand spare. Are you ready?"

"Am I fuck as like ready," Neil replied. "Me suit's hanging in me Mums room. I hope it bloody fits? I won't take long to get changed. I'll be ready, when these beauties kick in my system haha." He looked down into his tea.

"Suit? You're wearing a suit?"

"Yes I am," he explained, grinning wildly. "My new grey suit. It's my special suit. I even have a hat that goes with it." He beamed.

"Oh ok? I hate suits. Only wear them at weddings, and funerals. Highly over-rated, in my opinion. Anyway Neil, don't slide away from the subject. There's not a lot of, erm that funny stuff in the tea, is there?" What was It called again? and come on, tell the truth Neil?"

I looked down at my full china tea cup, and then the lager in my hand. The cup seemed to look straight back at me and say *'I'm going cold here'? What you waiting for Hamill? It's the lager or me. Make your choice."*

Or maybe that was just my subconscious mind, knowing what swimming there-in.

THIRTY-TWO

Now to be blatantly honest, and all things considered. At this juncture in my life, I'm young, fit & reasonably healthy, and possess a pretty good constitution, alcohol wise. I can stomach, pretty much anything, I deem fit enough, to pour down my neck stupidly, too. Granted, I'm a nineteen something, veritably seasoned drinker. But when it comes to mind-altering, or hallucinogenic drugs, and their ingestion. I'm pretty much lost. Ergo: I have no bloody idea what I'm doing, nor dealing with.

"There's bugger all in there it Ste. honest, four mushrooms juice, five tops! It tastes of nothing. It doesn't last long either, and your body builds up a tolerance, to the effects. Over time that is."

"Mmm, that's exactly what I'm worried about Neil. Your tolerance is probably shit-hot, and sky-high! Mine is bloody non-existent. Look, I'm not being funny, but I'll drink half of the cup. You say there isn't much stuff in It. So, you can have the rest of mine too, ok pal."

I'm happier with a pint of lager or nine, Instead.

"No problem Ste, just leave what you don't want. I'll gladly have it haha. I'm gonna go get ready. I won't be long. We can have a pint in the 'Honeysuckle' before we go the pier. I really like that Jill, we were dancing with, the other week. I might even ask her out later? Let's see how it goes."

"What! when we're off our faces on beer and psychedelic drugs, and I'm talking to a chair, in some corner. Oh, I'm sure that'll go down brilliantly Neil. Which reminds me, I just met a lovely girl on the way here Neil. In the Bold, her name was Tilly."

"I'll look after you Ste. It's not as bad, I mean, as weird as you think? People just have halos, and glow a bit, that's all really." Neil left the room.

"Oh my God! are you fuckin serious?" I shouted through the door. I glanced down again at the beckoning cup of tea. Nah, Bollocks to this, I thought. I looked at the cup, Neil had drunk out of. It was just less than half full. I looked around the room. It's a shame, he doesn't have any plants that need watering, I thought. I looked at my cup again.

'Oh, just give him your full cup, and you have his half one,' my good tempter advised.

"Bugger it! drink the lot, and party off the roofs" the devil tempter cackled. I took another swig of lager then switched the cups. *'You big pussy!'* said the bad tempter. *'Switch them back, and down it in one!'* No chance, I thought? I'm not tripping into next week and getting arrested for stripping. Waking up down a well or talking to any chairs either. Even if they have a winning personality. Fuck it! His half cup will suffice. I picked up the cup, swished it around, as if looking for Invisible nothings. "He puts plenty bloody milk in his tea" I muttered. "Oh, stuff it, bottoms up Stephen!" I necked the half cup, gulped and waited. As if expecting the room, to start to spinning and the four Beatles to appear knelt in a circle singing 'Lucy In the Sky with Diamonds' right away.

Mmm. Nothing? bloody nothing? Maybe I'm a bit previous, it's only been seconds? At least give it a chance to get to your stomach, I thought. Maybe when he made it up, he got the Lion's share of the psychedelic swirling stuff?

I was sat still, and cross legged on his carpet, waiting for Dorothy and Toto to appear? At least 'Glenda the good' or the scarecrow man. Yes Stephen, I thought? You've just drunk mushroom tea. "If you only had a fuckin brain!"

I put the empty cup back down on its saucer and reverted my thoughts back to the music. I slid Ian McCulloch and the bunnymen, back into his sleeve, and replaced him with The Adverts 'looking through Gary gilmour's eyes'. A record, I didn't on, and hadn't heard in forever. Mmm? I wonder if I'll be looking through his bloody eye's later? Probably not. What a waste of time all that mushroom crap was. Talk about colossal failure.

I decided to tidy up a bit while I was waiting for Neil. I matched the record sleeves, with the right artwork, and correct cover, with the right record. Swigging my can as I went. By the time Neil came back into room, everything was neatly returned to its original covers, stacks and places.

As the door opened, I was crushing, and placing my harp can, into his empties nest.

I looked up from the floor at Neil. He was again ear to ear smiling. My mouth fell wide open, and I felt my eyes slightly, pop out of my head. I instantly thought the hallucinogenic tea had kicked in. Possibly for both of us.......? I blinked and looked again.

"What d'you reckon Ste? d'you think I'll be the belle of the ball haha?"

"Sweet Mary and Joseph Neil! where In God's name, did you fuckin acquire that?!

As true as I was sat there, Neil was sporting a full grey, German issue, Nazi SS, uniform. Or as he called it a suit! Complete with boots, and the death hat! I quickly stood up. It had black, eagle embroidered sleeves, and badges, dotted all over it. Embroidered SS collars, and leather jack boots. He laughed again. "Look at the hat man? It's brilliant! I don't know if I should wear it. I mean, take it out? I'll probably end up leaving it somewhere? Putting it on someone's bird's head or losing it.

"Oh yeah Neil. That is a fair point mate? Fuckin hell! You might lose it? You might lose your fuckin teeth too pal? Are you completely off your nut!"

He just continued to grin. "It's well made too. Look at the quality of that embroidery?"

He pushed the death hat toward me. "Oh yeah Neil, well that makes all the difference, when you're found lying in a pool of blood, doesn't it pal? Fuck me! I bet they were thinking, exactly the same when they invaded Poland! We have lovely embroidery, on our murdering uniforms! I honestly can't believe you're even going out like that! Where on earth did you get it?" I stupidly placed the hat, on his gelled spiky head, for effect.

"Affleck's Palace' in Manchester. It's genuine. There's still name badges in it." He grabbed his harp can. "They had loads of different ones. I wanted the black one. It's more striking. Plus, the black suited oppressors, did the worst stuff, in the second world war. But they didn't have my size, and I didn't want to wait. I decided on the grey instead. I think it's smart? It even goes with my grey lager can haha." He held the harp lager can up, against a lapel. Then took a swig.

"I really am lost for words Neil? I really think you must have a screw-loose. But full marks for blatant effort pal!" I drank your half cup of mushroom tea. The full one's still there. I'd get it drunk, If I were you. It might lessen the effect of the pain later, when you get dragged into an alley, and garrotted haha'.

"Oh, don't be so over dramatic Ste. The war's over. It's just a piece of clothing. What did you say when I went out the room? You were meeting a girl tonight?"

"I suppose it is just a bit of clothing Neil. I just didn't expect it that's all. No, I said I met a girl, a girl called Tilly, on the way down here. She's great. I'll tell you all about her later. Are we making tracks or what?"

"Yeah. I think I'll leave the death hat here. I'll wear it when I go to Placemates night-club in Manchester, next week.

THIRTY-THREE

After we arrived in the Honeysuckle. I bought the round of lagers, and I could feel something changing. The mushroom tea had slowly started to take effect. As did Neil's, Nazi uniform? When Neil went to use the toilet, three punters walked out of the bar, in disgust after seeing him. He was affronted, and threatened by a forth, while we playing pool. The bar man seemed to blur in, and out of my vision. When I ordered, he seemed to be both shouting, and whispering, all at the same time. I had to stop playing the game of pool as I couldn't focus correctly on the balls. They seemed to be randomly changing colour, in front of me. Being in the honeysuckle, is the last solid thing I remember. After that point, I don't remember anything clearly at all? I don't even recall being in the Pier? Seeing, or talking to anyone? Walking, moving, drinking, Zilch? To this day, the only thing I can remember of the night, after the Honeysuckle...... is finding myself walking down the canal tow-path, toward home. Mumbling, and wondering to myself, that I was piss-wet, through soaking, from head to foot. and wondering how I'd got that way.

My mind was a complete blank. My purple jumper's sleeves, had doubled in size, due to being completely sodden, with water. The only other thing I can still recall, that remains indelibly imprinted on my mind, is standing still, turning to my left, and looking down, at the dark, black water in the Leeds-Liverpool canal lock. Realising, that I somehow, I must have walked, or fallen into it. Even more confusing to me, is that thank God, I'd somehow managed to get myself out of it too! I was in shock, for the rest of the brain-blurry walk home. When I finally made It home and into the house, I silently half emptied, the plastic washing basket, stuffed my wet clothes in, and covered them up, with the one's I'd taken out. In a fearful attempt, not to have to explain anything to me mam or our John.

On a Lighter note. The only silver-lining of the night was, I'd made a new and important, Tilly.

THIRTY-FOUR

Next day I woke up, just before eleven. I could still feel, the stupidly induced, Alcohol and Psilocybin after effects of the night before. Not my greatest idea in life so far. Legal and Illegal drugs, to destroy my bodily functions and the rest of my life thus far. The Tippings and lad's early beer shift was being given a miss, by both Eric and myself today. Things to do, people to see. Not like we were some kind of 'yuppie' entrepreneurs. There was a Saturday delivery, which was a first for 'Churches'. First for our John and Eric too. Paul and Tony couldn't make it in today. Other commitments. H was supposedly making a rare appearance though? Unbeknown to Eric, Peter was going to offer him the job, to replace Tony finally. The alcohol day-rest, would hopefully give my body, fair chance to recover too.

Mam was always religiously, out shopping on Saturday's. But our John was home. I could hear ELO, blaring from the lounge stereo. I went downstairs and walked into the kitchen. Opened the bread bin and pushed two pieces of 'sunblest' into the toaster. The patio doors were open, and the green garden hose, was unravelled, and lying across the flags, in a pool of water. Mmm? must be cleaning his 'new' motorbike, yet again I concluded. There'll be no paint left on It, if he carries on like this? I walked over to the 'swishing' patio doors and leant on them.

The sun was out. Making random glint's, in-between the wind dancing clouds. Shamus was relaxing, lying on the grass, near Mam's reading 'hot' spot. Watching the fountain, and the fish darting about in the pond. He lifted his big head off his paw, as he spotted me. Probably smelling the toast too. He quickly jumped up and galloped toward the kitchen, wagging his big fluffy tail. I moved to one side, out of his way, and he slid across the tiled floor, and 'crumpled', straight into the cooker, in his attempt to stop. "Hello lad." I stroked his long mane as the toast clunked up. He stood up on his hind legs and rested his front paws across my skinny chest. Once, at the fruit market, H had once, openly cracked a joke, saying I had the worst case of an 'In growing' chest he'd ever seen! The scouse swine! As I bent over, to get the stork margarine out of the fridge, he jumped back down. Due to the possible promise, of food and scraps, his tail was now set on 'constant' wag. As I spread the margarine on the toast, he dropped his back end, looked up at me, and waited patiently. In his 'sit' position he'd unknowingly, also become a canine, 'ACME' tile shining machine. His tile sliding and wagging had instantly reminded me of a much happier 'canal' experience, I'd had donkey's years ago.

It was in the middle of winter. Years before last night's brain-blurred, and unexpected drug induced sabbatical into the canal water. Eric, Ian, Paul, Chris and myself had decided (as you do) to go walking on water. Literally. What a brilliant Idea, we thought.

The Leeds-Liverpool canal was, for the first time frozen over. In truth, every single stretch of fresh-water, throughout the Lancashire area was. The nearest flashes, to our housing estate were; Greenwaters, Waddickers, Turners and Scotsman's flash. They had some six inches and more, of thick ice on them. Shamus had decided (as dogs do) he wanted to join us. We climbed down onto the ice, and 'safety' checked its rigidity and 'crackability' for ourselves. Well, you can never be too careful, when risking life and limb in these matters. Eric shouted, "Bring him on too Ste? Come on, don't be tight! You can't leave him up there on his own, that's just cruel?"

Once I got down on the Ice, Shamus and I were almost eye-to-eye. Me stood the ice, and him on the canal bank. He yelped and even tried to jump onto me few times. I cupped my arms, under his hairy hulk, and lifted his doggie-mass up, off the canal bank. Receiving multiple free 'face licks' as I did, and plopped him down icebound, to join us. Straight away, his doggie legs did the splits..........! After a short while, when he felt sort of, accustomed, and at ease on the ice, He was a picture. For the next few hours, he was our own, personal canine version of Robin Cousins, or John Curry. As we ran and slid across the ice, he was like an animated Scooby doo. Slipping, running and clammering, on the spot. Until eventually, after constantly trying, his claws would dig in, or he managed to gain some kind of paw-grip, to try to catch us up he was usually buggered. When we dug our Adidas 'samba', or in my case Dunlop 'green flash' in the ice, and quickly drew ourselves to a stop. Shamus had no other option, but to continue sliding. He certainly chased some sticks that day. A couple of times, he slid into the canals edge bulrushes, where the ice was dangerously thin. It would crack and collapse, and his paws and front end would disappear up to his dog chest. Do dogs have chests?

We would hear and see, the constant puzzlement on his face, and his yelps. He couldn't really suss it all out. But then, he was a dog? We all agreed, he'd enjoyed himself almost as much as when we took him 'clamp' dingy summer-swimming in Greenwaters. We'd even ice walked on there once too. Eric was the unfortunate casualty, who disappeared waist down, into the freezing water and ice that time. But that's another story.........................

"Toast lad? Want some? Course you do.... You're a canine, waste disposal unit like Denver aren't you...? You 'ACME' turd machine! I poured myself a cold glass of milk, put the toast onto a small plate, and went into the garden. Rested the plate on top of the glass, and walked over to the fish pond, closely followed by my toast hoover. The pond was in more than serious need of a complete cleaning overhaul. It was filthy green and teeming with algae all around the edges. It had the same green film, on the surface of Its plastic, right down to the bottom. Since Dad had left home, John, and I had only attempted it twice? We didn't have the first clue, how to do it correctly It was Dad's 'baby'. I'd helped him a couple of times, but always lost Interest. Really must get around to cleaning that soon? I'll do it before winter.

I bit into the toast and spat it the floor for Shamus. He didn't mind, he wasn't proud. I could hear John on the driveway, singing along to 'Mr Blue Sky', and walked over to the open back gate, and silently lent on the house gable end. He was happily tending his pride and joy, for all he was worth and, didn't see me at first. Knelt down, he was precisely rubbing 'Duraglit' onto any and every, possible chromed and silver orifice of his new white Yamaha RD350 lc. Shamus 'woofed' and walked toward him, smelling the duraglit tainted exhaust pipe. In doing so, the smelly white, cleaning metal polish rubbed off, onto his nose. He 'dog' sneezed.

"Shamus, come out the way you daft get! Look, It's all over your nose now? Come here!" John picked up his cleaning rag, spat into it, and grabbed Shamus around the jowls.

"D'you want your conk sprucing up too?" He gave Shamus almost as much care and attention, as his silver dream machine, and wiped the polish clean off his nose, then spotted me watching him. "Fuckin hell, It's creepin Jesus!" I crunched another mouthful of toast.

"Good morning to you, too John?"

"Morning? it's bloody afternoon. I was In the Tippings looking for you last night? Did Alan tell you?"

"Erm, yes he did bro. What was all that about?" John lied on his back, moved further under the exhaust, applying the duraglit gunk, underneath.

"It's about tonight. Dad want's us to meet him at the Derby Arms. He said it's Important Stephen?"

"Oh, he does. Does he? What for John?" I asked. "How very fuckin courteous of him, to let us know in advance. Yet again, the selfish bastard!" How very, I don't think. I mused.

"Well I won't be there John. I've got plans." Mmm, even if I didn't have any plans, I would make alternative plans! I wasn't going. Last time Dad and I'd met up, a full-scale battery of arguing, crossed words, *burn in hell*, and *get to fuck's*, had been exchanged. You know the sort. From all barrels and both sides. I wasn't putting myself through all that bullshit again. Maybe he just wants to apologise? I humoured myself. Or maybe he just wants to give me some more of the same? I pondered and looked down at my concrete wriggling brother.

"What time is this bollocks supposed to be occurring then? And how the fuck are we gonna get up there?"

"Eight o'clock. Taxi. He's paying for it. Asked me to make sure you're there.

"He's paying for it Ste."

"Well blow me down John? Knock me down with a fuckin balloon."

"Oh, shut up Stephen, you moaning get. He gave me twenty quid on Thursday night when I went over to see him!" Want's us together when he tells us. And no, I don't have a fuckin clue either? John had now wriggled, like a concrete 'limbo' dancer, completely under his bikes chassis, and was almost out the other side.

"What time's this wagon drop this afternoon anyway Stephen? Me and Elly are having a ride to Rivington barn this afternoon."

"Oh, you might see Paul and his Karen there?" I replied. "He said he was going to that thing. And his brother Mark too. What's on there, anyway?" I put the last bit of toast into Shamus's eager jaws. His flicked his head to one side, and his huge tongue flopped out of the way to receive it gladly.

"Nothing Ste. It's just a biker get together. There's a car boot sale on, the pub's always stays open, and a hell of a lot of bike buying and selling. I'm taking Elly on the back of this. I'll make him shit in his leathers, by the time I've finished haha. He's taking a load of dosh with him. Hoping to ride back with a new bike today?"

"What? exactly the same as this thing?" John stood up, replacing the ball of 'duraglit' wadding, into the bold red and silver tin.

"Nah, we've had loads of arguments about that. He wants a Honda, CB250? I told him to get a Kawasaki? Doesn't really matter what he gets. I'll race him anywhere, on anything and anytime," he smiled. "This beauty will blast anything off the road. So, when is this French wagon coming then?" He stood back, looked at his bike and admired his cleaning handy work. "I'll leave that to soak in a minute, before I rub it off'."

"Erm, Peter said the wagon will be in around two o'clock? He's usually always wrong on purpose though. Just to make sure, we're definitely gonna be there. I'll ring Gerry at the Liverpool stall, when I get to the market. After it's left there, it's coming to us, and then on to Preston market. Eric's coming up too. Think we're gonna have a couple of beers, In the Hawk or the Ben Johnson, after we've done. Depends how we get on?"

"It'd better be on bloody time. I'm not cancelling this trip to Rivie barn. I'm not hanging around when it gets there either. Elly will be right pissed off If we don't get to rivie barn today?" John bent down and rubbed his finger through the dried white polish.

"Alright John, bloody hell, calm down. Don't shoot the messenger!"

"That should do. Do me a favour Ste. Go get me one of mam's clean tea towels. I'll rub this shit off with this rag and use that to polish off."

"She'll go nut's if she finds out you've used one of her tea towels for that John?

"She'll never know? Oh, I'll buy her some new ones, if she finds out. I need a new rag for under the petrol tank, anyway." He knelt down at the side of his bike. Shamus joined him and tainted his nose again!

"Alrighty. Back in a minute." I said walking to the kitchen. "I'm putting the kettle on John, d'you want a cup of tea?"

"Yeah, I'll have a brew! Turn me LP over on the stereo! Oh, and wrap that hose up for me too?" He shouted from outside.

"Erm, no, fuck off John! Do It yourself? Stick the hose up your arse!" I shouted back. I walked into the lounge, flipped the record over, and walked back into the kitchen. Filled the kettle under the tap and clicked the button down. Opened the cupboard near the dining table, and pulled a folded, clean, cotton tea towel, off the shelf. I Looked down at my purple jumper, sandwiched in the washing basket, as I did. Closed the door, and slid myself on to the Formica worktop, in between the kettle and tea-mug tree. Shamus strolled back into the kitchen to have a food nosey. Jumped up beside me and placed his paws on the worktop edge. I unfurled the tea towel and put it over his eyes.

He playfully shook It off his head, onto the floor, and jumped back down. I pushed myself off the worktop and grabbed it from the floor. Spun and twisted it around to create a small, but deadly 'flicking' device and commenced, to chase him around the kitchen. Randomly flicking, re-twirling and flicking again. After a series of direct head hits, he playfully lost his rag. Growled, woofed, and came at me and the towel. He sunk his teeth clean through the cotton, pulled back, and bent away from me, on his front legs. He had a teeth tight hold, and continued growling, shaking his head, and pulling it away from my grip. It began to rip and tear. I goaded and egged him on. Pulling his head from left to right, and up and down, with my grip with his teeth still firmly, embedded through the material. His paws slid, on the tiled lino in his attempt to yank it away from me. The kettle clicked, I let go laughing. He'd won! After a few growls, and unhindered side-to-side shakes, of his big head, he relinquished his grip, and let the tea towel, drop to the floor. He pawed up onto the Formica again, to help me make the cups of tea.

A minute or two later, we were both back outside, watching John, covering the new tea towel with muck from his machine. "What time is it Stephen?" He asked, blowing on his tea.

"Just after eleven. Don't you be late for the market bro? I need your fork-lifting brilliance."

"I won't! I'll be done here shortly. Gonna nip up to the paper shop and get this week's Motorcycle News."

"Get my NME, while you're there will you? I'll put the hose away for you, if you do?"

"Haha ok, no problem. I'll call at Elly's on the way up. See if he's all sorted for later? So, it's me, you, Eric and Peter then?"

"Yeah, I don't think Peter will be getting his hands dirty though? Probably not. He'll be too busy smoking, or fuckin about upstairs in the office? He might even bring his two sons with him for a trip out? Take the piss out of the wooleybacks the scouse bastard! Might even the bring his wife?" I sipped my tea.

"I don't give a shit what happens, as long as we get done quick," John assuaged.

"Did I tell you he's gonna offer Eric a full-time job, in place of Tony?" I looked up at the darkening sky.

"Eric's worked there, cash in hand loads of times, anyway. He knows the job, and he'll be ten times better than Tony.

"My thoughts exactly. Right bro, I'll get that hose away. Stuff to do upstairs yet. Shut the back gate when you piss off." The sky had quickly dulled over, and the sun had completely disappeared, behind a mass of black rain clouds. "It's going to rain John?" I felt a spot hit my cheek. 'It's fuckin raining John!'.

"I fuckin know! and me bikes spotless now, typical!" I took John's empty cup off him and quickly walked back into the kitchen.

Within a minute, the heavens had opened, and it was pouring down. It was thundering too. Shamus ran into the kitchen, half frightened and half wet. As I swished the Captain Kirk patio door, John had run into the garden and also grabbed it from the other side, overpowering me. "Here, put that lot under the sink."

He handed me mam's, plastic cleaning basket, as he fastened the chin-strap on his helmet.

"Don't fuckin get my NME wet. It'll be ruined if you do. Jam It down your leathers."

"Do I have dickhead written across my forehead cunt?"

"Erm sometimes, bro." He annoyedly rushed out the back gate. Purposely leaving it ajar, for me to close It, and get soaked. Three motorbike revs later, he was gone. I ran outside latched the gate and swished over the door. I went back into the laundry cupboard. Pulled out a clean towel. Sat on the dining suite bench and towelled down Shamus's back.

THIRTY-FIVE

The ELO music had finished playing in the lounge. I carefully lifted the LP up from the stereo, and delicately returned it into its sleeve, and colourful gatefold cover. John firmly believed, Jeff Lynne was a musical God and treated all his records, with the same care he afforded his bike. He was right too. I used to dip into his ELO records, and Lynne's production intricacies, genius and sheer musicianship, when he wasn't around. I never told him so. God forbid he knew he was right. As far as I was concerned, Lynne was on a par, with Trevor Horn, Tony Visconti or Paul McCartney.

"Right you, In your basket." Shamus frantically shook himself, after his towel rub and curled up in the corner, and looked out of the patio, watching the pouring rain I dispensed of the hair ridden towel, into the wash basket, made myself another cuppa, and headed upstairs to my room. Mmm, quarter to twelve. I'll give Eric a bring in a bit. I'd better have a look through some of my music stuff.

I probably won't get another chance. I did promise Tilly, for next Saturday. Wish it was this Saturday Instead? I suppose I'd better go with John later. He did say It was Important? Better find that Casio keyboard charger too? Not used it in ages. Not used anything in ages? Bet I can't even play the bloody keyboards anymore? I got on my knees and lifted up the quilt. On all fours, I peered under the bed, and reached into the darkness. Mmm, a mug? a glass? another cup? I was wondering where that one went to. Two empty crisp packets.... a 'Mars' wrapper.... bloody hell... Yeuch! a green mouldy sandwich. Oh yeah... I remember eating the other bit weeks ago. Where the hell can It be? Might have to get some batteries for it if it doesn't materialize. I'll take the dirty cups downstairs in a bit. I conceded. I reached a little further under. Aah, There's the CZ101, full of dust as expected. It's not too heavy. I'll be in a taxi so, It's not too bad.

I opened the bottom bedside cabinet drawer. Inside was scribbled notes and scraps of paper. An A4 pad, and right at the bottom 'The Keyboardists picture chord encyclopaedia'. My own fault for not learning properly, off the alcoholic snuff taking tutor. Mmm, anything else I need? I could take the drum machine just to impress Tilly? Nope, this lot will do. I'm not going completely mob handed. I'll just stick them in my rucksack. May as well put some music on. On my turntable was 'songs to remember'. That'll do.

Just as I put the needle down, familiar over revving outside, told me John was back. I grabbed the rubbish and cups and ran down the stairs. I ran some hot water into the sink, as he walked into the kitchen, then dropped the dirty cups into it. "Bloody hell John, the floor." The lino had water footprints. "These leathers do the job. They keep out the water and keep away the bruises too'. He took off his helmet.

"Alright, alright. I'm never gonna live that down, am I?" He put his helmet on the table and unzipped his Belstaff leather jacket.

"No! none of you are, you fuckin idiots! Here's your shitty music paper." Shamus food sniffed him, then returned empty mouthed to his basket.

THIRTY-SIX

About three years ago, I was out at night with the lads. Just generally dicking about, with nothing to do. We hadn't even qualified, for legal entry into the Tippings. John had bought his first motorbike and was proud as punch of the fact. Like a dog with two dicks, he rode it constantly around hawkley estate, for no other reason than to show it off, and race his arch nemesis, Steve Conway. Steve had an Identical model. Bought at the same time too. Virtually identical, except for two in-discrepancies. Steve's was roughly knackered white, to John's shining-pristine blue. Steve's abused engine to John's impeccably tuned and looked after.

Me and the lads thought it would be a brilliant Idea to block the bottom of Fulbeck avenue off, with a bright yellow, eight-inch, plastic gas pipe, we found at the side of the road. The gas board had left a stack of them, for a new local diversion. To newly feed new houses being built further up the hill. We hid, smoking in the bushes, expecting some OAP driver to come sauntering slowly down the hill, and have to get out, and move the pipe. Oh, what fun and giggles? How wrong could we be...? Both their motorbikes engine's revving, almost sounded similar too. All we heard from the top of the hill, to the bottom, was the gear changing revs.......... then, a long, loud thump!.......... a pretty lengthy bang!... And finally, a loud clatter and smash! We weren't even sure what we'd done and didn't hang around to find out either. Until I woke up the next day......... John's prized Suzuki ER50 was, 'written off' in the back garden. Smashed to pieces. Never to grace the streets again. John wasn't much better either.

He told me, after impact he'd done about eight somersaults, both on and off the bike which almost ended up in Mr Kay the milkman's, front garden. A battered, twisted and mangled shadow of its former glory. He was ok though. His bruises and pride soon healed, when the insurance finally paid out, and he was able to buy his new monster steed, now sitting on the driveway. He'd got his own back on me too. One night, in his bike-less interim, he decided to borrow my MOT-less Vauxhall viva, for a quick illegal, and uninsured trip to Hindley and promptly wrapped it around a lamp post! Granted, it was never going to be road worthy to start with. Just a wistful pipe dream, of owning my first car. He really enjoyed telling me, after the fact, how it crumpled like a concertina, when he hit the street light. As a direct result of his continuing catalogue, of near misses and accidents, he'd taken the CB radio name of *'Bionic Man'*. A homage to Steve Austin, the Six Million Dollar Man.

"Thanks Bro. Hey, bro." It was wee wind up time. "My NME's almost as crumpled as your Suzuki and my car haha."

"Oh, fuck off Stephen, you idiot! Right, I'm off again. Elly wasn't in. His mum said he'd nipped to Millers bike-shop? If he rings, tell him I'm at Karen's. Then ring me at hers. Don't forget, or I'll forget about the caulis! See you later."

"Okidoki John. I went back upstairs, sat on the bed, leaned forward, and put the needle on the vinyl.

Unfolded my paper to see Morrissey staring back at me with, the headline; *'Morrissey's Smiths scoop best group spot, in readers poll, full results inside'* Mmm? Mozza, Brilliant! wonder if there'll be an interview? Probably not. They just stick a God on the cover, to sell oodles of copies.

At the bottom in smaller print, it said; *Husker du, Roy Orbison, Peter Weir.* Who the bloody hell's he? I wondered. *Robert Plant, De Barge and Katherine Hamnett.* Never heard of her either? She's probably in fashion? Glorious Bowie Instantly barged into my brain, and out of my mouth, as I flicked the pages in sync... to the music; *"Fashion...! turn to the left... fashion... turn to the right... Ooooh... fashion.... I am a dickhead and I'm coming to town... beep beep!"* Mmm, another total let down again. Not one decent Interview.

Morrissey probably told em to fuck off too, amongst other things? The pure legend! Another shit issue. Gonna stop buying this crap. I randomly flicked through the pages. Still humming the Bowie beat.

I soon ended up at the back page, music 'one' ads where last year, I'd acquired my Juno106. Bugger all here either. Boring! What a waste of sixty pence that was.

On the second to last page, I quickly scoured the 'wanted ads'. *Bass player wanted... Lead guitarist needed for rock band.... Keyboardist required for tribute act.* Just as I was about to ditch it, the 01942 Wigan telephone code caught my eye. *Singer needed ASAP, for rock/pop band. Studio work and gigs to follow for right person.* Mmm, rock pop? Interesting? It's the first time I've even seen an 01942 number in here? Nope, just the same old shite. I dismissed It. Threw the rag on the bed and headed downstairs. But the ad was subconsciously, etched on my brain.

As I reached the bottom, the hall phone rang. I picked it up before its second ring. "Alright Elly, he's up at Karen's. I'll give him a bell now."

"What? Inge It's Peter," came the scouse twang. "It's H."

"Oh, alright bossman. Sorry I was expecting someone else. What's up?" I could hear him talking to someone and taking a draw of a cigarette.

"Just ringin about the delivery. They've just rang me. Half-past three. The wagon got stopped, and searched when It came off the ship, at the docks?"

"What the fuck for H? it's a locked and sealed unit?" John's not going to bother his arse now I thought.

"I kno it is. Don't tell me my fuckin job Inge." I'm not gonna make it down today either. The youngest is in hospital. He's got appendicitis. That's where I'm ringing from. Fuckin hate these places.

"Bollocks! oh erm, sorry, is he.... Are you. So, do I?"

"Let Eric kno the score. No! give me his number. Have you got it? I'll speak to him myself." H chronically coughed. Smoke almost filtered through my ear-piece.

"Yes H, 01942 32575. he might not be in though?"

"If he aint, I'll ring again tomorrow. Make sure you tell him though. Dinner time. I want him started and working next week, while you're off, and rid of that ginger prick once and for all! Listen, I gotta go."

"Right H. John's not gonna be coming now. I'll have to get someone else? H are you there?" He was gone. The receiver had already been put down? Tut! I'll have to ring John up and plead with him now? Nah, fuck beggin him? Not a chance. The phone rang again.

"Hi Elly he's not here........"

"Elly? who's Elly? Are you seeing someone else?" Linda asked.

"Am I fuckin hell! Jesus, you're bloody paranoid Linda! I thought it was our kid's mate Andy. His nicknames Elly, cos his surname's.... Ellison.... Oh, never mind! How are you sweetheart? to what do I owe the pleasure?" I'm glad she's rang. My mind said.

"Hiya oh, I'm ok. Bit of hay fever today. Can't stop sneezing. Just ringing to see what you're doing tonight?" She sniffed loudly.

"We'll, I'm.... erm.... What are you doing this afternoon sweetie pie? Oh, light of my life?

"Oh, here we go again. What are you after now Stephen?"

"Nothing, my little pin cushion of pain. My darling of death. The phone went dubitably quiet for a second or two. I broke the silence with a laugh. Linda concurred.

"What d'you want? And keep the bullshit to an acceptable level. I burst out laughing again.

"Bloody hell, potty mouth, what's up with you swearychops. Come up the fruit market with me today. Drive the forklift. It's really easy. I'll show you what to do. You knew you were going to end up giving me a lift sometime. That sometime's today. Our kid was gonna do it, but he can't now. Go on... you'll be doing me a massive favour. There's a tenner in it for you. Go on, please... I'll be your servant... no! your sex slave for a day."

Linda laughed. "You're a piece of work Stephen, you really are. Ok then. If we can go out somewhere later then?"

"Well erm, we can yes. As long as you don't mind some company. I've gotta go to Hindley with our John. Meet me Dad. I wasn't gonna bother but apparently It's Important?"

"Your Dad really? I thought you two weren't talking? Oh yes, it'll be nice, to meet him." she added.

"Good stuff. Thanks Linda. You're an Angel." She didn't seem the slightest bit phased about the prospect of meeting me Dad. Let alone driving a forklift, being constantly laden with crates of cauliflowers. Haha, she doesn't know what she's let herself in for.

"I've gotta ring Eric and our John. It's a quarter to one now, D'you want to meet me there at about half-past three?"

"What about going out? I'm not wearing my best stuff, to drive a forklift Stephen?"

"I know you're not, and I know you like looking your best, but have a day off Linda, just this once. You look great in your jeans, anyway? It's not as If we're going clubbing Is It? Me mam'll cook us some tea. Or we can just go for a pub-lunch, or MacDonald's? I'll stick an empty carrot sack on the forklift seat, then you don't get a wet arse haha!?" I shouldn't have said the last bit.

"WHAT!' She screeched. Oh Shit, everything's going to fall flat on its face now.

"I'm joking. Having you on."

"You'd better bloody be? I'll just bring a top with me then. No, I'll bring some spare jeans, just in case. I don't trust you. Not sure about this forklift thing either? What if I hit something? I've only had four driving lessons, and I'm not very good at that?"

"You'll be fine Linda. I'll be with you all the time. Promise......"

"Oh, what the hell. It might be fun. I'll see you there then. You'd better not be late?"

"Or you Linda! Right, see you there then. I'm gonna ring Eric' I blew a kiss down the phone. Pushed the handset button down, then dialled his number. It was engaged. Mmm, talking to H, I expect? Better ring Karen's too. I repeated the telephone moves. Engaged? Fuckin hell. Everyone's always busy, when you want em, I groaned. Who now? Maybe I should ring that NME Wigan number for a laff? I could do with one at the moment. I've nothing to lose? Oh, fuck it why not! I ran upstairs and grabbed the NME. Ran back down and sat on the bottom stair. Turned to the back pages. They automatically opened at the same page? I looked at the bottom. *Contact Phil or Tony on 01942393776.* I stood up to dial the number. The phone rang again? I yanked it to my ear. "I've not fuckin rang you yet, you rock/pop bastards!"

"Stephen, who the bloody hell are you talking too?" It was me Mam.

"Oh erm no one. Sorry mam. I was just messing about. Trying to arrange the fruit market. Nothing...... Just waiting for Eric to ring.

"Messing about on the phone? I hope not? I hope you're not ringing out? That last phone bill was way over budget? I have to budget for everything.... It's really hard you know? There's very little money coming In as It Is. That's why I've taken on these extra, Saturday mornings, I don't want to do them... I do enough, during the week as it is? I'm going to get the phone taken out, if it's that dear next time......! This budgeting...." I moved the receiver away from my ear, up into thin air, and sat back down on the last stair.

Bloody budget. Budgeting? Who does she think she Is? the Chancellor of the exchequer? I grinned listening. I could've gone to the kitchen and made a cuppa, knitted a jumper or even baked a cake. And she would still be going......! and I can't even knit!

"Mam.... mam!" I interrupted. "Just listen for a minute. I'm working in a bit too. Just waiting for Eric to ring that's all. What did you ring for? I need to put the phone back down. If it's engaged, he might not ring again?"

"Oh, it doesn't matter now Stephen. I wanted our John. Never mind. But just think on, next time you use the phone. That's what the little red, money kiosk is for, at the side of the phone. To put money in when you bloody use the thing Tara!"

"I know I know. I'll put some money in it now mam." She was gone? I tried Eric again. "Eric, Is that you?"

"Yes Ste. I've got a fuckin job. Don't have to go back workin at woolhams again. Brilliant!"

"I know you have mate. Listen, I'll see you up there, In a bit. It's been put back. Half three now. Linda's coming too. John's jibbed out. Tell you about it later," As I talked, I stared again at the advert.

"Oh, has he? Now there's a surprise. Ok then. What time is it now? It's five past one. I'll see you there Ste." I looked at the advert, then at the phone and sighed. Picked it up, then put it back down. Oh, what are you waiting for Stephen? I trapped it between my shoulder, and ear and twisted the dial. '01942... three, three, nine, six, seven, seven, six. "Here goes nothing?"

THIRTY-SEVEN

"**A**fternoon Haywood's, Rosemary speaking."

"Oh, erm hello. I'm looking for a Phil or Tony? *Did I dial the number right? I appeased myself.*

"Our Phil's not here today. He's over at the video shop. Tony's at the cash and carry. He's due back anytime. I can give you the video shop number?" She sounded just like Linda?

"Oh erm, they don't really know me. I'm Stephen. I was just...... Oh, go on then. Yes, you can give me the other sh............"

"Oh, he's back now. He's was just outside, locking up the van. Why didn't you tell me he was back George? Just a second love."

The phone clunked as if it was dropped on the floor. I listened intently, to the background voices:

"Right you are Beryl. George, how much is this washing powder again? What have I told you about labelling stuff? Thanks Irene, I will." She returned to the phone. "He's here now love, sorry about that. Tony, The phone? Someone called Steve... no Stephen. He asked for our Phil?"

"Hello, Tony speaking." bloody hell, he sounds familiar, I frowned. "Oh, hello Tony. Sorry to bother you, I'm ringing about your advert?"

"Oh, they've all gone now, erm Stephen. Sold the last one this morning. There's only the Mother left now. I wanted to keep the little one, but Janette wouldn't let me. said there was enough shit in the yard."

"I'm sorry? the advert in the NME. For a singer?" What the bloody hell's going on here? My brain was almost turning in to a cauliflower now?

"Oh, that advert. I thought you were talking about the puppies, haha sorry, we had crossed wires cracker!"

Crossed fuckin wires? Did I fuckin mention puppies pal? No? you bloody did? This isn't going well at all. Maybe I shouldn't have bothered. I contemplated putting the phone down. I composed myself.

"That was fast!" He said "The NME only went on the shelves today. You're quick off the mark Stephen. Well erm, what can I say. There's four of us in the group at the moment. Our Phil on guitar and keyboards. Jeff on drums, Phil on lead guitar and I play the bass. We've got two Phil's. Phil number one, is from Hindley green. Phil number two, is from Ashton. I play lead guitar too if I have to. We can all sing, but Roy, the lead singer just walked out on us, the bastard! We had a mate's studio booked too? I'm doing lead vocals at the moment. I'll have to stay there, if we don't get someone soon? I don't want to be the singer. Happier just playing bass. Our Phil's the main songwriter. He can play anything. I must admit even though he's my brother. He's very talented. He's got more talent in his little finger than I'll ever have.

We've decided to have one final stab at it, and If It doesn't work this time, that's it! Time to hang up the guitar strap. Or use it for a dog lead haha." I was lost for words. Bloody hell, these lot sound way out of my league. Really professional? Think I should just casually decline. The whole time he was talking, other voices, bumps and bangs, were constantly coming from the background down the phone.

"Oh erm. Well, I think you've just, about covered everything there Tony."

I had no Idea what to say. "Excuse me for asking, but are you in a shop?"

"Haha top marks, cracker. Yes mate. I'm in the family shop In Pemberton. Just up from the Carnegie Library. What about you Stephen? tell me a bit about yourself? Are you from Wigan? You have a Lancashire accent. I hope you are? Let's just say, it would help to practise."

After hearing about his bands individual talents, I was at the moment, feeling almost like a triangle novice, or kazoo beginner. He can't see me squirming anyway, I thought. I decided to be a tad more 'voice' positive. After all, he wouldn't be any the wiser.

"Erm, yes Tony, I'm a Wiganer. I know where your shop is too. Been past it loads of times. I live over at hawkley hall. I do my own music. I really love music. I was lead singer in a band called 'Target' a while ago."

I was fading, before I'd even started, and helping myself fall back down the hill too.

"Well, that was actually, just after school. I play keyboards when I can. I have a Roland, Juno106, a four track and some other bits and pieces. I haven't done anything for a while though." The words *'haven't done anything'* seemed to echo in my empty head, and down the phone. I'd totally dried up.... nothing left. I gritted my teeth. 'Erm, My Dad's a singer too', I piped up. "He does the working men's clubs. Has done for years." Tony was silent. Probably totally unimpressed, or he'd just fell asleep. Mmm, as long as I had a hole in my arse. I'd never make a Stephen, salesman. Let alone a singer.

"Yes love, you can get three, for the price of two on those. It's a Limited offer." Came down the phone. Jesus Christ? Is he even listening?

"Sounds good Stephen, so you're Interested? Why don't you come over, and audition tonight?" Fuckin hell Tony I thought, aren't you gonna let me fail miserably first? Or at least let me start begging?

"Tony, call me Steve. Please, It's shorter and less well.... just less. I'm positive, I've spoken to you before? Maybe In your shop? Sorry erm, I'd love to come and audition. Thanks, that's great. Where do you audition? I mean practice? Above the shop?" I took a wild guess.

"Oh no, that's where the folks live haha. We use the function room upstairs, In the Red Lion in Hindley. Ashton Phil's Dad runs It. So, we get it free. We try to get together there, either Saturday or Sunday, every couple of weeks. But our Phil's got some new songs. We're working them out at the moment."

"That's a bit weird Tony. It's more than weird? I'm actually going to meet my Dad, at the Derby Arms, In Hindley tonight."

"That's over the road from our mate, Paul's studio. LA Sound, Halfway up, Castle Hill road. Look Steve. I'm gonna to have to go. The shops completely mobbed, and my Mother's giving me the evil eye here. I've gotta empty the van from the cash and carry, and people are waiting in the shop for stuff off it. We'll be in there later, from eight o'clock' onwards. I'll tell our Phil you're coming."

Mmm? Mothers and evil eyes. Mam'll give me the whole phone bill, if she finds out I've been on It this long. "Ok Tony. Just one more thing. Well, two. I'll have the girlfriend with me. Is it ok if...?"

"Of course, pal, no problem," he Interrupted. "Our girls will be there. They always are, she can keep Janette, Lisa and Claire company. The more the merrier! We'll try out the new songs on them. They're going to be really good when we work them out properly. I really must dash. See you tonight. Don't let me down now. Bye Steve."

The phone went dead yet again. Every bastard has done that to me today? Mmm, he was a nice bloke. Sure, I know his voice? I bet he's that bloody bald Dj I spoke to at Maxims? Mind you, all Wigan folk sound much the same. He did say cracker? Oh well, If It is him. I'll be meeting him again later, anyway. Bloody hell, I thought. The reality of what I'd done, just hit me. I've just bagged my first ever audition, as a singer. I hope I don't screw it up? Not sang in ages. Only in the shower when the house was empty. Shit, not sung in front of an audience for years either? Oh, what the hell, I'll get a few Dutch courage beers down my neck, I'll be fine. If they've got a

few beers down theirs, they won't know the bloody difference either.
I giggled. How hard can it be? I'll ask me Dad for some tips later.
Hope Linda'll will be proud? Shit what's the time? I went into the
lounge. Oh shit, ten past two. I've been on there almost an hour.
Mam'll crucify me! I'd better stick some coppers in the red money
box, before I leave. Bollocks to our john. It was engaged when I
rang, anyway. No, that was Eric's phone? Oh well, Stuff our john.
He did say, he wouldn't come, If I didn't ring. I'd better get moving.
Sharpish!

THIRTY-EIGHT

The rain had eased off before I'd left the house. But was threatening to start again the whole way up the road to work. As I reached the top of the dual carriageway, I looked at my watch. Five to three. Everything else today, was going to be by taxi, so I'd left the push-iron at home. I glanced over at the Ben Johnson. I felt the loose change in my pocket. Mmm, might as well partake in a quick pint while I'm early. I happily reasoned. I crossed over the road and pushed open the door. The pub was busy. Being a fly-by-night customer, I didn't really know any of the regulars. As I waited at the bar to get served, I spotted one, solitary face throwing darts, I recognised. Martin Abbott.

We were in the same class at Marus Bridge, middle school. I don't think I'd even seen him since then either. At least I couldn't recall If I had. He had red hair, like mad Tony from work, a ginger top, and hadn't changed one bit. He walked toward the dart board, to retrieve his darts and one handedly, plucked the cluster succinctly out of the pig skin. Turned back, to face the bar and walked across toward the hockey. He walked to one side, picked up his half empty pint off his table, as his throwing opponent stood up, to take his turn. It was Mark, his older brother. I hadn't seen him in years either. As they exchanged patter, Martin lowered, and was about to sit into the seat Mark had just got up from. Just before he did, he spotted me, and stood In Marks way. "Get out the way Martin, d'you want a dart in your other eye." He smiled and continued to beckon me over. Martin had been involved in a serious pellet gun accident as a kid, and almost lost the sight, in his left eye. His pupil bore the scar.

Mark turned around to see what the fuss was about. I don't think he recognised me. Well, it was donkey's years ago, when me and Martin knocked about.

I pointed at the bar, feigned drinking an invisible pint, gave him a smile, and thumbs up acknowledgement. He returned the gesture and disappeared below the bar onto the seat. All that remained visible from my vantage point, was the top of his head. His ginger curls. Mark took his place at the hockey. That was nice of him, I thought. Not seen him in years, and yet he still Invited me over.

Once I was served, I made my way around the bar, and through the double adjoining doors, into the games room. As I walked into the room, Martin was throwing again. Mark looked up, from his pint, and nodded at me. The horses were on telly, and various, afternoon punters were doing much the same as John from the Tippings. Loudly giving each other 'certs' for the day, and swapping general, alcohol banter based, one-upmanships. Much the same as everyone does as laid down in all and every drinking folklore imaginable. From Miami to Timbuktu. Once, I'd been told there are three subjects that you should never talk about, or even utter, in any hallowed, drinking establishment. Football, religion and politics. Yet all around me, they were being fervently discussed, defined, negated and deliberated on. It was just the pub way. Martin returned to the hockey, to take another throw. "Alright Ste, how the hell are you? How many years is it mate? Won't be a sec." He threw his darts. They landed to the left of treble twenty.

"We got sick of 301, so were just playing around the board now. I want double nine. Probably won't even finish at this rate. I'm crap at darts anyway haha. We're just waiting for our coach. We're off to the Manchester bierkeller. It's bloody late too Mark?" Mark looked up, again. "Three o'clock they said. It probably will be late, cos they've got four pickups before us lot in here. At least we'll be first off, on the way back. Which is just as well? We won't have a bloody leg under us haha."

"What you up too Ste? He walked toward the board as Mark stood up.

"Not much really mate. Still working at the fruit market, just over the road. Been there since I left school. That's where I'm off too now. Gotta go unload a wagon. Paul Ingam works with me, d'you remember him?" Mark threw his darts. "I can't say as I do Ste?" Martin scratched his head.

"Eric Hemingway works there too. He was at our school. Least he will from next week. He'll be over the road in a bit too. Giving us a hand with the wagon. What are you doing Martin?"

"I work for that slave driver haha" Martin winked at me. "You, cheeky twat!" Mark said, as they changed positions. "What number are you on now?" asked Martin.

"My first double, then Bull," Mark confidently said, picking up his lager from the table.

"M & A kitchens in Pem, d'you know it Ste?"

"I do Martin. That's your place is it Mark?" I asked, as he pushed his flights securely down into his darts, then passed them to Martin. "Yes Ste, started the company when I left school too. Brought our Martin onboard when he left as well. We're not doing so bad. It keeps the wolfs from the door." As he said that, the room went considerably darker. Followed by long, cumbersome brake screech. Their coach had arrived outside, blocking the daylight, parked across the window.

"That's you two sorted, you jammy sods," I jealously conceded, as they smiled and necked their lager. Along with another five or six blokes in and around the room. Martin finished first, and three handed the darts into the board, then walked toward the bar, with his empty glass. "Well Ste, I suppose I'll bump into you again, in another five years, haha. Just kidding mate. If you ever need a new kitchen, give us a call. Come on slow coach, we've got gallons of authentic Bavarian beer, and an Oompah show to get too heehee."

"Have a good night then" As they disappeared out of the games room door, they were happily followed out, by about eight others.

Almost subconsciously, forming a dancing line. One happy departee, feigned playing a Tuba, as his mate laughed after him. Foot stomping and thigh slapping as he went. The lucky sods I thought. I'd been there with Eric, and a few others on a coach once too. A drinking gargantuan of fun. Huge 'two for one' Steins of Haus, and Hollandia Lager. Topped off by the green clad, brass playing, Oompah band. I was heading over the road to welcome 300 crates of caulis to our shores. What a complete bloody let down. Quarter past three. I downed the last of my lager and headed out the door. The coach was still there. I ran across Warrington Roads first carriageway and looked over my shoulder. Martin and Mark, were at a steamy window, halfway down the packed seats. He saw me and gave a smiling thumbs up. I waved back, and crossed the last of the dual carriageway, into Wheatlea road, Industrial Estate and the Market.

THIRTY-NINE

The market was like a mini, ghost town. I don't usually see it like this. Except In the morning darkness. It's always bustling with customers, cars, vans and wagons. I walked down to old John's incinerating shed, and grabbed the hidden stall keys, from under the brick. Throwing them up in the air as I walked back to the stall. I pushed the brass key, into the rusty lock and pushed open the shutter door. I walked into the office and placed them on their hook. Grabbed the onion stall key and slipped it into my jeans pocket. I edged myself through a gap in-between a row of white 'Perlim' apple boxes, and open-topped water melon crates. Last week, Tony had taken one out, and thrown the water melon up in the air, for no other logical reason, than to watch it implode, and decimate on the concrete, at his feet. "Ooops, Butterfingers!" He crazily affirmed. "Dickhead!" I frowningly agreed. The one 'short' crate was still comfortably hidden, at the bottom of the stack. "Wheee!" I grinned, sliding myself across a small pallet of stacked shallots. Displacing a sack onto the floor as I did. I quickly replaced it, as I rose to my feet, and unhitched the second shutter lock, and pushed on the doors. These were finicky at the bottom, and always took some severe, pushing and side-to-side thrashing to open fully. They'd be belted by forklifts on dozens of times, which didn't help. *"Come... on... you... awkward... bastards!"* I assuaged, intermittently between every push, until they were fully concertina'd, out of harm's way. I was now panting from the shutters. I yanked out the forklift charger cable, threw it over the racking, and plugged the end, into its under-seat batteries. After turning the key, I silently whirred across the wet concrete, and up to our onion stall, at the side of Conroy's. I spun the three wheeled, green forklift around to within, six inches of the doors, almost level with the lock. Still sitting, I turned the key. The hasp dropped open. I placed the keyed lock, into the recess at the back of my seat. Now slightly off-skew, from the Identical shutter doors, I put my palm, on the main door facia. Ever so slowly, I drove forward. As I did, the left door clicked its segments together, until it reached the wall, and I stopped. I spun the forklift around, and repeated the same manoeuvre, until both doors were wide open. *"Forklift drivers.... Shit em!"* I laughed. To be perfectly honest, it was a trick I'd learned from forklift-moulded arse, Our John. I turned the wheel and machine backward, through 45' degrees, then drove into the dark, half empty stall. Skewered a sizeable stack of empty pallets, onto the shiny forks, and reversed backwards out of the stall, and down across the empty market, and whirred back to the main stall.

I reached in to my jacket pocket, grabbed my cigs and lighter and lit up. I slid down in the seat, and lifted my both legs up, to rest either side of the steering wheel, on the forklift safety frame in front.

It was almost three thirty on the market clock. Mmm, it's due anytime now, I hope. As I waited, I thought about getting myself a coffee from the machine. Nah, my stomach's already been lined and libated with the lager. That would be just yeuch! Eric soon appeared from around the corner. He was smiling, then randomly started chanting "I've got a job, got a fuckin job!........... I said, I've got a job, got a job got a fuckin job!" I started laughing.

"Fuckin hell Eric, you're not on the terraces watching Wigan rugby now?"

"I know I'm not. But it doesn't matter because...." He paused, then continued...........

"I've got a job, got a fuckin job I said....... I've...." As he carried on, he alternated his voice between a whisper and almost a roar. It became strangely, and slightly Infectious. He danced around the forklift like a Maori warrior. I was almost tempted, to change the words, and concur back at him. "You've got a job, got a fuckin job" But I was laughing too much. Then I contemplated, totally changing his chant for myself. To Something along the lines of; "I've got an audition, a fuckin audition.... But It wouldn't go......? It simply wouldn't fit in his chant. Too many adjectives or nouns. Bad Idea, I thought. I'll keep shtum. He's happy, In his own job glory. I really wanted to tell someone though?

'Go get yourself a free coffee Eric. You know where the key is, leave it on free vend. He was still chanting........?

Above his chanting, I heard a loud wagon engine, and air brakes commotion, behind the stall on Wheatlea road. This must be for us, I thought. A bit later than originally planned, but reasonably on time for a change. Eric came back from the coffee machine, still smiling, but he'd got bored chanting. Mind you, He was the type who would resume at anytime. Just Like Ian and his, 'kebabs'. I got off the forklift, as the artic turned across the market, and in front of the stall. I looked at the barely, visible cab driver, and pointed at the market, in front of him. Beckoning him where to park. Eric stood at the side of me, sipping his coffee. "He's like me him?"

"What?" I asked "Has he got a new job too?"

"Nah, he needs a couple of cushions under him, the short-arsed fucker, haha. Here's your sweet-heart Ste," Eric announced. A red crusader taxi, pulled into the market, and stopped right at the side of us. She was on time too? Good, this might be a quick turnaround, I thought. She waved at us through the glass, then paid the driver.

The wagon driver turned off his engine, opened his door, and jumped down, on to the concrete, with his consignment note in his hand. He vexed at the taxi and walked slowly towards us. Linda jumped out of her taxi and slammed the door. It Immediately sped off. She had a plastic Tesco bag, and her red purse in her hand.

"Hello Eric" She smiled, and greeted him, as she kissed me on the cheek. "Alright Linda"

He answered.

"Alright Honey pie" I smiled. "Ste, he looks confused as fuck? It's not fuckin rocket-science pal?" Eric said, as If the Frenchman was going to understand him. Eric spoke to him. "We're gonna off-load you pal...... I said off-load you? You mutton clown!" As if he Frenchman was now deaf too. "Then you can get the fuck out of our face! Oh, just get back in your cab, where you belong, you stupid sod! Sorry Linda. You tell the daft old bugger Linda?" Eric jokingly added, jumping on his forklift.

Linda silently handed me her Tesco bag, Smiled, then turned around to face him.

"Excusez moi, mes amis. Volonte decharger votre vehicule. Comme rapidment pour vous. Vous boite s'asseoir cabine. Bien?"

She took his note from his hand and patted him on the back. He gladly smiled at her, said something in his native tongue. Turned around and happily walked to the back of his wagon.

"You clever sod Linda! I proudly proclaimed. I didn't know you could speak French? That was genius. Oh my God, haha. What about that Eric?" Eric Smiled at her.

"Yep, that was pret... ty cool." He spun his forklift around, and headed for the back of the truck, where the bloke was undoing the ropes, on his tarpaulin curtain. Eric had already unclipped it at the bottom, and it was now slightly blowing in the afternoon wind. Eric jumped back onto the forklift, and put his empty pallet stack, at the side of the wagon.

He'd left one on the forks, ready for blast off, and was motioning and coaxing, the Frenchman to stand on it. Pointing up at the curtain, and down at the pallet, as he did. Eric looked over at me, and raised both his hands in the air, but remained silent. The man, clearly wasn't sure what Eric intentioned. I laughed intently and decided to leave them to it. Fully incommunicado.

"I'll put your stuff in the office sweetheart. Do you want a coffee?" I briefly put my arm around her shoulder, and we kissed again. "Yes please. Eric makes driving it look easy. I hope it is?" I walked into the office and put her bag on the desk. "Coffee's around there, just help yourself." She followed me and I pointed to the machine. "I'll go see what they're up to Linda? If they're ready, I'll make a start. Eric can come and get the palletizer truck, then give you a crash course, on the forklift." I headed back outside. "What's a pallet truck Stephen? oh that's it there, isn't it."

"You're not just a pretty face, sweetheart," I smiled. "I'll have some more of that sexy French talk, off you next time were in bed haha." She looked over her coffee at me.

FORTY

Back outside, Eric had fork lifted Charles Aznavour man, to the top of the wagon, to secure his curtain out of the way. As I approached. He was slowly descending him, back down to the ground. The Frenchman, was holding on for dear life. As I got to the side of the forklift, he was still six-foot shy from the ground? I could see the devilment in Eric's eye's. He smilingly refrained himself. Once firmly on the ground, the Frenchman turned to me." 300, trois cents." Gave me the universal gesture for 'ok', and disappeared like a frightened vole, back to his cab.

"The stack's about halfway down the wagon Ste. He'll have virtually nothing left on, when we've taken ours." I jumped onto the pallet, Sasha Distell man had just got off, and Eric lifted me up and drove forward. He slightly dropped the forks leaving both me, and the pallet safely on the wagon. I pulled the pallet from the floor of the wagon and thread my arm through it. Dragging it into the wagon, at my side. "See you in a bit Eric." I shouted. He reversed back and disappeared.

I dropped the pallet onto the wagon and kicked it into the centre. Grabbed the first crate and threw it to the far side of the pallet. The crates were ergonomically designed, to hold 24 individual cauliflowers inside, and always created a perfect 'five' stack, corner to corner, across the length, and width of a standard 40' by 48' by 5' wooden pallet. A pallet happily took 25 crates, leaving two feet clearance, from the wagon roof. There was some noise or commotion outside, not currently visible, due to me, being fully enveloped, or cocooned inside the wagon's body, and full-length curtain. I regardlessly carried on stacking. Mmm, it's only Eric, showing Linda how to forward, and reverse the forklift. Putting her through an *enough education to perform* speed induction. He'll be back here soon, I figuratively assumed.

After about six minutes I'd thrown the last crate up, onto the pallet, and had warmed up, more than considerably. "Phew! I'm a bit out of condition today." Usually with two bodies, you could pass and 'haymake' the crates, but on your own, it was a wee bit harder. All the time you created a stack, the source gets further away. The pallet truck wasn't here yet, to deter the increasing gap. As I finished, I took a few deep breaths, and walked past the first departee pallet, and looked out of the wagon, to see how the *throw her in see if she can swim'* progress was getting along. Hope he's not tapping her up, I smiled? Explaining where his carrot and two radishes fit. I popped my head around the arctic's curtain, as if I was an actor, peeping in a theatre, checking for a full audience, in a west end re-run of Victor Hugo's, Les Miserable's. Complete with napping French driver. As I peered around, being careful not to walk off the edge, and fall on to the concrete below, as Paul had done a few weeks earlier. I was gobsmacked to say the least. I looked twice. There were four motorbikes, and H's Capri. Eight of them stood there, casually having a conversation, as if they were on a random 'day out' or warts and all, excursion to the fruit market. Complete with a full day itinery, and full passenger duty of care to experience, the rich and interesting history, of Wigan Fruit and Vegetable market, with H, as their day-trip representative.

"What the fuck" I thought. Just then, our John walked out of the stall, with a tomato box lid tray of coffees? Not a one of them were giving the current offloading task, a blind bit of notice, or even a second thought. Just a regular everyday Jolly, swapping banter and chat, and general 'pleased to meet you's'. I didn't say a word, and just quietly sat myself down on the back of the wagon. Well, H seemed to be in charge of the throng. Who am I, to Interrupt his glory day, I thought.

I glanced over again. There was, H, his wife and one son. A mini replica of his Dad, obviously without the mouth cigarette. Eric and Linda. Paul and Karen. John and Elly, on probably his new motorbike? Swapping Idle chatter. Just when I thought, it wasn't going to get any weirder. Ginger Tony came revving around the corner, on his motorbike. Oh brilliant! I grinned to myself. This is going to throw the cat amongst the pigeons? I might finally get this wagon unloaded now. As he 'vroomed' across the concrete, their heads spun around. I put on my best Rupert Carrington, posh voice, and sarcastically Interjected. "Eric! old bean, would you forklift the dear palletizer truck over for me, would you? There's a good fellow. If it's not too much trouble old boy?" Eric knowingly grinned, and shouted back,

"Of course, I will, my dear man, on the way old chum." The day out, ad-lib trips, mini conference ceased immediately, and was just about to turn into an unmitigated, multiple frowning "What the fuck's he doing here," interrogation. I walked back into the wagon.

In less than two minutes, the wagon was crawling with bodies. Two minutes after that, the regular off loading, contingent had been formed. Eric continued on forklift duty, as Paul and myself, were shoulder to shoulder stacking as usual. "What's going on out there Paul?' I inquired.

"H's took Tony in the upstairs office. Your John's pulling wheelies, with his mate. Linda and Karen were talking clothes when I left. Oh, and Peter's wives sat back in his motor. Have you got any money on you Inge? I could do with a sub mate?" He politely asked.

"Fuckin hell Paul, you'll never change, will you haha. Wait til after we've done mate."

"Thanks dude," he replied. "We should be out of here, in half an hour or so, I reckon?" He added.

"Tony'll be out of here permanently, when he gets out the office haha." We both laughed. "Thank fuck for that too," Paul acceded. "Oh, what a life. What you doing after this Paul? Fancy a couple of jars, over the road?" He threw the last crate. "Why not? Only a couple though. We're due at Rivie barn, teatime. Having a meal with our Mark, and his fat bitch."

"Yeah, I'm heading up to Hindley later, with Linda and our kid, to meet me Dad." Eric jumped onto the back of the wagon, to pull the pallet out of the way. "I've got an audition up there too. Should be Interesting to say the least? With a pop-rock band. They sound really professional. I won't get it?" Eric spun the palletizer around, as Paul grabbed another empty pallet. "You've got an audition Ste?" He asked, jumping down to the forklift. "Bloody hell, good luck mate."

"Thanks pal... Bevy over the Ben Eric?"

"Is the pope Catholic?" Eric replied, reversing and disappearing. Fifteen minutes of sweaty, humping, and throwing later, Paul and I were sat on two crates, catching our breath. Eric appeared again, balanced a pallet up, and rested it onto his knees.

"We've one pallet left to do" He launched it onto the wagon. "Fill that fucker, and we've finished. 300 boxes!" I turned to sweating Paul. He stood up, and ran to the back of the wagon, like a man possessed. Grabbed the pallet, and skull dragged it back toward me. Pushed it over, thumping it down with his trainer. The wood 'bang' resounded, all around the almost empty wagon canvass.

"That'll wake the French fella up!" He exclaimed. Eric waited patiently, forklift bound. As we filled the last pallet, Karen and Linda appeared at either side of him, to have a delayed nosey. "Stephen, Eric told us, you've got an audition?" Linda shouted down, through the wagon.

"What took you so long, I panted. I thought you were going to jump on and give us a hand haha?"

"They've been talking shop, haven't you?" Eric said, looking at them. "This is their last pallet" Eric said. I pumped up the palletizer.

"That's it! Take it away Inge!" Paul shouted collapsing back onto the remaining crates. Five minutes after that, I was alone again, putting the stall keys back under the brick.

FORTY-ONE

It was a quarter to eight, walking up market street In Hindley. Linda and I had decided to head up here, a bit early. Well, not long after the market wagon, had been finished. We'd just been suitably filled up, with a bar snack, and a pint at the Red Lion. I'd just taken a notion to familiarise myself with it, before I was due, to be back there, for the audition later. Linda had never met my Dad. He'd never met her either. He doesn't even know, she's going to be with me. That should put an Interesting, slant on things If he turns up, I mused. Probably the first time I've seen him for months. "Wonder what's so Important about tonight Stephen" Linda quizzed.

"I have no Idea Linda. That bar snack was good, didn't think we'd get as much, as that did you?"

"Yes, it was nice. I'm glad you had something, before you started drinking though. You usually do It, the opposite way around." She smiled. "I hope you're not going to have, an all-out war, like you told me you had last time?" She said.

"Nope. If I was planning that, I wouldn't have you with me. I'm just here to see what he's got to say. I really can't be bothered, with any arguments either. To be honest, I wasn't even thinking about it. I was thinking about the audition. Been thinking about that non-stop, since I spoke to Tony, on the phone. To be honest, I'm a bit bloody nervous now."

"You'll be fine Stephen. Can't wait to hear you sing too?"

"Oh, don't you start putting me under pressure."

We came to the end of Market street, onto bridge street, and started the final walk, up castle hill road. "I'm glad we decided to walk now. Revving up the metabolism, will help burn off that food we just had. How much further Is it now Stephen?"

"We're nearly there Linda. D'you see the blue sign, up the hill on the right." She bent forward and squinted her eyes. As she did, a white van beeped its horn, as It drove past us. Soon followed by a GMPT orange bus. "I bet that was my him, driving that van, Linda? Trust him not to bloody stop."

"We're nearly there now anyway Stephen." The white van slowed, just before the pub, indicated right, and disappeared from view. I looked at my watch. Two minutes to eight. As I continued to look up the hill, he appeared from where the van had gone, waving his arms up, In the air. He disappeared into the Derby Arms, on the corner of the road junction. "That was him in the van Linda. He's just walked into the ale-house. Wonder what he'll make of you, sweetness haha?"

She turned to me. "If he's anywhere as cheeky as you, he'll get a short, sharp kick in the goolies." She stopped walking and started personal straightening duties. Pulling her black skirt down, and around into its correct, ass buttock sitting place. So, the slit at the back, was correctly parallel, and in the centre of her legs. Then, she undid a button on her white blouse, put her hands individually into it to pull, twist, and re-position her bra and also her boobs in the process.

"Linda, we're on a main road here? D'you want me to do that for you?" I laughed. "I'm quite capable." she smiled. She jiggled about her boobs and shook her shoulders. Once she seemed happy with her 'tit' re-positioning, she re-fastened the blouse button, and then started on her hair. Wetting the nails of both her hands and running them both, uniformly together, and tucking it neatly behind her ears. Then, she flicked her fingers through her fringe, and shook her head. She was just about to start on me. Just before she did, I grabbed both her hands. "Oh no you don't lady! I don't even know why you bothered with yourself? As soon as you walk in there, you're gonna head straight into the loo, and do it all again, anyway. Or at least lipstick your lips. You may as well, have just waited til then. He's not gonna bother his arse, what the hell you look like."

"I don't care If he's bothered, I'm bothered! Oh, and get me an orange juice, when we get in there. I don't want him thinking, I'm some kind of raving, alcoholic, psycho either."

"Haha, Oh my oh my. And I thought I was nervous, about the audition."

"Well", she flicked my fringe across. "I don't know, what you've told him about me do I?" You could've told him anything about me? She pulled my denim coat together, wet her finger, and rubbed It, into my chin. "Ouch! What the hell are you......?"

"You had some sauce there!" Oh, don't be a big baby Stephen."

"Right. Come here, you mad woman, while I've got a chance." I grabbed both her shoulders and kissed her, full on the lips. It lingered slightly longer than I'd anticipated, and I felt It was really meant. By both of us. Just as I pulled away, I sucked a little, to make a big slapping noise, 'MWAH!'. There sweetypoos, haha "You can go and put your lipstick on now."

As we walked into the pub. Dad was standing at the bar. He turned around. "Hello Stranger." *Hi sarcastic features I thought.* "Alright Dad. This Is Linda.... Linda.... this Is my Dad."

They smiled at each other. Linda even curtseyed and bowed her head?

As she did, I Instantly began to grin. I wanted to say something like, *'he's not the fuckin Queen'.* But as she looked up, she went visibly red. As I quietly looked at her, I decided to keep my mouth, well and truly shut, because by now, the look I was currently experiencing, coming from both her body language, and whole facial demeanour, and Instantly told me, that when she'd eventually, managed to wriggle and squirm herself, out of this present, embarrassing situation, and had me completely on my own, she was going to kick the living shit out of me. Possibly even twice. Or at least until she didn't have the use of her legs anymore.

"Call me Cliff love." Dad said to her. "What are your both drinking? Linda, what can I get you both?"

'Oh, quit with the fuckin false charm dad, you know what I'm drinking. what I always fuckin drink, a pint. I wish you'd just go jump off a fuckin cliff sometimes Dad, you asshole.

"Oh, erm thanks Dad, I'll have a pint of carling please. Linda's on......."

"Orange juice Cliff" She smiled at him as she smarmily, finished my sentence for me.

"You'll have to excuse me Cliff, I'm just going to..."

"Yeah, the ladies room to put some more lipstick on." I returned the favour and finished her sentence back.

Well, you fuckin started It I thought. It may as well, be fuckin war paint, if you're gonna carry on like this, I convinced myself. In fact, I'm not putting up with any more of this shit from the pair of you put together. If this fuckin bollocks carries on, I'm outta here. I digressed....

Dad always seemed to bring out the worst in me, in recent years. He was hardly around, in my youth. and now not around at all. It's not that Dad chose 'not' to be around. I just don't remember him being there a lot of the time that's all. If he wasn't there, around the house. He was always, working or singing. Bringing home the bacon, so as far as I was concerned, that was ok. It was forgiven. Maybe I was just out playing when he was at home. To be honest, I don't really know. I think most of the singing rashers, stayed firmly in his pants pockets.

Doing the clubs, is pretty much being at work too. Except with the bonus of being able to down a pint, or three while you're there. When I was really young, I didn't know much about it. We were parped off to Nan's for the night, or a babysitter was brought in, if mam went with him. As we got older, John, and me fended for ourselves. Thinking back, a lot of DIY was done at home too.

Probably more than the average household. Which was great as I usually, had a helping hand in it somewhere?

I think Dad really enjoyed the feeling of a 'Draper' claw hammer in his hand, and a pencil behind his ear. At all times If possible. He always had plaster somewhere, on his hand and a black nail too. Sometimes two! A couple of cuts, or bruises for good measure. Consistently for years throughout my youth, black nails? He must have been a terrible aim?

But I digress....

FORTY-TWO

"It's just down there Linda. To the end, and just take a right love." Dad said to her.

"Right, thanks Cliff. I erm won't be long. Just before she walked down the corridor, she gave me a look that would burn wallpaper off. Granted, I'd slightly gone a little overboard, with my lipstick comment. I silently mouthed, sorry at her as she walked away, down the corridor. As I did, she stuck two fingers right up at me. She wasn't fooling about either. This just made me laugh to, myself even more. If she doesn't watch her fuckin step, she'll be bumped and dumped, in favour of Tilly, I mused to myself. I might be better on my own, anyway? Best thing about being alone, is that there's no one else to let down. I'll leave the fuckin pair of them in here, on their own, if this shit carries on. Why the fuck does people put falsities, niceties and heirs and graces on. It really is beyond me. Does my fuckin head in too? What's wrong with being yourself, I thought.

"So, what you doing with yourself Ste. Are you still at the market?"

"Dad, why are you asking me a question, you already know the answer too?"

"We'll, I haven't seen you have I" He said, accepting his change, and lifting his drink from the bar.

"No, you haven't taken the time to see me. Not now, not ever Dad." I grab Linda's, and my drink from the bar, as we look for a table "There's no surprise there either, is there, Dad?"

As he was just about reply, or to continue, I firmly cut him off. "But you've seen our John. In fact, you see John every two, fuckin weeks, don't you dad. Without friggin fail! In fact, where Is that bloody brother of mine? I thought he'd be here by now? So anyway dad, back to your original question. You're not going to stand there and tell me that you don't ask him about me, are you? Or don't you genuinely bother to ask? Cos that wouldn't fuckin surprise me, In the least bit either." He blankly looked at me. "Listen lad, let's go get a table. we've a lot to talk about," He led the way, and we headed up some steps, from the bar to one of the empty tables, looking out, onto the main road. I carried on talking as we walked.

"No, you listen to me dad. Have you come here to harass, me with your positive mood, or something?" He quietly looked at me as I continued. "Maybe we have some un-said things to say, and some scores to settle. As far as I'm concerned about things, that in my humble opinion, that have gone unsaid for a long, long time. In some ways, they should have long been said and sorted, Done and dusted."

"Well, yes, your right son, I'm sorry. I was just being pleasant. I know you're still at the fruit market, cos I've asked John. I ask him all the time, and before we go any further, I'm sorry to you both, I'm not around anymore. And for all the time's, I haven't been around for you both. In fact, this why I've asked you both here tonight. It was going to be, an apology. This Is me saying a big sorry, to both of you. I wish you'd have come on your own. I didn't know you were coming with your girlfriend. But that's ok. You weren't to know any different."

Just then, Linda made her way back down the hallway, from the toilet. "She's coming back, Dad." I motioned over in his direction and speeded up my voice.

"I'll listen to what you say, if you have the decency to listen to me, I still have an axe to grind but not now. Not tonight! I didn't know anything about this. If I did, Linda wouldn't be here with me, and as long as she Is. It's not happening. She doesn't need to be subjected, to all that crap." Linda spotted us at the window, as she got to the bar. I lifted her orange up from the table at her. "Just bring your niceties back, for the moment, for tonight. We'll talk about this, at a more appropriate time. Let's just be men enough, to push It to one side, under the carpet, at least for the moment, agreed?" We both took a sip of our pints. As we did, he offered up his glass. The glasses clinked together, above the table.

"Of course, we can lad. Agreed Stephen. We're both grown adults. She's here now."

he quietly said.

"And besides everything, I'm not missing my first ever bloody audition for a heart to heart either. If we got into all that bollocks, we'll be here all bloody night Dad, won't we!" As Linda sat down, I feigned a laugh. he quietly nodded.

"Yes, erm we would. Alright love?" He smiled at Linda. She smiled back at him, and then over at me. "Sorry I took so long. I got stuck in the cubicle. Trust me! Well, the lock got stuck. Took ages to loosen It. I thought I was going to have to start banging on the walls, to get out. I snapped a nail too, look at that Stephen." I looked at her, grabbed her hand, rubbed the nail, and clasped our hands together, on my knee under the table, and quietly smiled.

"But there is something else, I need to tell you both." Linda looked up at me, from her missing nail. Sorry, not you Linda. Our Stephen and John I mean." He said. "Where Is he Stephen? I thought you were both coming together, In a taxi?"

"There was a change of plan dad. We came early, cos of the audition. Just tell me? If he doesn't show. I'll tell him, when I see him next.

"Well it's erm. It's a bit." He looked tense.

"Cliff, if you want me to go?" Linda said "Tell him on your own, I really don't mind, erm Cliff?" We all looked at each other. My grip on her hand tightened, as If to say, "Your staying right here at my side, with me, sweetheart."

"No, Linda don't be silly." He assuaged. "Nobody needs to go anywhere at all. It's just some unexpected news that's all. It's nothing to fret about either." The table went silent.

"Oh, come on then, Dad," I said. "For God's sake, let the cat out of the bag."

"It's Christine and me. We're having a baby." The table fell silent yet again. Linda squeezed my hand back. "Well erm Dad, I don't really know what to say. Except, congratulations and well done." I lifted my glass off the table to give another toast. But this time along with Linda's participation too. "Yes, erm congratulations Cliff." She smiled across at him.

"How the fucking hell, have you managed that dad? You dirty old, bloody trout. What age are you now?"

"Stephen, don't be so rude." I burst out laughing and smiled at them both. Mmm, that's really nice news, I thought to myself. "I'm not being rude Linda. This Is him, we're talking about." Linda didn't really understand. Despite our personal grievances, with each other. Deep down, dad and me, were the best of pals. Literally. We weren't like father and son at all. We treated each other as an equal. We had a lot of mutual respect too. Just then, our John and his motorbike, went flashing past the window. "Oh, bloody hell, our gob-head's here now," he said.

"Well Dad, like father like son." he looked across at me, took a sip of his beer, laughed and headed to the bar. "I'll go get him a pint in. Are you two ok?" He pointed a ten-pound note at us.

"We're fine dad. Really. Get your own, we're going to be leaving shortly. Auditions to do."

"Oh yeah, your audition, you'll have to tell me about that lad? Yes love, erm a pint of lager and a Worthington's bitter please." He said to the barmaid. John walked through the front door pulling his crash helmet off. "Sit down lad. I'll bring them over. Our Stephen's up there with his girl."

"Ok dad. Sorry I'm late. Elly got a flat tyre at Rivington." He said, stuffing his scarf into his helmet.

"That's ok lad. Just sit yourself down. I've something to tell you too."

In the short space of 40 minutes, we'd established a hell of a lot of things. And not an angry, or crossed word was spoken, in the process either. Dad was having a daughter, and John and me we're going to be getting, a baby step-sister. His drilling and sawing business, was going virally through the roof. So much so, that he'd just offered us both, a full-time job on the spot. Even Linda had been offered an interview as his new secretary. Tilly had to be asked about that too? I'd also agreed to, commandeer his new white van, for a working trip to London on my holidays off, from working at the market. We'd for at least once, made some little kind of family peace. We had all even solidly shaken each other's hands, when Linda and I left, the pub. Things were certainly looking, on the upside. I was on holiday from tomorrow too. All I had to do now, was sing my little heart out, and get this audition cleanly in the bag. Now, that would be a result. I wonder where life will have taken me this time next year?

. . . .

THE END!

Earth Angel Media

S C Hamill

schamill.com[1]

---

1. http://schamill.com

• • • •

Other Titles

Saving Eden. (Ecology Romance)
The Market Lads and Me. (Adult Humour)
Brick Lane. (Communal living Comedy)
The Time -Travel Twins. (Time Travel Tale)

Children's Titles

Magnus and Molly and the Floating Chairs.
A Birds Tale.
Zak and Zara and the Invisibility Ball.
The Alphabet Zoo.
Windy and Wendy get bendy and Fly!
Ace has an Accident!